Perera, Pathak and Kumar have rescued the idea of South Asia from its statist straitjacket and infused it with a new and rich cultural meaning. Their imaginative essays collectively beckon a better future for a beleaguered subcontinent.

Sugata Bose
Gardiner Professor of History, Harvard University

This volume represents the first serious attempt to move beyond an artificial and policy-driven definition of South Asia. By analysing the many ways in which the region has assumed an autonomous cultural, intellectual, political and economic reality, the authors have lent it a strategic and historical weight that points towards a new kind of future for its peoples.

Faisal Devji
Professor of Indian History, University of Oxford

Weaving together myth, folklore, art and politics, this volume views the region from the perspective of an experiment in transnational cooperation—The South Asian University. It is probably unique in that it locates the academic programmes of the University at the heart of the discussions on the region. It is an important contribution by a group of sociologists to the study of a region that tends to be dominated by political scientists and defence analysts.

Roma Chatterji
Professor of Sociology, Delhi School of Economics, University of Delhi

Geographical regions are evolving and unfolding entities, not only politically and strategically, but also in all other human manifestations. South Asia is no exception as it remains both radically vibrant and soothingly conservative. This volume is an unconventional and bold attempt at revisiting and reimagining South Asia in all its diverse perspectives. The attempt is timely and refreshing. It will intellectually stimulate and empower the readers at the same time.

S.D. Muni
Professor Emeritus, School of International Studies
Jawaharlal Nehru University, New Delhi and
Former Ambassador and Special Envoy, Government of India

In the age of nation, nationalism and nationhood, becoming a South Asian or practicing South Asianness is no easy task. This is as much an issue of physical boundaries as it is of the boundaries of the mind, indeed, nurtured zealously by the state and society in the different countries of South Asia and beyond. Yet, South Asianness is very much a part of the civilisational quest of the people of this region. It may not have found its expression in politics and hardly celebrated in the corridors of power, but it is ripe in music, gastronomy, film, travel, art, myth and in the manifold ideas of South Asia. This book will interest both proponents and sceptics of South Asia, not only in understanding or inversely nullifying the viability of South Asianness in the future, but also in flagging its strength and weaknesses in the past. And to do this, the authors of this book have made an effort to coalesce the empirical and the non-empirical, knowing well that only a post-disciplinary approach could create 'knowledge without borders' and make us 'think like South Asians' for the peace and prosperity of the people of South Asia.

Imtiaz Ahmed
Professor of International Relations and Director
Centre for Genocide Studies, University of Dhaka

Against the Nation

Against the Nation

Thinking Like South Asians

Sasanka Perera

Dev Nath Pathak

Ravi Kumar

B L O O M S B U R Y

NEW DELHI • LONDON • OXFORD • NEW YORK • SYDNEY

BLOOMSBURY INDIA
Bloomsbury Publishing India Pvt. Ltd
Second Floor, LSC Building No. 4, DDA Complex, Pocket C – 6 & 7,
Vasant Kunj New Delhi 110070

BLOOMSBURY, BLOOMSBURY ACADEMIC INDIA and the Diana logo are trademarks of Bloomsbury Publishing Plc

First published in India 2019
This edition published 2019

Bloomsbury Academic
An imprint of Bloomsbury Publishing Plc

ISBN: HB: 978-93-88630-22-1; eBook: 978-93-88630-24-5

2 4 6 8 10 9 7 5 3 1

Typeset in Minion Pro by Manipal Digital Systems
Printed and bound in India by Replika Press Pvt. Ltd.

Contents

Preface and Acknowledgements

The overall expectations, approach and the politics of this book are clearly spelled out in our introductory note, which we have called, 'Beginnings.' But at the most fundamental level, this collection of chapters can be understood as an attempt to explore South Asia beyond the state and nation-centric approaches that predominate the academic and policy discourses at present. We find these approaches both stale and extremely limiting, and would not offer a broader perspective to comprehend South Asia in a nuanced manner with reference to its multi-layered complexities. Instead, we have attempted to find other ways to understand South Asia by privileging culture. By culture in this context, we mean myth, folklore, travel, memory, visual and performing art, politics, pedagogic innovations and so on. In this sense, this book is not merely a cartography of what we think is possible, but also an invitation to other like-minded colleagues and friends to consider seeing the region differently.

This book has been possible due to a number of often unplanned as well as planned intersections of personal and collective histories and institutional arrangements. Our ability to collaborate on a number of intellectual projects including this book was made possible because of our accidental meeting in 2011 as the result of all of us coming to South Asian University. That is, we came to the university to establish an institution of higher learning, literally from scratch, from different educational, cultural and political backgrounds, but with sharable academic and intellectual interests. This is despite our individual differences in pedagogic approaches, ideas of political intervention and politics more generally. We have never tried to erase any of these differences, and some of these differences and personal positions come to the fore in what we write. In this sense, without South Asian University providing the kind of intellectual forum and space it has, for relatively unburdened thinking at a time when the public sphere is shrinking, this book would not have been possible.

We are also very thankful to our students from different parts of South Asia who have taken us on guided tours of their cultural and social worlds and into the discourses of their political dilemmas and upheavals, allowing us a first-hand look at what they have seen up close, which we had missed. The intellectual and sometimes emotional encounters with them in the classroom and beyond have provided some of the core building blocks that have made this book possible.

Also, our own expansion of focus from our own 'national' contexts of work to the region more broadly and other 'national' and sociocultural contexts within the region with which we were not familiar have broadened our intellectual horizons and academic canvas. All of this was possible entirely due to our location at South Asian University, and our own willingness to experiment with our thinking and approaches in these circumstances.

We are extremely grateful to Professors Sugata Bose from Harvard University, Faisal Devji from Oxford University, Imtiaz Ahmed from University of Dhaka, Roma Chatterji from University of Delhi and S.D. Muni, formerly from Jawaharlal Nehru University, for very willingly providing endorsements for this book and indicating their collegial solidarity towards the approach we have undertaken. Their words have offered us considerable encouragement.

We would like to thank *The Wire*, Primus Books and India International Centre Publications in New Delhi; *Ground Views* and Theertha International Artists' Collective in Colombo; 1 Shanti Road in Bengaluru; *Daily Observer* in Dhaka and *Fair Observer* in the US for readily giving their consent to republish a number of essays we had initially published in their forums.

We must very specifically note our appreciation for Mr Chandra Sekhar at Bloomsbury for pursuing this book with us and providing us the relative freedom to undertake something we were comfortable with. This book comes in a format that we think is easier to read that we would not have thought of this soon on our own without Mr Sekhar prodding us along. We note this level of flexibility is rapidly disappearing in the world of publishing as well as in the world of academia. We also thank Ms Shreya Chakraborti and Ms Guneet Kaur for their help.

We sincerely hope colleagues, friends and students who would read our book as it enters circulation in South Asia and beyond, would be willing to work with us in times to come, to make the region more culturally and politically legible.

Sasanka Perera, Dev Nath Pathak and Ravi Kumar
Dakshin: South Asia Research Group
Department of Sociology
Faculty of Social Sciences
South Asian University
New Delhi

15 March 2019

Beginnings

Against the Nation and Thinking Like South Asians

Sasanka Perera, Dev Nath Pathak and Ravi Kumar

Genesis

Mountains are intriguing and often inspiring places, as are they difficult to reach and leave. It is perhaps in this context that William Blake had once noted, 'great things are done when men and mountains meet.'[1] In that sense, this collection of chapters in the present form has much to do with climbing a mountain, and the vistas of possibilities it indicated both metaphorically and in reality.

According to Christian belief, Jesus Christ delivered his 'Sermon on the Mount' possibly from Mount of Beatitudes located in present-day northern Israel. It is Jesus' longest discourse in the *New Testament* and contains some of Christianity's core teachings. Closer to home in the extended neighbourhood we call South Asia, mountains have been equally important in myth, history and matters of faith. In Bhutan, popular belief holds that Guru Padmasambhava, popularly known as Guru Rinpoche visited the country in the eighth century or so, and defeated evil spirits that were harming the people, and essentially 'cleansed' Bhutan. To do this, he is believed to have initially flown on the back of a tigress to the mountain known as Taktshang Goemba or Tiger's Nest and began his quest by subduing a local demon. In mythological terms, this effectively marks the entry of Buddhism into Bhutan, which decisively impacted the social and cultural evolution of the country. In Sri Lanka, popular belief suggests that *Arahat*

[1] https://www.brainyquote.com/quotes/william_blake_145040 (accessed on 7 March 2019).

Mahinda flew through the air from the general area we now refer to as India with a small delegation of disciples carrying the message of Buddhism from the court of Emperor Asoka and arrived at the mountain known as Mihintale, close to the ancient Sri Lankan capital, Anuradhapura. Sri Lanka's history too changed radically in cultural and political terms with the introduction of Buddhism. Hindu mythology constantly refers to Mount Meru as do Jain and Buddhist mythic references. Mount Meru, in all these systems of faith, is believed to be the centre of physical, spiritual and metaphysical universes. And there are abounding narratives of similar significance from various parts of the Himalayas dotting the landscape in India, Afghanistan, Nepal, Tibet and beyond. In all these narratives, embedded deeply in mythology, mountains generate notions of faith, versions of history, the genesis of cultural domains, and above all, the travel of culturally coded ideas.

This is the reason why poets have ruminated on and about mountains in many ways, including admission of an effortless flow of mind in the face of mountains. If Blake attributed the dawn of grand ideas to mountains, Sachchidananda Vatsyayan Agyeya, the Hindi poet wrote, 'as my horse gallops ahead, leaving marks behind; beholding riverine orbiting around the hills and peaks, I move ahead as though yet another thing in the larger picture.'[2]

In this context, perhaps this collection of essays would not have found its genesis if not for a mountain and more specifically, Tiger's Nest once sanctified by Guru Rinpoche. In February 2018 (20 February to 24 February 2018), we had travelled to Thimphu, Bhutan, at the invitation of colleagues from Sherubtse College, Royal University of Bhutan, to help revise their syllabi in political science and sociology. This exercise was well within the mandate of the South Asian University with its slogan of 'knowledge without borders' and, more importantly, squarely embedded within our own ideology pertaining to how South Asia should be seen and experienced. At the end of the training, one of the Bhutanese colleagues, Leki Sangay,

---

[2] Sachchidananda Vatsyayan Agyeya: http://kavitakosh.org (accessed on 14 December 2018). Translated from Hindi by Dev Nath Pathak.

volunteered to take us to Tiger's Nest. It was a tough trek for us, unused to the climatic conditions in the area as well as the steep ascent and descent. But, it was done. In the slowness of the trek and the many rest stops and accompanying conversations, preliminary ideas for two books had emerged! One was a reflection on higher education in South Asia, which would not only survey the landscape of formal knowledge production and learning in the region but would also attempt to theorise on how to explain this landscape and its intrigues. The other was a possible collection of chapters we had written at different times that deal with the idea of South Asia. It is this latter idea that has now become the present volume. We have reworked many lectures we had delivered at different places, restructured academic papers written earlier and essays specifically written for popular outlets as well as notes we had written for ourselves for future reflection. All these have been re-edited and restructured keeping in mind the politics of ideas we have envisaged for the present volume.

Academic Knowledge beyond Academia

We fully agree and know well from experience that the circulation of academic writing is limited. But that is in the very nature of the academic enterprise globally. What we usually write is not meant for popular or mass consumption. But as a group of people, we are interested in scholarly knowledge as a form of politics, as a source of power and as a means of social and political transformation, as well. In this context, we have believed for a considerable time such knowledge needs to shed its ivory tower sensibility at certain times, it should transgress beyond the limited and limiting ramparts of academia and enter the broader discursive spaces of the society at large. This does not mean that all academic knowledge could be made available for unrestricted mass consumption. In other words, it does not mean that a journalistic piece and an academic reflection could be forcefully made to read the same. Instead, we believe it to be self-evident that specific elements of knowledge we produce formally must necessarily travel to domains inhabited by enlightened people who may not be academics, but might agree with what we have to say, on the basis of our own politics of knowledge. Or, they might also not agree with us. Nevertheless, we hope such knowledge would form a basis for conversations. However, in making this shift, we are also mindful of a potential 'unbearable lightness' of things, a populist compromise on depth and breadth of an argument or the comprehensive nature of an observation we might have to make. We tend to enlighten our lightness with critical insights, conceptual and theoretical formulations that we hope are more readable, with some help from canons of social sciences in the background. This enlightened lightness, we hope, is not unbearable, overly simplistic and an undue compromise on the rigor of reasoning. The chapters in the volume are, at the same time, invitations for engagements with larger theoretical-political questions that have historical origins, which continue to affect contemporary conditions.

In this context, we know that by and large, most discussions on South Asia so far have been limited to policy or conventional academic discourses and have seldom touched the cultural and political domains beyond these. This is one reason why a more inclusive idea of South Asia as an approach to politics or research and way of thinking has not had much success at the popular level beyond academic circles. Kanak Mani Dixit explains this situation in his book, *The South Asian Sensibility*[3] where he notes, 'it is imperative to think of regionalism as going beyond conference rooms and airport lounges' so that regionalism might ignite 'the imagination of the masses rather than only well-meaning elites'.[4] It is in this context that S.D. Muni's observation, 'South Asia as a geo-political entity and concept has constantly been evolving and re-imagining itself',[5] makes sense. That is, the possibilities the region offers cannot be seen as something static and it is endlessly interpretable. In our present effort, we hope to join Dixit as well as other predecessors, such as Ashis

[3] Kanak Mani Dixit, ed., 2012, *The South Asian Sensibility: A Himal Reader*, New Delhi, SAGE Publications.

[4] Dixit, 'Introduction,' in *The South Asian Sensibility*, pp. xiv–xv.

[5] S.D. Muni, 'Reimagining South Asia: An Intellectual Agenda for the Next Generation of South Asians,' *Contributions to Contemporary Knowledge Lecture*, 2014, p. 9, New Delhi, Faculty of Social Sciences, South Asian University.

Nandy, Sugata Bose, Imtiaz Ahmed, Shiv Vishwanathan, S.D. Muni and so on, in doing precisely this. But as far as we are concerned, this is merely a preliminary step towards making our writing and thinking more accessible not simply among fellow academics with an interest in the region, but more so among enlightened people who may be based in art studios, colleges, schools, corporate offices, stakeholders in the culture industry, publishing houses, diplomatic circles and so on. Our academic background is not something we are willing to camouflage or shed and cannot see any reason to do so. At the same time, we are convinced that very background can more sensibly inform what we are trying to do here, somewhat differently. As a result, many of the chapters in this collection are more simply written and relatively shorter than our regular work. That is why we do not shy away from utilising in these chapters poems, creative prose, fiction and other cultural texts vis-à-vis cinema, theatre, music and so on. When the intention is to drive an argument of academic nature to the wider readership, the submission cannot afford to be bound to what is considered 'empirical' in social scientific orthodoxy. In these chapters, the empirical and the non-empirical seamlessly coalesce to accomplish a dual hermeneutic goal—explanation and an understanding. Likewise, the art of reasoning and polemic also unfold together without hiccups about the legitimacy of this cocktail. We tend to share a basic disposition with Karl Popper, and we do not concern ourselves too much about the types of sources that inform us. Instead, we invite our readers to falsify us. Through these essays, we understand, and we persuade our readers to see the merit of our understanding, if any. Similarly, any profundity in these essays would stem from our keenness to straddle many worlds, primarily, academic and non-academic.

All of us have also intervened and commented on matters of importance to us in public forums beyond our academic work at different times in our individual careers. In that sense, the present effort as a method is not new to us. What is new is that we have collated some of our recent writings and lectures so far presented in disparate places into a single collection. In these essays, we have opted to explore South Asia through music, film, violence, pedagogy, travel, art, myth and ideas more clearly located in the messy and often indefinable domain such as culture. That is, we have pushed the conventional ways in which ideas of regionalism are studied in our universities, in disciplines that vary from sociology and social anthropology at one end to international relations and political science at the other end. We are sure our colleagues in more established departments of sociology or universities more generally would be horrified at this approach and would pose that perennial question often posed to irreverent practitioners within the discipline: *This is not sociology! How is your work sociological?* For them, our answer is a simple counter-question: Why is this not sociological? After all, we are dealing with society, politics, art, culture and so on in the extended area we call South Asia. These are products of human interaction, which essentially make them relevant to sociological inquiry. The fact that some domains of knowledge become 'sociological' such as caste, class and gender in the case of South Asia and other domains such as art, music and film somehow have to be studied beyond sociology makes no intellectual sense to us. It is a reflection of the intellectual regression of the region's formal sociological enterprise. Besides, we are amply sociological in another sense. These essays are deeply informed by sociological and anthropological canons, as are they by many other disciplinary sources. In many instances, this reality comes through in these essays, but we seldom waste our energy on, what might well be a conservative-obsessive-disciplinary disorder.

Politics of Knowledge

Everything we have presented is informed by our research, thinking as well as our sense of 'politics' broadly defined. We take it as axiomatic that in an effort like this, the clinical objectivity of sociology as well as the empiricist rationale of social research needs self-conscious reassessment. It is not that we would insist myth is considered empirical fact or that a figment of imagination be considered grounded theory. However, in this intervention, our readings, our thinking, our formal research as well as what we see, hear and smell as individuals in our travels and quotidian existence would also inform what we have to say. History as much as present-day politics inform our ideas. We do not fear utopias and instead embrace them at a time dreams are in short supply and might be considered hallucinations. In other words, biography as well as research and a particular kind of idealism, have pushed us in the direction we have taken. These essays are a testimonial to the larger intellectual objective of bursting the 'safe' territory of academia open for much needed risk-taking, a kind of out-of-the-box thinking. While the worshippers at the altars in the established ivory towers may deem something hazardous about what we have done, we consider it essentially an ideal act to be performed, frequently and feverishly, in social science literature. In short, one must be truly angry with issues, genuinely in love with things, passionately affected by matters, and yet writing about them as cogently as possible. Is this not what Bertrand Russell envisaged to be the hallmarks of good writing? No, we have not achieved it in fulsome. We don't have sufficient arrogance to present this book as an ideal instance of the kind Russell celebrated. But the essays in this book might often remind one of Russell's ridicule about the problem of writing in sociology. He says that sociologists might write like the following:

> Human beings are completely exempt from undesirable behaviour-patterns only when certain prerequisites, not satisfied except in a small percentage of actual cases, have, through some fortuitous concourse of favourable circumstances, whether congenital or environmental, chanced to combine in producing an individual in whom many factors deviate from the norm in a socially advantageous manner.[6]

This whole humbug can be simply put, without a care for political correctness, as Russell does in the following observation:

> All men are scoundrels, or at any rate almost all. The men who are not must have had unusual luck, both in their birth and in their upbringing.[7]

At times, through acrimonious polemic laced with instance-based reasoning, the chapters in this book call a scoundrel a scoundrel, and at times let loose the rawness of energy, emotion and intellect.

---

[6] Bertrand Russell, 2009, *The Basic Writings of Bertrand Russell*, edited by Robert E. Egner and Lester E. Denonn, with an introduction by John G. Slater, London and New York, Routledge.

[7] Russell, *The Basic Writings of Bertrand Russell*, p. 35.

Why 'Against the Nation'?

The title we have given to this collection, *Against the Nation: Thinking Like South Asians* might also lead to some anxiety in the general climate of fearing 'others' and populist sentiments of 'anti-nationalism' and being 'unpatriotic' that have become a part of the political landscape in South Asia. Any criticism of any nation is instantly, and cheaply, dubbed anti-national or unpatriotic. It may range from the sublime to the ridiculous, from the sacred to the mundane and from the important to the banal. For example, if one says one word against the imposed practice of standing up for the national anthem before a movie begins in a theatre, it may be considered anti-national. Likewise, if there is a critical idea about the state of development in the development of the state, it may be thought of as anathema in developmentalist societies. These are extremely superficial notions that call for the submission of citizens' will, people's thinking and electoral subjugation. Our approach to nations in South Asia solicits a more nuanced treatment of patriotism without falling prey to what Tagore warned us in the heydays of cultural–political nationalism. As one of the most erudite poets and thinkers of modern South Asia, Rabindranath Tagore[8] tried to show through metaphors that modern political nationalism warrants us to belong to the unison produced by a mechanical and coercive power loom, whereas culturally there has been an idea of belonging to the hum and rhythm of a handloom.

In our writing, we seek to restore this sense of belonging, to the region and its nations in tune with the handloom. A more organic version of belonging, which does not prevent a critical comprehension of the problematic politics of belonging, is pivotal in our scheme. The gloss, erasure and finesse produced by the power loom of nations could be detrimental to the organic evolution of people's belonging. In short, they give rise to a variety of identity politics foreclosing the possibility of dreaming and enacting those dreams beyond boundaries. While we appreciate the sentiments in favour of a landmass described in poetry

[8] Rabindranath Tagore, 2017, *Nationalism*, London and Delhi, Penguin, p. 9.

and music of a nation, we are wary of the divisive lines deepened by them too. While we may love to hum our individual national anthems, we are anxious of the Machiavellianism behind the impositions engineered by state apparatuses. Though there is no denial of the significance of national flags in the popular conscience, one cannot dismiss the hegemonic emergence and impositions of the same too. The region of South Asia has been a witness to the politics of national flags, acquiring all sizes and spectacular manifestations.

Being aware of all this does not mean a cancellation of the nation, the state and the reality of state apparatuses. There is a discomfort that we encounter while looking at the contemporary politics being almost exclusively defined within the frame of a nation. 'Nation' appears to us in myriad forms in these kinds of politics. However, our perturbation emanates out of the uncritical, blind and violent employment of the term called nation. In contemporary times, it makes much sense to be aware of Tagore's idea that 'nationalism is the training of a whole people for a narrow ideal; and when it gets hold of their minds it is sure to lead them to moral degeneracy and intellectual blindness.'[9] He attributes violence, massacre and conflict to the 'Nation'. We are also aware of debates on the nation grounded in the context of anti-colonial struggles and how it is being debated in light of globalisation debate and the rise of transnational capital. It is the vast body of work around the nation and nationalism that informs our discomfort with it when we posit it vis-à-vis the idea of the region. This is what has led to our discomfort in looking at South Asia as a region defined primarily through the prism and framework of nation states. South Asia is much more than the simplistic relationships between nations. It is rather about connections across people over time. In this sense, we have not attempted to divide our chapters among the nation states in the region. That is, we do not count nations in order to be South Asian. Instead, as we think like South Asians, our ideas usher in nations as well as stories from them when they make sense in relation to what we have to say.

---

[9] Rabindranath Tagore, 2017, *The Complete Works of Rabindranath Tagore*, Delhi, General Press.

We take the nation as a given in this region and beyond. We have not dispensed with our individual citizenship or passports. And we see no reason to do so. But we do believe that the days of pilgrims and travellers like Hiuen Tsang or Fa Hian who traversed the region relatively freely without too many restrictions based on 'national' origins is perhaps a much better ideal. We also believe that a vast and far more interesting world of possibilities awaits us if we can think beyond the limits of the state and the nation and transgress into an area that is broader, more open, more replete with ideas and certainly more exciting in general. This is what many of the pilgrims did before the dawn of the official modernity in South Asia. After all, they were the ones who concretised the idea of sacred geography, connecting the dots from Anuradhapura to Varanasi, Kandy to Kochi, Peshawar to Patiala, Kathmandu to Calicut and Kabul to Calcutta. People moved across the boundaries as small traders, sellers, artisans and craftsmen. And if one can join Ashis Nandy,[10] mercenaries have been more successful in crossing boundaries, even though for the wrong reasons. The sociocultural underworld of South Asia is, therefore, more successful in showing us the way forward. But beyond this underworld, there were missionaries and intellectually hungry wanderers who paved the way. Who can forget Anagarika Dharmapala in this regard who came from Sri Lanka in the latter part of the nineteenth century to re-establish what he considered was the lost Buddhism in India and also to champion his idea of a 'united Buddhist world'. And among many others, Rahul Sankrityayan was renowned for crossing boundaries in various guises, as a monk or as a ready-to-be converted mind or as an eternally keen traveller, a *ghumakkad*, willing to witness the world.

And that is South Asia. That is the sum of the spirit of South Asia that conditions our way of thinking like South Asians.

What we have written is an invitation to experience that possibility.

---

[10] Ashis Nandy, 2007, 'The Idea of South Asia: A Personal Note on the Post-Bandung Blues,' *Inter-Asia Cultural Studies*, Vol. 6, No. 4, pp. 541–545.

I

'Official' Imaginings of South Asia and Its Contradictions

1

SAARC Setbacks and Thinking beyond the Boundaries of Its Nation States[1]

Ravi Kumar and Sasanka Perera

In September 2016, four member states, namely Afghanistan, Bangladesh and Bhutan led by India withdrew from the South Asian Association for Regional Cooperation (SAARC) Summit that was to be held in Islamabad in the backdrop of an attack on an Indian army base in Uri in Indian-administered Kashmir, that was blamed on Pakistan.[2] This was later followed by withdrawal of Sri Lanka and the Maldives.[3] This mass boycott effectively scuttled the meeting as SAARC's fundamental principles mandate that all member states must agree to hold a meeting. At one end, this was a diplomatic victory for India's foreign policy while it was a disaster for the foreign policy of Pakistan, as it appeared completely isolated within SAARC. This has raised several important questions that range from the continued existence and overall usefulness of the regional grouping to the foundational concern of how to work out issues of regional cooperation. In this context, the idea of cooperation has focused on relationships based on territorial identities and geophysical spaces marked by militarised borders that have come to typify the general and popular conceptions of what is meant by nation states.

---

[1] An earlier shorter version of this chapter under the title 'As SAARC Faces Unprecedented Setback, Time to Rethink the Rigid Boundaries of Its Nation States' was published in *The Wire* on 7 October 2017. The authors would like to thank *The Wire* for its consent for republishing this chapter.

[2] For more information, please visit: https://www.huffingtonpost.in/2016/09/28/after-india-bangladesh-and-bhutan-withdraw-from-saarc-summit-in_a_21480662/ (accessed on 1 March 2018) and https://edition.cnn.com/2016/09/18/asia/india-kashmir-attack/index.html (accessed on 3 June 2018).

[3] https://www.indiatoday.in/world/story/saarc-summit-maldives-joins-india-pakistan-isolation-complete-344244-2016-10-01 (accessed on 3 June 2018).

This has allowed politics and economics of nation states to become the most significant dimension of the hegemonic discourses of 'regional cooperation'. That is, the nation remains the core point of departure and the final point of arrival in all thinking on collective matters, that hardly leaves any tangible space for a multilateral entity based on collective and common interests to work in any real sense. In this process, it loses track of the actual sites inhabited by people, which are the messy cultural and emotional spaces beyond the seeming clinically assigned to these territorial boundaries. This has become evident in the way states have to work through their own formal bureaucratic mechanisms, while the initiatives of the people and the imagination of scholars and creative people of the region have often been very different and more inclusive than that of the state.

In general, these non-hegemonic approaches have not been recognised at the level of formal statecraft and diplomacy. The obvious disconnect between the people and the nation is reflected in the constitutive character of SAARC itself.

In these general circumstances, it is important to see the disconnect between the people and the nation in the context of regional politics. It is the 'nation' (the bureaucracies, ministries and political players with power) that interacts with the others, and the idea of regional cooperation is framed only through the idioms in which they converse and in the initiatives they plan.

Most of these interactions—be they bilateral linkages or multilateral forums like SAARC—clearly indicate the inability of nation states in the region to transgress their rigid boundaries dictated by simplistic notions of sovereignty.

They do not debate the format of conversations that could take place among the different constituencies of South Asia, which would allow cooperation to become a less strenuous reality. To bring such considerations into the centre-stage of regional politics as well as the populist politics of nation states themselves necessitates a certain self-conscious dilution of the rigidity in the identities of nation states for the greater good of the collective.

It was in such a situation that an entity like the European Union became a reality despite its many fallacies and more recent ruptures as indicative of Brexit. States have their own structured internal and external political necessities, which may not concur with certain manifestations of the collective consciousness of the people who inhabit these countries.

The Sri Lankan Buddhist pilgrims who annually flock to Buddhist sites all over India, hardly interact with the nation state India, except at points of entry and exit at the airports—and a few places in between—due to mundane necessities, that are often negotiated by 'experts'. Some of these necessities are urged by consumerist tendencies to buy a few saris and other souvenirs, that too from selected stores in places like Bodh Gaya and Varanasi that are often facilitated by merchants who speak a smattering of Sinhala and sometimes also carry their store names in the same language to create a comfort zone for these pilgrims so that they can easily buy their non-essential wares. But in their travels in search of the places believed to have been sanctified by the Buddha himself, they traverse through a mythic and historic landscape that they see as Dambadiva (from the Sanskrit Jambudvipa) and not really India. In this process, they visit Rajagaha Nuwara and instead of Rajgir, Baranesa instead of Varanasi, Buddha Gayawa instead of Bodh Gaya, Kapilavasthu instead of Patna and so on. That is, what they see and consume mostly refer to the distant past than contemporary times.

Similarly, Hindu travellers who go to Sri Lanka to visit sites believed to have been associated with the story of Rama and Sita in the *Ramayana*, hardly experience Sri Lanka, the post-colonial nation state. Instead, they embed themselves in an ancient land of multiple meanings often lost to most local residents as they travel to local places such as Seetha Eliya and Rawana Ella believed to be places associated with the narratives of *Ramayana*. Their interactions with contemporary Lanka is as marginal as is the situation with Buddhist travellers to India.

In both cases, what these pilgrims do as they travel in search of historical and mythological pasts motivated by faith is to draw on the ground a complex cartography of the past layered with meanings which has no reference to the kind of borders and ruptures in travel associated with contemporary times. Though this cartography drawn on the ground emanates from beliefs inherited from the past, the travel itself is actually done very much in the present even though the gaze of nation states hardly befall travellers except at the margins of travel marked by issues of visas and so forth, which are routinely dealt with. But these kinds of possibilities that are offered by culture and recollections of the ancient past and mythological memories hardly form any serious bases for thinking about regional cooperation today. The mere suggestion itself might well be scoffed at as naïve imaginings of idealistic people with 'no relevance to policy'.

Hence, in situations of this kind where broad-based conversations have been absent, and where it is all too common to assume a few terrorists as representatives of entire nations, crises and distrust between nations can easily become a hallmark of interstate interactions that determine the futures and mindsets of entire generations.

Unfortunately, such negative possibilities also have popular currency in difficult times. This mistake persists because the simplistic instrumentalism of state-led cooperation does not give priority to the popular—their sense of belonging or their actual life situations. Rather, in a Debordian sense, 'everything that was directly lived, has receded into a representation', and the states seem to have worked hard to establish what Guy Debord called a 'pseudo-world' by presenting life as a spectacle, which 'is a concrete inversion of life, an autonomous movement of the non living.'[4]

Diplomatic moves, regular foreign relation measures, or the possible militarisation of some of these activities, are those spectacles that so succinctly transform actual human relations into unreal spectacles and performances of power with considerable popular appeal. Within this collective of spectacles and performances, ideas and possibilities of any real regional cooperation often get trapped and dismantled.

The consequences of this instrumentalisation of everyday life indicate the eclipsing of a great history from collective memory, the diminishing of massive possibilities of working with culture across borders and an important derailing of a collective counter-culture of solidarity. Irrespective of contemporary political spin, the reality of the region is not the persistence of violence, conflict and nationalist frenzy.

---

[4] https://genius.com/Guy-debord-the-society-of-the-spectacle-chapter-1-the-culmination-of-separation-annotated (accessed on 3 June 2018).

It is due to the negatively spectacular manifestation of it on many occasions in recent times, that the unreal and historical anomalies have become the overwhelming reality.

Under such circumstances, one often wonders if the connections between these nations can only be forged through instrumentalist mechanisms alone that aim to build formalised, ritualistic and bureaucratically understood bridges. It is our suggestion that in these kinds of situations, it is much better to be creative and think out of the box. For instance, why not invoke the spirit of Nazrul Islam who was writing 'Shyama Sangeet', songs in praise of Kali, and for the proletariat of the region as well when he composed *Sarbahara*? His Muslim identity had nothing to do with his poetry as he composed 'Shyama Sangeet' while his later identity as a Bangladeshi (after 1971) had nothing to do with his composition of *Sarbahara*. In both instances, he freely transgressed parochial identities of religion and nationality and opted to embrace broader cultural and political possibilities. But he would die in 1976, five years after Bangladesh was created as a man extremely angry and aghast at the violence and religious sectarianism devouring the region. Any culturally sensible regional cooperation would have to bring into conversation Faiz Ahmed Faiz, who would stir masses across borders through his poetry of love and revolution. Despite his national identity as a Pakistani, the sense and sensibility of his poems were not restricted to the geographic or cultural areas within the borders of that country. It is in his spirit of discomfort at the larger socio-economic milieu of oppression and deprivation that he would compose in '*Intessab*' (dedication) or would express his angst in a conversation with his beloved in, '*Mujh se pehli si muhabbat mere mehboob na maang*' (Oh my love don't ask me for the love I once gave you).

Similarly, the conversations between people across borders will also have to speak in a language that Sahir Ludhianvi was making use of when he condemned war in his beautiful poem 'Parchhaiyan'. Resurrecting more sensible older conversations which seamlessly and simultaneously criss-crossed geographic, national and cultural borders of the region and created new avenues of expression in the arts, poetry and other expressions of popular feelings, will have to constitute a more historically and culturally rooted sense of regional consciousness.

This would need to counter the often hollow and flippant mantra-like articulation of 'regional consciousness' and 'South Asian sensibility' that we often hear from forums of nation states as well as from SAARC. These are mere utterances without any sense of feeling or deeper meaning rooted in a clear historical understanding of our region. Any 'consciousness', if imposed as a mere political slogan, would cease to be a consciousness except in the sense of being unreal, hyper-real or simply nonsensical.

SAARC has created institutions, which can—in an ideal world—become effective in initiating the processes of forging a more organic and critical understanding of the idea of regional cooperation. In theory, the SAARC Cultural Centre in Colombo is one such institution, and the South Asian University in New Delhi is another. Both, again in theory, have significant possibilities to initiate conversations across borders between intellectuals, cultural producers, civil society groups and citizens in their formative years (students). In fact, this is what South Asian University's motto 'Knowledge across Borders' boldly proclaims.

But this would be possible only if these institutions can first unlearn how to think like nation states while recreating rituals of statecraft in the most colourless and uncreative fashion. So despite its potential, SAARC Cultural Centre works like an amalgamation of state bureaucracies, which thereby stifles the outcome of its potentially important work. In comparison, the South Asian University, in its knowledge production and student induction programmes, works independently, and offers far better results, though by no means anywhere near perfect.

Nations consisting of people in flesh and blood would forge a better understanding among themselves on the basis of experience only when there is an organic process of interaction binding them. But today, by and large, nations in our region have forgotten their own people. They get subsumed within the political compulsions of the nation and become faceless, nameless statistics. They lose their voice and their ability to converse.

In these general circumstances, there is an immediate need to begin conversations as militarisation and nation-centric politics will not work through these moments of anger and angst, particularly if regional cooperation is the preeminent ideal. We need to imagine South Asia differently in a new framework with a sense of hope and aspiration. As Ernst Bloch has noted, 'hope means venturing beyond'.[5] But venturing 'beyond' and looking for 'hope' is not something that the nation states in our region or SAARC could possibly do as clearly indicated in their own established track records. It is an endeavour that lies beyond these rigid and unimaginative structures. It was in such a context that Ashis Nandy once said, 'the more the scholars, artists and writers talk of the common heritage of the region, the more the functionaries in the region nervously eye their neighbours as enemies planning to wipe out their distinctive identities.'[6]

It is precisely this sense of self-conscious and deliberate subversiveness in the acts of reasonable people that is necessary to rediscover a more humane and politically sensible South Asia.

[5] https://www.marxists.org/archive/bloch/hope/introduction.htm (accessed on 3 June 2018).

[6] https://www.tandfonline.com/doi/abs/10.1080/14649370500316828?src=recsys&journalCode=riac20 (accessed on 3 June 2018).

2

Seeing Like South Asians

Moving beyond Narrow National Frames

Ravi Kumar and Sasanka Perera

In *The Hindu* of 23 February 2018, Shiv Visvanathan wrote an extremely optimistic and critical essay on how we should talk like South Asians.[1] His angst was most evident in placing in context how India has failed as a large state in its role in the region. According to him, 'India needs to see South Asia as a new imaginary if the idea of India and Indian foreign policy is to succeed.'[2] He is concerned with how India has been acting in the region through its 'obsession with Pakistan and China', that 'makes us [India] indifferent to other countries in the neighbourhood. South Asia as a place, as a bubbling culture of diversity, gets converted to space or at the most to turf or territory.'[3] Obviously, one may critique Visvanathan's foundational argument, which suggests that the anchoring of the idea of South Asia always rested on India. That process, however, did not create space for an agency for other states to play a creative role in the political and cultural making of South Asia in the present and the recent past. To put it more bluntly, even in Visvanathan's more accommodating if the paternalistic prescription for India in the region, there is no sense of equality in political or cultural action among the peers which makes the nation states of the region. In this regard, he offers nothing different for the future. The expectation of leadership from India and India

[1] http://www.thehindu.com/opinion/lead/talk-like-a-south-asian/article22828352.ece (accessed on 24 February 2018).

[2] http://www.thehindu.com/opinion/lead/talk-like-a-south-asian/article22828352.ece (accessed on 24 February 2018).

[3] http://www.thehindu.com/opinion/lead/talk-like-a-south-asian/article22828352.ece (accessed on 24 February 2018).

alone is a problem because it becomes a discourse of hegemony, and in this case, hegemony camouflaged with an outer layer of paternalistic accommodation, which in the present moment is already evident in the region's statecraft. Until the anticipation of the sole leadership role from India for all things South Asian is self-consciously stopped and a more nuanced way of imagining the region is worked out, what is left is an imagination of South Asia through a paternalistic framework.

Whatever Visvanathan's reasons are for imagining South Asia through the prism of India, he offers much sense as well. On the day his essay was published in *The Hindu*, which among other things presented the South Asian University initiated by South Asian Association for Regional Cooperation (SAARC) as a failed experiment, four colleagues from the University's Faculty of Social Sciences were conducting a workshop in Thimpu for colleagues from Sherubtse College of Royal University of Bhutan trying to revise some of their syllabi in the Sociology and Political Science teaching programme through a South Asian prism. Clearly, Visvanathan's expectations of South Asian University had been belied in the way it has progressed beyond its initial vision, but it has not necessarily completely died. He laments at its failure to develop a South Asian 'theory of culture and knowledge'. He says,

> One of the most exciting of these regional ideas was the creation of the South Asian University (SAU), with a faculty from all South Asian countries. While we have the faculty, what we lack is a South Asian theory of culture and knowledge, which should anchor this imagination. SAU looks like any other university, part of the embassy set in South Delhi. It needs a manifesto, which makes South Asia central to its imagination. Such a manifesto must transform ecology and culture into a theory of South Asian diversity and difference. The borderland, the frontier, the island, the riverine communities have to anchor a local imagination which diversifies South Asia as a region.[4]

He is absolutely correct when he argues for a manifesto that makes 'South Asia central to its imagination'. He prompts us to look for reasons why South Asian University does not have such a manifesto or in the very

---

[4] http://www.thehindu.com/opinion/lead/talk-like-a-south-asian/article22828352.ece (accessed on 24 February 2018).

least a programme of work that broadly follows its own mandate to create 'knowledge without borders' or what the university's public rhetoric refers to as a sense of 'South Asian consciousness'. True, 50 per cent of the university's students come from South Asian countries other than India while the rest come from India. Teachers and administrators, however, overwhelmingly come from India bringing with them very specific attitudes and work ethics, which do not necessarily jell with the anticipated ideals of South Asian inclusiveness. One cannot simplistically expect to herd such a group of people into a single concrete building, and expect them to somehow churn out a South Asian consciousness or a theory of knowledge and culture merely because the university's formal nomenclature carries the words 'South Asian'. But recruitment from diverse ethno-national sources as a way of creating a sense of South Asian belonging also needs to be qualified. It is true that the university's South Asian distribution among faculty is abysmal. But this is not due to a lack of trying. Often, what has been clear in interviews is that qualified individuals hardy apply for positions from outside of India or those very few who do apply do not fulfil basic requirements. In such a situation, creating a quota system for faculty would be the wrong path to take as it will end up merely creating a sense of political tokenism based on citizenship rather than quality in education or a 'theory of South Asian diversity and difference' as suggested by Visvanathan.

On the other hand, it is not that there have not been any efforts at trying to engage with the questions Visvanathan raises. Rather, such efforts have not been effective because in most cases they have been tokenist, rhetorical or reductionally representational as even a cursory look at the curriculum, pedagogy, admission and residential policies of the university would reveal. While we readily admit that South Asian University has not consciously dealt with the need to develop a South Asian theory of culture and knowledge, Visvanathan's levelling of complexities involved would imply an ignorance of the efforts that some individual academics and limited collectives of scholars within the university have been making though as a minuscule community of anxiety-ridden social scientists. These efforts, in general, have manifested in terms of research or writings that have become possible due to individual authors' location within the specificity of this university. There is a reason why a number of colleagues at the Faculty of Social Sciences, have been trying to argue for 'another' notion of South Asia, which should take into account issues of culture, history and popular religion in understating the region, rather than the hackneyed cartographic and geopolitical route taken by conventional Political Science and International Relations scholarship as well as diplomatic practice. One example of where this effort is self-evident is the collection of essays, *Another South Asia!*, edited by Dev Nath Pathak.[5] Similar attempts have also been made to explore how culture and political action in South Asia might be understood within the prism of performative politics as argued in the book, *Culture and Politics in South Asia: Performative Communication* edited by Dev Nath Pathak and Sasanka Perera.[6] Others have attempted to craft a South Asian understanding of issues related to gender, conflict and security as suggested in the essay, 'Gender, Conflict and Security: Perspectives from South Asia' by Shweta Singh.[7]

These are indeed the first disparate steps towards the kind of South Asian theory of culture and knowledge that Visvanathan refers to as well as a self-conscious attempt to move beyond the state-centric imagination of the region. But beyond these exceptions of individuals within the university, hardly any serious and concerted academic efforts have been undertaken by the university to transcend the statist notion of South Asia, which we had discussed in *The Wire* some time ago.[8] Any academic community whether in South Asian University or elsewhere, for this reason, falls prey to their own particular versions of jingoistic nationalist orientations, which they would bring to their work places from their individual habitus. But then, when it comes to SAU, this is hardly surprising when the nation states that fund the university and many of its decision makers have not made a newer and more inclusive imagination of the region a mandatory prerequisite in the way the university works, in

[5] http://www.primusbooks.com/showbookdetail.asp?bookid=179 (accessed on 24 February 2018).

[6] https://books.google.co.in/books/about/Culture_and_Politics_in_South_Asia.html?id=FfYtDwAAQBAJ&redir_esc=y (accessed on 24 February 2018).

[7] http://journals.sagepub.com/doi/full/10.1177/2347797017710560 (accessed on 24 February 2018).

[8] https://thewire.in/author/ravi-kumar-and-sasanka-perera/ (accessed on 24 February 2018).

the way it recruits faculty and staff or in the ways in which it is expected to undertake its outreach work in the worlds beyond Delhi. Despite all this, however, at least a few faculty members have joined the university with the kind of vision that Visvanathan argues for. They did not come to SAU merely for the higher salaries and blue number plates that would make them—albeit superficially—an extension of Chanakyapuri's embassy coterie. Instead, they came because they wanted to explore the possibilities of developing an episteme that goes beyond the national boundaries, and to become South Asian, but without being parochially regionalistic. Unfortunately, however, this is more the exception than the norm.

Disoriented Intellectual Formation

To a certain extent, one has to accept that the imagination of the university has been subdued by the narrow nationalist visions of each nation state, which contributes funds to it and dictates its policies. This is the result of a grand dream cherished by a group of sensible South Asian intellectuals becoming a colourless intergovernmental project understood not within intellectual or nuanced political terms, but in reductionist bureaucratic terms. As a result, organisationally, South Asian University hardly goes beyond the way the national universities work and function in the region. But beyond this serious structural limitation, the university's relative inability to live up to what its name means has much to do with the intellectual orientation of its faculty as well. There can be two ways to be South Asian:

1. The easier approach is the conventional and tokenist way within which intellectuals from different nation states are expected to sit together in a department with each other dealing with their own nation and national questions and issues. One can say this is how SAARC tries to be South Asian within its institutional arrangements.

2. The second approach suggests that scholars from different national locations come together to brainstorm on how they can transcend both disciplinary and national borders in their academic work by looking at issues and subjects of research. The same is true of administratively running the place as well.

Unfortunately, by and large, within the university, the notion of South Asia has been restricted to the first approach historically. National boundaries become the starting point as well as the end-point. This may not happen only due to nationalist jingoism; but it also happens because historically, most academics in the region have been narrow, blind and conservative in their intellectual formations.

To make it clearer, a student of sociology from Jawaharlal Nehru University or Delhi University hardly has any idea of what transpires in the sociologies of Bangladesh, Nepal or Sri Lanka. And students of sociology in Universities of Dhaka or Colombo hardly have any notion of the sociologies of India or Afghanistan. In general, neither do their teachers. The academic training and intellectual formation of faculty members who come to SAU have also been inevitably created via such a narrow methodology. This is also evident in the exoticised notion of South Asia in the western intellectual tradition. While there would be intellectuals working on some of the countries in South Asia, it is (*a*) limited to national frameworks and (*b*) the idea of South Asia often gets restricted to India only. A random survey of approximately 50 book titles published up to 2014 with the word South Asia in their titles (see Figure 2.1) reveals the obvious India-centric dominance in the prevailing intellectual imagination. It is clear that there is a much greater focus on India than on the rest of South Asia.

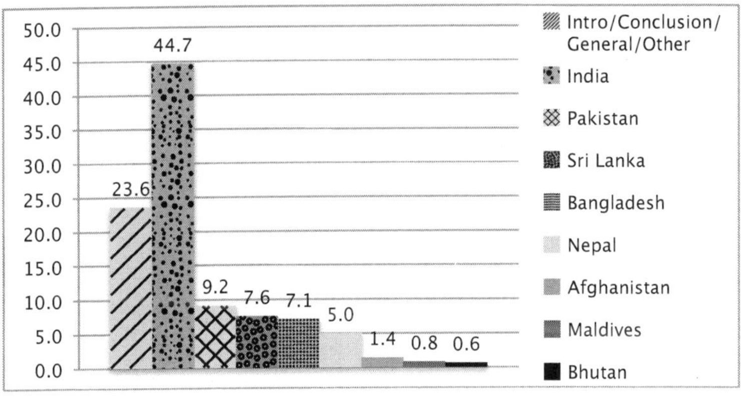

Figure 2.1: Country Focus of Books on 'South Asia'
Source: Authors.

It is precisely this same limitation with regard to the diminishing of South Asia in preference to India specifically within the excellent publication series, 'South Asia Across Disciplines' hosted by three US-based university presses that Sasanka Perera draws attention to in his chapter, '"South Asia" as an Idea and a Problem of Modernity' later in this collection. This is not about banishing India from intellectual considerations in South Asia, which in itself would be a ludicrous notion. But, is it simply impossible, to get to 'know' about the rest of the region in terms of knowledge that is regularly produced? The answer to this question obviously is, 'that it is entirely possible'. But to get there, one needs to advance this idea not from positions of power or national interests, but from positions of ideology and passion, anchored to the necessity of a body of knowledge rooted within the region about its cultural and sociopolitical pluralities.

Classrooms and Cafeterias: Challenges and Making of South Asian Epistemology

In an ideal sense, South Asian University should provide a unique opportunity to overcome the narrowness of being South Asian within the dominant state-centric cartographic understanding. Classrooms filled with students from different countries provide a way to realise how narrow we have been in our intellectual formations and outlook. Teaching social movements, stratification, political economy of the region, art and social transformation or social history in the context of Afghanistan, Nepal and Bangladesh emphasise how one can imagine the political economy of identity-formation, legal epistemologies, politics of art or working of economies in the region. Unfortunately, however, we have been either too slow or unaware of the need to go about working on such dimensions even within classrooms that could have produced an epistemology that challenges the narrowness of national knowledge. Though South Asian University's classrooms provide such possibilities, the obvious intellectual failure in general to do that implies a colonisation of knowledge rigidly bound to national boundaries and creating hegemonies of the kind that Figure 2.1 represents. Also precisely due to this intellectual failure, the experimental space these classrooms offer is routinely missed by teachers in preference to something easier and ordinary, and in the process would make these classrooms filled with potential seem like any other university space in the region where neither creativity nor other potentials are realised. Sadly, the need to transcend this parochialism is not something that students also demand except in a very few and rare exceptional moments.

Being creative is essential to developing any new framework or epistemology, and these also emanate from the way both our personal and professional lives are shaped. We have already shown how our academic lives can lead to a restricted and narrow intellectual horizon. On the other hand, it has also been amply proven how everyday life could have intrinsic relations that might help in imagining a new South Asia. Food, for instance, becomes an important part of such an exercise. It is impregnated with potential. As Eagleton has noted, 'if there is one sure thing about food, it is that it is never just food', and as a result, 'like the post-structuralist text, food is endlessly interpretable, as a gift, threat, poison, recompense, barter, seduction, solidarity, suffocation.'[9] Food is much more than this too. But like many other things, colleagues, administrators as well as students have missed the possibilities of food in a place like South Asian University which Eagleton's perennial commonsense alludes to. The nature of our food habits, tastes and the way food is cooked are more than our personal choices. They are also reflections of our openness or closed mind-set in accepting the habits of others. A South Asian journey of food reveals how people, habits and ideas have travelled over a period of time and how some foods have re-invented themselves in new places after travelling from another place. A university like SAU is an apt example of how this can become a topic of conversation about societies and histories, not just in classrooms, but also in the canteens in terms of what kind of food is available. In fact, the rules that govern the operation of SAU's two eateries have at least partially taken this possibility into account when they refer to the necessity

---

[9] https://www.timeshighereducation.com/features/edible-ecriture/104281.article (accessed on 2 June 2018).

of making available regional cuisine. But the unchecked practice of offering only the most basic of North Indian cuisine over the last six years has killed this possibility, and the university community, by and large, has come to accept this as the only possible reality.

A cafeteria with different food items transcending geographic and cultural boundaries not only tells us about how we may look at the idea of South Asia, but also how through that avenue we might explore the way national hegemonies of food choices dictate the lives of different nationalities or whether one can have an open conversation about particular societies through food. This is both symbolic and real in knowing the region. After all, there is a complex politics that can be understood by using food as a vehicle of one's individual as well as national and societal sensibilities. Marianne Elisabeth Lien in the book *The Politics of Food* notes,

> What appears to be a carrot or a piece of meat is indeed a product with a history and implications more complex and profound than most of us even want to think about. This gap between what we actually know about the food we eat and what we could potentially know (and even act upon), makes transparency a key issue. Thus, the politics of food is also a politics of silence and exposure, a quest for the power to control what will be declared, what will be the focus of public debate and what will remain unspoken.[10]

But it is heartening to see that a South Asian food festival initially organised by the Department of Sociology as part of one of its student initiatives, *Jatra*, in 2014 amidst considerable opposition from the university administration, has now gone beyond the Department and has become a popular annual student event facilitated by the university itself. In order to develop a South Asian theory of culture and knowledge, one will have to question everything from our own intellectual formations to our readiness to develop transcendental curricula and pedagogies and to rethink our everyday lives, which are being made more and more closed and conservative.

---

[10] Marianne E. Lien and Brigitte Nerlich, eds., 2004, 'The Politics of Food: An Introduction', in *The Politics of Food*, Oxford, Berg, pp. 1–18.

As academics, an essential part of the ideal job is to dream and look forward to newer and adventurous intellectual frontiers. Unfortunately, in contemporary circumstances, many of us are subservient to the states and their agendas when it comes to developing a notion of South Asia itself, where adventures have no place, where free imaginings and dancing with histories are thwarted by citing bureaucratic rules. These complexities have to be understood and thought through seriously to move further as Ernst Bloch notes in *The Principle of Hope*:

> Thinking means venturing beyond. But in such a way that what already exists is not kept under or skated over. Not in its deprivation, let alone in moving out of it. Not in the causes of deprivation, let alone in the first signs of the change which is ripening within it. That is why real venturing beyond never goes into the mere vacuum of an In-Front-of-Us, merely fanatically, merely visualizing abstractions. Instead, it grasps the New as something that is mediated in what exists and is in motion, although to be revealed the New demands the most extreme effort of will. Real venturing beyond knows and activates the tendency which is inherent in history and which proceeds dialectically. Primarily, everybody lives in the future, because they strive, past things only come later, and as yet genuine present is almost never there at all.[11]

[11] https://www.marxists.org/archive/bloch/hope/introduction.htm (accessed on 24 February 2018).

3

The Idea of South Asia

Beyond the Intellectual Dependence on the Statist Perspective

Ravi Kumar

It is said that Hitler wanted to create a *Greater Germanic Reich of the German Nation*. My concern is not so much about the historical veracity of efforts towards achieving this kind of a goal than about the intent to create an empire by 'annexing' modern nation states, leave aside the cultures and differences across huge geographical spaces. The idea of South Asia, in my imagination, does not represent this kind of intent. It is largely an idea that acknowledges the 'differences' and tries to map the 'commonalities' that exist. I also acknowledge that South Asia has been seen in a variety of ways—as a region, a civilisational entity, a modern alliance of nations struggling to have economic relations, and even as a 'consciousness', etc. Even though it would be interesting to see how these commonalities came into existence, this is not what I would explore in this chapter. I am only trying to argue that the geographical space defined through an instrumentalist entity called South Asian Association for Regional Cooperation (SAARC) has possibilities of being conceived as one unit for a variety of purposes. It is also my intention to indicate that the possibilities of a South Asian sensibility must be rooted in the weakening of increasing instrumentalism of nation states. Once this happens, it would be up to the intellectuals to get beyond their disciplinary limitations imposed by the nation states and stop teaching in their classes how great India and its religion has been in creating both South Asia as a space and its cultural terrain. In other words, intellectuals would be required to be free from their parochialism, nationalism and the farcical idea of tolerance.

SAARC-defined South Asia merely remains an instrumentalist convenience in the short term and not a nuanced ideal.

Sadly enough, there are efforts to destroy even the SAARC-driven instrumentalist idea of South Asia. This destruction of the idea emanates from the obstinacy of some states to impose their hegemonic ideology on the other states. With this, the popular will of South Asian people also gets dampened as within some of the states there are internal political dynamics that link religion to national identity and then identifying nations along religious lines. So the internal politics gets reflected in the regional geopolitics. This culminates in the centrality of a xenophobic nationalist project that rests on the rhetoric of superiority of one nation over the other. Recently, there has been a revival of the idea of *Akhand Bharat* riding on the wave of a nationalist frenzy that seeks to establish the hegemony of India. This became clearer when a political leader said: 'The Rashtriya Swayamsevak Sangh (RSS) still believes that one day these parts, which have for historical reasons separated only 60 years ago, will again, through popular goodwill, come together and Akhand Bharat will be created.'[1] And this has taken the form of a well-conceived campaign. If one googles the word *Akhand Bharat*,[2] one would be bombarded by a mesmerising basket of fictional ideas of how certain nation states in South Asia would have to be brought within the umbrella of India. There might be many more such hegemonic imaginings though I will not reflect on these here. I am merely trying to argue that South Asia has the potentiality to become a unit that would have far-reaching sociopolitical and economic bearings even though my interest is not in the kind of hegemonic India-centric imagination that 'Akhand Bharat' represents.

The other chapters in this book clearly show how the instrumentalist visions of the nation state can only impede South Asia to be considered as a unit because their premise is based on the validity of the competing entity of the nation state. If one looks closely at what impedes the

---

1 See https://www.thehindu.com/news/national/akhand-bharat-india-pakistan-bangladesh-will-reunite-one-day-says-ram-madhav/article8031920.ece (accessed on 3 April 2018).

2 *Akhand Bharat* is an exclusivist political concept that literally means 'undivided or un-fractured India'. It assumes that India in the past was a large sociopolitical and cultural entity that spatially subsumed most of present-day South Asia.

emergence of a cohesive and inclusive South Asian unit as a political and sociocultural space, it becomes clear this is largely due to the dynamics of the relationship between states. The states 'assume' the responsibility to represent the masses inhabiting within their territorial boundaries. This jeopardises the possible encounter between people across the region. This existing model is operationalised through instruments that ensure people across physical borders cease to interact. In real terms, these instruments manifest all around us in the form of censorship, stringent or whimsical visa regulations among other things. One may simply ask: What harm would it really do to the nation states if my colleague or any student wants to go across to Pakistan or Sri Lanka from India and talk to somebody or present a paper at some conference or vice versa? I do not see a systemic upheaval taking place due to such an interaction. Besides, such interactions happened as a matter of routine until the Indian Independence or soon thereafter, a useful byproduct of colonialism and the idea of the commonwealth. Indian traders went and set up shop in Sri Lanka and Burma while Sri Lankan traders did the same in Burma, Singapore and Malaysia.[3] The elites among those we refer to as Pakistanis and Sri Lankans today sent their children to colonial schools in Dehradun and elsewhere in present-day India throughout the colonial period. Parsi theatre companies from Bombay casually crossed the Palk Straits and enthralled Sri Lankan audiences in the late nineteenth and early twentieth centuries, thereby also positively impacting the evolution of Sinhala theatre in early twentieth century. Except for long-term friendships that continued across international borders that became more entrenched and militarised over time, no systemic upheaval took place because of these interactions that happened without the mediation or intervention of the nation state.

There are different ways in which people have imagined South Asia as a unit. There are many other examples that go back deep into the region's cultural history that demonstrates how Sufi and Bhakti

[3] One can look at works such as Sunil S. Amrith, June 2009, 'Tamil Diasporas across the Bay of Bengal', *American Historical Review*, Vol. 114, No. 3, pp. 547–572; Ravindra K. Jain, 1970, *South Indians on the Plantation Frontier in Malaya*, New Haven, Yale University Press; S.N. Arseculeratne, 1991, *Sinhalese Immigrants in Malaysia & Singapore, 1860–1990: History Through Recollections*, Colombo, KVG De Silva & Sons.

traditions transcended the boundaries and people across what today appear to be distinct cultures spanning across different countries. These interactions, like the ones outlined previously, took place freely and without the impediments we see in contemporary times. There are scholars trying to outline the ancient linkages between what is now India and Sri Lanka. The *Mahavamsa* would chronicle how Prince Vijaya landed on West Coast Sri Lanka with his followers around fifth-century BC. According to the myth and belief, he is credited with establishing the lineage of present-day Sinhalas.[4] Irrespective of its historical veracity, this implies the connection that existed across this region even in mythic contexts. But *Mahavamsa* itself provides considerable historical information on such interactions in historical times including the bringing of Buddhism to Sri Lanka. One does not even need to go too far down the memory lane to see how mobility across the region was extremely easy. It is in such a context one would see how individuals who wanted to escape from British colonial policing, would move from one place to another in the region.

This kind of mobility diminished drastically when the nation states in their current form came into existence. Ever since colonial times,[5] there have been strands of thought that have maintained that the region should be unified because at some point of time in history the region was 'governed' through one religion, and once other religions came in, a sense of 'separation' led to the later establishment of other nations on the basis of competing religious identities. Conceptualisations such as Hindu India and Nepal, Buddhist Sri Lanka and Muslim Pakistan, Bangladesh, Maldives and Afghanistan emanate from this understanding. This idea has been voiced by leaders of political formations as well as their think tanks in India.

---

[4] Unfortunately and intriguingly, the same example is cited by right-wing activists in India to argue that at one point of time a Hindu king ruled Sri Lanka, and it was taken away from the Hindus subsequently. It is in this context that they argue in favour of re-establishing the 'Akhand Bharat' framework. But as historians such as R.A.L.H. Gunawardana have outlined, the peopling and ethno-religious identity formation in Sri Lanka was far more complex. For a good discussion on these issues including Gunawardena's essay, one can read: Jonathan Spencer, ed., 1990, *Sri Lanka: History and the Roots of Conflict*, London, Routledge.

[5] It is important to emphasise that 'colonialism' for me means British colonialism.

In this context, at this time in the twenty-first century and also in the context of a serious assessment of cultural and political history in the region, the idea of a homogenising trait based on religious dominance or in the name of specific cultural traits becomes antithetical and unpractical while imagining a more nuanced and inclusive South Asia.

So, if difference is so significant, why not allow different nations (made up of their own complex internal cultural and economic politics) to exist as they are? Why should one even imagine an entity like South Asia? One option, of course, is to remain imprisoned within the nation state model. My belief is that historical experience, commonalities in the way people live their lives in this part of the world and ideals of common good for the future suggest that a collective formation such as South Asia offers much more freedom for the region's citizens in terms of ideas, culture, travel and so on. But 'ways of living' is not a literal concept here that is tantamount to everyday rituals of life. It implies the way in which societies, polities, economies and cultures are designed and have altered over a period of time. To concretise this, one needs to understand that homogenisation is a dangerous project not only because it comes at the cost of liberty and freedom, but also because it censors conflicts, contradictions and desires of transcendence (from the given order of things). Therefore, what one needs to acknowledge is that history has placed before us a situation where I, belonging to nation 'A', must hate 'you' because you belong to nation 'B' and vice versa. This happens with differing intentions depending upon the political and economic exigencies of nation states, and more precisely due to the interests of their ruling classes. In this process, history is invented and re-invented. Social and cultural mores get defined and redefined. Everything is reinterpreted to demonstrate how animosities between people of nations 'A' and 'B' have been perennial, and therefore inevitable and a necessary part of the nature of things.

The idea of South Asia therefore, cannot even be looked at in an abstract manner as a relationship between two or more nation states. It has to be located within the history and cultural memories that the people of these nation states share. Some of the contexts have been homogenised, thanks to the insatiable appetite of private capital and its expansionist designs. They have also been homogenised because of the internal class politics and matrix of conflict that are expressed through ethnicity, caste, race and gender. Across this region, there have been many secessionist movements, increasing pauperisation of masses, while gendered violence can also be seen across borders. Radical assertions against the ruling classes and dominant hegemonic interests are also common across the region, whether it is by strands of the militant left such as Maoists and Marxist-Leninist formations in India, Maoists in Nepal or formations such as Janatha Vimukthi Peramuna (JVP) in Sri Lanka and so on. On the other hand, one can also see a commonality in the collapse of traditional anti-systemic movements characterised across these nations. Repression of democratic movements, attacks on the freedom of expression and censorship are becoming the order of the day. Representative democracy is increasingly moving towards a corporatised democracy and many more such tendencies cutting across polity, society and economy can be seen. In fact, the question should be asked whether the definition of South Asia as put forth by SAARC is sufficient, or whether one should move towards Myanmar as well.

This is how South Asia in contemporary times might appear, and in such a situation one often wonders if 'defiance' and 'solidarity' can be the ways in which South Asia can be imagined. There has been some work arguing how a common shared past is an example of how this region could be historically imagined as one unit. But we need to bring to the fore how struggles of the masses, the poetic and artistic creations and their imaginations of a better world have also been a common thread that binds these nations. There have been conversations that take place when the plight of struggling masses of different countries finds expression in the words of Faiz Ahmad Faiz, when he universalises the idea of exploitation and resistance, and says:

Bol, ke lab azaad hai tere;
Bol, zabaan ab tak teri hai,
Tera sutwan jism hai tera—
Bol, ke jaan ab tak teri hai.

Dekh ke aahangar ki dukaan mein
Tund hai shu'le, surkh hai aahan,
Khulne-lage quflon ke dahane,
Phaila hare k zanjeer ka daaman.
Bol, ye thora waqt bahut hai,
Jism o zabaan ki maut se pahle;

Bol, ye thora waqt bahut hai,
Jism o zabaan ki maut se pahle;
Bol, ke sach zinda hai ab tak—
Bol, jo kuchh kahna hai kah-le!

(*Speak, for your lips are free;*
Speak, your tongue is still yours,
Your upright body is yours—
Speak, your life is still yours.

See how in the blacksmith's shop
The flames are hot, the iron is red,
Mouths of locks have begun to open,
Each chain's skirt has spread wide.

Speak, this little time is plenty
Before the death of body and tongue;
Speak, for truth is still alive—
Speak, say whatever is to be said.)[6]

Habib Jalib, the Pakistani poet, makes this even stark when he connects the region and argues that both Pakistan as well as India belong to all of us. However, USA has entrenched itself here as well. And he shows what connects these countries and makes them one is the fact these nations belong to the workers and the oppressed. He is concerned that across these countries, American imperialism has converted these nations into their playground in collaboration with the local ruling classes. In other words, Jalib ceases to be a poet of a nation here as he crisscrosses a regional concern in the context of how imperialism has been operating. As he writes:

---

[6] Translation is from Faiz Ahmed Faiz, *Poems by Faiz*, 2000, translated, with an Introduction and Notes by V.G. Kiernan, New Delhi, Oxford University Press.

Hindustan bhi mera hai aur Pakistan bhi mera hai
Lekin in donon mulkon mein Amrika dera hai

Aid ki gandam kha kar ham ne kitney dhokey khai hain
Poochh na hamne Amrika ke kitne naaz uthai hain

Phir bhi ab tak wadi-e gul ko sangeenon ne ghera hai
Hindustan bhi mera hai aur Pakistan bhi mera hai

Khan Bahadur chhodna hoga ab to saath Angrezon ka
Ta bah gareban aa pahuncha hai phir se hath Angrezon ka

Macmillan tera na hua to Kennedy kab tera hai
Hindustan bhi mera hai aur Pakistan bhi mera hai

Yeh dharti hai asal mein, pyare, mazdooron dahqanon ki
Is dharti par chal na sakegi marzi chand gharanon ki

Zulm ki rat rahegi kab tak ab nazdik savera hai
Hindustan bhi mera hai aur Pakistan bhi mera hai

(Hindustan belongs to me and Pakistan belongs to me
Both of these, however, are under American hegemony

American aid gave us wheat, as also their deceit
Do not ask me how long we've suffered their conceit

And yet the bayonets are all around this flowering valley
Hindustan belongs to me and Pakistan belongs to me

Khan Bahadur, do not follow the English, from them better keep away
Once again they are holding you by the collar, you are still their prey

Macmillan was never thine, Kennedy can never be
Hindustan belongs to me and Pakistan belongs to me

This land, in fact, my dear, belongs to peasants and workers
Here, will not run the writ of a few clannish marauders

The dawn of freedom is heralding the end of tyranny
Hindustan belongs to me and Pakistan belongs to me.)[7]

---

[7] The translation is from the website of *Revolutionary Democracy* journal available at http://www.revolutionarydemocracy.org/rdv9n1/jalibpoems.htm (accessed on 10 June 2018).

What is significant here are the people across borders who have been struggling against exploitation at the hand of local as well as a global capital. It is a universalist sentiment that emerges from the historical experiences of people in this part of the world. It is an act of defiance against the tyranny of particular kinds that has always been at the heart of an imagination that captured the attention of people across borders. This is not limited only to poetic sensibilities and appeal, but one encounters the dissipating borderlines of nations in the works of visual artists as well.

There is pain, anxiety, angst and anger at the way politics of ethnicity and history within nations have led artists to dwell on the life of soldiers or the way politics and religion have led to the collapse of a pre-existing and more inclusive idea of religion. The works of Jagath Weerasinghe from Sri Lanka is an apt example where he politically engages with the consequences of the civil war between Sinhala and Tamil military formations. His work demonstrates what a regime can do to its people—the inhuman aggression inflicted upon its own citizens. What he does is to locate the violence within the larger sociopolitical context. He has argued that artists cannot become subservient to the system, but have to become a catalyst of change. There have been trends in Sri Lankan art in the last decades of the twentieth century, as Sasanka Perera observes, which mark

> the most dynamic period in contemporary art since the advent of the 43 Group, even though much of this dynamism took place in the backdrop of extreme social and economic upheavals specifically marked by the militarization of the inter-ethnic conflict involving segments of Sinhala and Tamil people, as well as the attempted insurrection staged by the JVP and the counter-terror campaign of the state unleashed to contain that situation.[8]

One can locate works of art in areas of conflict in other parts of South Asia, which makes efforts to create spaces where repressed expressions could be shown to the world. In fact, what Weerasinghe and the

[8] Sasanka Perera, 2016, *Violence and the Burden of Memory: Remembrance and Erasure in Sinhala Consciousness*, New Delhi, Orient Blackswan, p. 212.

politically active artists of the 1900s Trend explain for Sri Lanka through their visual narratives are equally valid across the region in much the same way as the poetic narratives of Faiz and Jalib speak across borders.

These are spaces of solidarity as well as defiance that are not subsumed and rendered voiceless in the instrumentalisms of the nation state. This is because they also challenge the idea of governmentality that bases itself on control and repression. These are only two instances of how people across borders can converse with each other to create possibilities of a South Asian sensibility. They dissipate the territorial parochialities and restraining paradigms of 'cooperation'. However, this dissipation of borders does not lead to the creation of Greater India or *Akhand Bharat* and therefore does not subscribe to hegemonic Indian political assertions. Instead, it leads to similarities in the stories of people who might speak to one another about creating solidarity that brings people together for the greater good despite the borders that presently separate them. Those who want to converse, those who want to share, those who want to build solidarities do not desire to leave their compatriots even if they speak different languages and adhere to different faiths but would seek to cross over the visa queues and security checks.

4

Anxieties of SAARC

An Experiential Reading through South Asian University[1]

Sasanka Perera

Approach

The South Asian Association for Regional Cooperation (SAARC), established in 1985 has now reached 33 years of existence in 2018. From the beginning, the organisation's Charter had mandated that SAARC should hold one meeting each year in one of the member countries. But by 2016, only 18 meetings had been held. This means that 15 had been cancelled due to the disagreement of one or more countries. The most recent of these cancellations was the 19th Summit scheduled to be held in Islamabad in 2016 that was called off due to a boycott initiated by the government of India, which was supported by all other members. So let alone deliberating crucial economic, political or diplomatic imperatives, the organisation has not been able to even perform its most basic of annual rituals. It is perhaps taking into consideration this abysmal failure of SAARC as an organisation that the former minister of External Affairs of India, Yashwant Sinha, called it 'a complete failure'.[2]

[1] This text is an edited, updated and expanded version of the presentation made at the panel discussion, 'SAARC in a Globalizing World' organised by the South Asian University on 8 December 2014 at India International Centre, New Delhi. A version of this has since been published with the facilitation of India International Centre under the same title in Rajiv Kumar and Omita Goyal, eds., 2016, *Thirty Years of SAARC: Society, Culture and Development*, New Delhi, SAGE Publications, pp. 153–162. The author would like to thank India International Centre Publications for their consent for republishing this chapter.

[2] https://thediplomat.com/2016/11/saarc-is-dead-long-live-saarc/ (accessed on 3 June 2018).

In these unenviable circumstances, it is an opportune time to explore its relevance, take stock of its present status and ponder over its future. This chapter proposes to pose these broader questions by taking an approach quite different from what is usually adopted by scholars of International Relations and Politics. My interest is to explore the regional manifestation of two kinds of imaginations and explore what these imaginations mean for SAARC. These two imaginations are:

1. The imagination of the nation state when compared with the imagination of the multilateral collective. Each country, including the eight that make up official South Asia, inevitably expresses an imagination of the state in the manner in which it deals with itself, as well as with each other.

2. The imagination of the multilateral collective as it ideally should manifest in the manner in which an entity such as SAARC is expected to work.

In this context, what would the implications of these twin imaginations be for SAARC in the midst of relentless globalisation at the present moment of the twenty-first century, particularly if these imaginations play contradictory roles?

To think about these two imaginations, I propose to take the readers on a less trodden journey through three specific experiences of my own, as well as my students and colleagues at South Asian University (SAU). This will be my point of departure. The selection of this somewhat peculiar vehicle for exploration has very clear reasons. After all, every individual who works for SAU is a citizen of one nation state or another in the region, while all of them work or study in an entity, created with the agreement of all eight nation states that constitute the region, funded and ultimately realised through SAARC. This is one of the few projects of SAARC that still continues and had the support of all member states of the organisation. Besides, the university, in its present form, is a metaphor for the region's aspirations, its hopes, its successes, its geopolitical realities and its anxieties. Crucially, lived experiences of individuals are a reliable measure to gauge how perceived ideals and rules actually work on the ground. These experiences are located in the intersections of the two imaginations to which I referred earlier, which, in real terms, is a grey zone in International Relations. More clearly, this area of intersection is a kind of regulatory Bermuda Triangle, where the shadows of the nation states' imagination of themselves and the imagination of the multilateral collective, which in this case happens to be SAARC, are cast on each other in an enduring discourse of relative confusion and liminality.

In its most ideal and basic form, nation states are supposed to be independent entities with a clear sense of their borders and a pronounced sense of their sovereignty, irrespective of the fact that these sensibilities might at times be contested. When a multilateral collective, such as the European Union (EU), Association of Southeast Asian Nations (ASEAN) or SAARC is formed, that collective can work well only if the nation states that constitute the collective can achieve the following three basic preconditions.

1. They should have the ability to pragmatically redefine some of the ways in which their own sense of statehood is generally defined and allow for the personality of the collective to manifest and emerge on the ground. For instance, if this is possible, it would also be possible at least in theory to rearrange one's own notions of sovereignty to some extent—to put in place a more open visa regime applicable to at least citizens of some countries if it cannot be applied across the board.

2. They should have the ability to halt bilateral issues from becoming a hurdle in the workings of the collective. Without making undue comparisons, EU is clearly the best recent example of this ideal kind of political arrangement that has become very successful despite long histories of war and mutual distrust. SAARC in comparison has an unpractical agreement to be guided by mutual and complete consent for any decision to be taken making it virtually impossible to make any major decision.

3. The availability of adequate political will and wisdom among political leaders to surpass locally and bilaterally contentious issues and political parochialities to work towards the greater good of the collective without compromising national interests, including security. Again, South Asian political leaders have never shown their ability to be statesmen or stateswomen as opposed to being mere politicians.

If we cannot address these issues successfully, it is quite likely that the imagination of the nation state and its rituals of statecraft will shackle the collective from realising its potential and anticipated goals. Perhaps it is in such a context that *The Hindu* described SAARC prior to the 18th Summit (2014) as 'bursting with potential, burdened with disappointment'.[3] The experiences of my students and colleagues, and my own, that I want to narrate, can also be broadly located within this untapped potential and its relentless disappointments.

Experience 1

In 2011, while making preparations for coming to Delhi to start work at SAU, I applied for what was then known as the 'SAU Visa'. It is a special category of visa that the Indian state, in its wisdom to move towards better realising the ideals of SAARC, had created for the benefit of South Asian citizens who were likely to come to SAU to either work or study. This was essentially done on the basis of the provisions elaborated in the following three documents: (*a*) Agreement for Establishment of SAU signed between the foreign ministers of all SAARC countries on 4 April 2007; (*b*) South Asian University Act, 2008, No. 8 of 2009, passed by the Parliament of India; and (*c*) the Head Quarters Agreement signed between the Secretary-General of SAARC and the Secretary of the External Affairs Ministry of the Government of India on 30 November 2008. The actual creation of this visa shows the ability, when necessary, for a nation state to work towards the benefit of the collective by changing some of the ways in which it usually works and is related to the first issue I had flagged earlier.

The SAU Visa was conceived as a hassle-free long-term residency permit with a number of privileges. When the visa system was initially introduced in 2010–2011, even for Pakistani students and colleagues, the visa allowed hassle-free travel throughout the country, which was very unusual, compared to the city-specific visas with entry and exit restrictions usually granted to Pakistani citizens. This was a clear example of the

[3] http://www.thehindu.com/opinion/blogs/blog-suhasini-haidar/article6632431.ece (accessed on 27 November 2014).

potential that was possible when political will existed. In my case, however, it became like any regular long-term visa due to two restrictions imposed on it: (*a*) Mandatory registration with Foreigners Regional Registration Office (FRRO) and (*b*) an entry restriction of three times per year into India. Taken in the general scheme of long-term residency visas, none of these conditions are out of the ordinary. But according to the agreements that were in place, both restrictions should not have been imposed on my visa and were in fact violations of these conditions. The FRRO registration was not so much of an issue, except that it required considerable time and patience in a generally unhelpful government office. It was an annual ritualised and institutionalised occurrence. However, Article VIC of the Head Quarters Agreement notes clearly that such registration is not needed for SAU Visa holders. But neither the university nor the Indian High Commission in Colombo or the FRRO office in Delhi showed any interest to be guided by these rather obvious rules. What it meant in real terms is that the sense of South Asian collegiality that the university and these specific rules were supposed to institutionalise were negated by these 'nationalised' performances of statecraft.

Beyond the first requirement, the second requirement related to entry restriction was a very serious problem. As a foreign national, I had to plan carefully as to which family and personal obligations had to be given up and which official or intellectual assignments I could attend abroad and those that had to be sacrificed. The personal and professional impact of this imposition was quite pronounced for me as well as for others in similar circumstances. Naturally, it is not easy to deal with the demands and challenges of building an international university with such debilitating restrictions haunting one's routine activities. But, analytically speaking, this was a simple case of the nation state's shadow eclipsing the personality of the collective even when that very same nation state had formally agreed to very specific rearmaments of its visa regime.

Experience 2

In 2013, the Department of Sociology at SAU, having looked at the ongoing and planned activities of the SAARC Cultural Centre in Colombo, thought that it would make sense for the two entities to collaborate with each other. After all, both were created by the same parent organisation. Besides, some of the activities of the Cultural Centre seemed quite interesting in theory. More significantly, it appeared that a number of departments in SAU could positively contribute to these activities. These included numerous conferences, research programmes and photography and art competitions. The University's Faculty of Social Sciences in particular and the University more generally, were well placed intellectually and in terms of what might be called a South Asian sensibility, to collaborate in these events because they were very close to our research interests and personal passions. At the time, in the Faculty of Social Sciences alone, there were scholars from four South Asian countries with research interests in at least five of these countries.

Colleagues in the Cultural Centre were open to collaboration. But they indicated that SAU academics from different SAARC countries had to apply for participation in various events through the respective External Affairs Ministry of their countries. Even the photographs for a SAARC-wide competition had to be channelled through this route. So despite my working at SAU in New Delhi, any submission from me had to be channelled through the Ministry of Foreign Affairs in Colombo. These were very time-consuming rituals of statecraft. In this situation, it was quite evident that one SAARC entity simply could not collaborate with another directly, without having to go through the rituals of power generated by the stately imagination of itself by each country in the region. While SAU from the beginning did not succumb to this kind of cumbersome bureaucracy at least in academic works, the SAARC Cultural Centre was a willing prisoner of this system. This meant that even academic conferences on important themes organised by the Cultural Centre could not necessarily attract the best possible minds as opposed to those drawn from lists maintained by each state apparatus. Again, the imagination of the nation state was self-evident in this situation, while the imagination of SAARC, the multilateral collective to which both our organisations formally belonged, could not be seen, could not be perceived and could not even be sensed. As a result, the SAU has not collaborated with the SAARC Cultural Centre on even a single project up to now.

Experience 3

All students who come to SAU from other countries in the region are supposed to get SAU student visas for the period of their study. Despite some difficulties, this seemed to work from 2010 onwards when the university initially started operations. But from 2014 onwards, students from Pakistan who came to SAU were given SAU visas for 730 days with pre-defined entry and exit points. More significantly, the visa restricted them to Delhi during their stint at the university. Under routine circumstances, there is nothing unusual in these kinds of restrictions. Often, when Indian citizens travel to Pakistan for specific reasons and when Pakistanis come to India, most of them get city-specific visas. So, this is a taken-for-granted practice regularly utilised by the nation states of India and Pakistan in their bilateral dealings. But how does this make sense when taken in the context of collective interests of the multilateral collective?

As a university of SAARC with the mandate to offer knowledge without borders and to create a South Asian consciousness, it becomes very difficult to uphold these lofty ideals if a group of our own students is restricted to Delhi during its tenure as students and is deprived of learning from the vastness of experiences that India so readily offers. From 2014 onwards, many other students from Sri Lanka, Bangladesh and Afghanistan were getting very different kinds of visas, instead of the SAU student visa for different durations, these required regular renewal that was both time-consuming and expensive. Particularly for the Department of Sociology, it became impossible to take its MA students for field training outside Delhi if the class had students from Pakistan. It took much effort for the Department to negotiate with the Ministry of External Affairs of India to get our students across insignificant local borders for simple class work. I am sure there must be official reasons to explain this. But for an academic community and for a university of this kind, this does not help. It impacts our sense of collective identity, and our teaching, while creating an unhelpful sense of anxiety and unease. By 2017, the six students who were admitted to SAU from Pakistan did not get any visa at all, openly violating their right for an education as well as the basic tenets on which SAU was established. Though the university did raise this matter with the Indian government formally more than once, the governments of the countries whose citizens were affected by these violations were not known to object to this dismantling of the university's basic operational principles.

Until very recent times, Pakistani colleagues, even if they did get the special SAU Visa, could not open a bank account in India. They had to resort to pre-modern and unsafe practices of informally storing their salaries, which becomes a problem when they attempt to take their savings back to their home country. Again, it appears this also has to do with unresolved bilateral issues between India and Pakistan and is a matter of reciprocity. But it is indeed quite sad that a mainstream SAARC organisation cannot resolve such fundamental issues despite the multilateral agreements through which the university was established.

Interpreting Experiences

The common feature running across these three experiences indicates how the aspirations of a multilateral organisation, and the dreams of individuals who subscribe to these ideals, get curtailed because the very strong imagination of the nation state continues to impact negatively upon the evolution of the ideals of the collective. This happens despite the existence of overarching agreements among these countries designed to prevent such outcomes. As we know quite well, the imagination of the collective did not suddenly emerge from an unknown universe, disrupting the nation state. Instead, it evolved carefully and over time, with the consensus of the contributing states. It is this state of affairs that Subramanian Swamy, Chairman of BJP's Strategic Affairs Committee, articulated at the Lalith Atulathmudali Memorial Lecture in Colombo on 26 November 2014.[4]

> First, SAARC is off and on in limbo. Thus, the first issue is this: how to grapple with SAARC's uncertain future and how to put it back on the rails again, and not permit in the future, international political changes affecting the functioning of SAARC.

---

[4] http://www.thehindu.com/opinion/lead/a-case-for-saarc-reforms/article6630591.ece?homepage=true (accessed on 5 December 2014).

> Second, SAARC has to resolve whether essential economic cooperation in an increasingly globalised world economy can be achieved despite continuing political conflicts. The issue is whether political differences—beyond vital national interest issues—can be set aside by each member country while a more harmonious environment is created through healthy economic cooperation.
>
> Third, is SAARC so fragile that it cannot survive if bilateral controversial political questions are raised in its deliberations without undermining its utility?

It seems to me that Swamy has captured the centrality of the same issues I have tried to explain with regard to my own circumstances, but with particular reference to economic cooperation. As in this case, political leaders often understand quite well what needs to be done with SAARC. However, these analyses seldom get translated into tangible outcomes on the ground. It appears that countries in our region are so deeply drowned in the intoxicating imagination of the nation state that they cannot imagine the collective as a viable, empowered and necessary, political reality. The gradual pace at which SAARC has generally evolved, as well as its inability to come to terms with most of the anticipated agreements at the 18th SAARC Summit in Kathmandu in 2014, clearly places this unenviable situation in the larger context. This is what Prime Minister Narendra Modi meant when he observed in the 18th SAARC Summit, 'as SAARC, we have failed to move with the speed that our people expect and want'.[5]

Concluding Comments

In the context of the experiences narrated, as well as the history of SAARC itself, which is now part of South Asia's larger corpus of general knowledge, we may ask what the relevance of SAARC is in the context of the relentless globalisation that typifies our global existence. It is self-evident that SAARC is nowhere close to realising its potential

[5] http://www.narendramodi.in/text-of-prime-ministers-speech-at-2014-saarc-summit-in-nepal/ (accessed on 5 December 2014).

or its original goals. Many of the hurdles in achieving SAARC's ideal goals have come about due to its inability to get out of the shadow of the nation state and embrace the imagination of the collective. In the context of what I have outlined so far, let me make two propositions to conclude my thoughts.

My first proposition is, if I am to be self-reflective, I would admit that SAU has many issues that need resolution. Even so, despite its many lapses, it is a much better model for SAARC itself to emulate. And I say this with a serious degree of responsibility. After all, no one asked me or any of my colleagues, what our citizenship was when we applied for employment. We were also not asked to apply through the Ministry of External Affairs or other government entities in our respective countries. We were not asked to bring letters of introduction from the Prime Minister, the President or some MP in our countries. We approached the university as individuals and were recruited only on the basis of training and competence. Since our inception in 2010, we have done our best to admit students from all SAARC countries despite considerable difficulties. Students from outside India now constitute nearly 50 per cent of our student body, although some countries like Pakistan, Sri Lanka, Bhutan and the Maldives, remain under-represented. It is this relative success to which the SAU anthropologist, Mallika Shakya from Nepal, refers to in the following words in a 2014 essay:

> My current employer SAU is partly Nepali. The class I teach at SAU is also partly Nepali, but more importantly, it is only partly Indian, while being also partly Afghani, Bangladeshi, Bhutani, Maldivian and Sri Lankan. I am a lot more at home with this class than I would have been if it was just one of any of these nationalities.[6]

But we have not been as successful in maintaining this sense of balance in the recruitment of faculty and support staff. Of the 55 regular faculty members, only five or so come from countries other than India. This is a serious issue which obviously needs to be addressed in all future

[6] http://recordnepal.com/perspective/search-humanistic-south-asia (accessed on 5 December 2014).

recruitment drives. Even so, by regulations, and by taking into account the existing pattern of employment of senior administrators, the university is obliged to ensure that its Director of Finance and Registrar, the two topmost administrators come from different countries. In 2014, it had one Deputy Registrar from Pakistan, Bhutan and India each, while the Registrar is from India. Its librarian is from Bangladesh, while his assistants are from India. It has one Assistant Registrar from Nepal, while the other is from India. It has an architect from Sri Lanka and an IT specialist from India. Rule 6.1 of the university mandates that at any given time the president and vice president(s) of the university must be from different countries even though this has been routinely violated as a simple matter without any sanction from the University's Governing Board.

All these suggest that SAU is far more serious in terms of rules, and often in practice as well, to work towards an imagination of South Asia beyond the shadow of the nation states that fund the university, so that a more humane and reasonable South Asia might be imagined and hopefully achieved. This does not mean, however, that in the minds of students, colleagues and officials, the shadow of the nation state does not exist. In fact, it often does as rhetorical articulations of competing nationalisms. But this is to be expected given the almost natural emergence of nationalism in human consciousness. What is important, however, is that such sensibilities are not given official or formal recognition. However, the inability of SAARC to achieve its larger goals and to evolve its multilateral sensibility in the long term might also spell a bleak future for an institution like ours, though it is clearly one of SAARC's very few success stories. In real terms, given the university's wider signification of South Asia in numerous ways, its lack of success in the long run, or its eventual collapse, would essentially signal the end of SAARC as well.

My second proposition is the restating of an obvious fact, even though it is often lost in the formal and official discourses on South Asia. That is, SAARC is not the only discourse in, and on, South Asia. For me, SAARC is simply one of the many platforms and discourses on South Asia while it might be the official, more audible and more visible of these. In this context, there is a need at the level of our collective perception and discursive practices to delink South Asia from SAARC when necessary. As all of us know, there are other histories, memories, discourses, networks and efforts in the region that have allowed for a more humane, more equitable and more reasonable imagination of South Asia to emerge, unshackled, from the shadow of the nation states and the debilitating non-movement of the multilateral collective itself. I have in mind the networks of writers, filmmakers, scholars and artists who are actively engaged in creating cohesive networks of international relations across the region, but often away from the public gaze.

Take, for instance, the South Asian Network for the Arts, which came into existence at the beginning of the present millennium. It created a viable network of artists from across the region. These artists met regularly in different countries and engaged in art-making and artistic experimentation that placed in context the issues of local relevance as well as matters that cut across the region and beyond, within the discursive practices of these emerging trends of art. As a result, I strongly believe that South Asian art today is a serious discourse on the region's ongoing political and social transformations. The point I want to make is that these networks have emerged precisely because SAARC's own were not available or were not viable.

Many of us have dreamt of a better integrated, more connected and a more humane South Asia for a very long time. In my case, this has been going on for at least a decade and a half before my formal association with SAU. Scholars and thinking people in our region, such as Ashis Nandy and Shiv Visvanathan from India, Imtiaz Ahmed from Bangladesh, Kanak Dixit from Nepal, Zia Mian from Pakistan, just to mention a few, have immensely contributed to this self-reflective and out-of-the-box thinking on the region. Some political leaders have taken this thinking to a more visible political level. It is in such a context that India's former Prime Minister, Manmohan Singh in January 2007 publicly articulated his dream of a South Asia where he could have breakfast in Amritsar, lunch in Lahore and dinner in Kabul.[7] But we know quite well that that dream was never realised. It is this existing, unenviable ground reality that Narendra Modi very subtly articulated

---

[7] http://archive.indianexpress.com/news/amritsar-breakfast-lahore-lunch-and-a-kabul-dinner/20468/ (accessed on 5 December 2014).

in the 18th SAARC Summit in Kathmandu when he noted, 'nowhere in the world are collective efforts more urgent than in South Asia; and, nowhere else is it so modest'.[8]

I think it should be axiomatic where exactly SAARC stands at the global stage today. For me, until SAARC comes of age and decides to reinvent itself away from the discomforting shadow of the nation state, the future is elsewhere. And that is in the consciousness and goodwill of the region's people, and their ability to imagine and create their collective space beyond the limitations of both the nation state and SAARC.

[8] http://www.narendramodi.in/text-of-prime-ministers-speech-at-2014-saarc-summit-in-nepal/ (accessed on 5 December 2014).

5

South Asia

Between Dream and Actuality

Ravi Kumar

The term, 'South Asia' invokes myriad images—from inter-governmental bodies such as SAARC, talks of how this is a geographic region to even discourses of its peculiarity and uniqueness. Some scholars feel that '... South Asia is not just any region, but an ancient, well-established and important one.'[1] In this context, there are institutions caught up in an effort to transform the region into a playground where nation states are trying to build across nations some kind of bridges, mostly to do business and now increasingly also to realise security goals. Beyond this, there are intellectuals who see the need to emphasise the historical unity that has characterised this space or the civilisational connections, which gives it its sense of continuity. As social scientists, what interests us cannot be tied up within the confines of the national and security interests of the eight nation states that have now become the most dominant and formal defining feature of South Asia. When we refer to South Asia as a region constituted by eight nation states, it is merely used as a reference of convenience and an interim point of departure. In the long term, we would like to retain the possible expansion of the spatial expanse of South Asia itself, in addition to bringing history, culture and people into the centrality of defining it. This is a task for the future. But it is nevertheless a very important one because it challenges many notions about how politics and history are

[1] Adil Najam and Moeed Yusuf, 2013, *South Asia 2060: Envisioning Regional Futures*, London and New York, Anthem Press.

understood as impacting the present. As an illustration, Guneratne and Weiss[2] argue,

> We focus on the five major countries of the region—Bangladesh, India, Nepal, Pakistan, and Sri Lanka—as they are the primary political actors that influence regional power and power relations. We've chosen not to include Bhutan and the Maldives, tiny independent states whose combined populations are smaller than many small cities in the major countries of South Asia. We have also excluded Afghanistan, which is not usually considered in academic discussions of the politics of the sub-continent.

In an age and time when epistemological notions of enlightenment are being challenged by ideas of decolonisation and when we recall how colonialism employed its power to construct a notion of 'unenlightened' and 'enlightened', it becomes a dangerous reproduction of such violent ideas by whimsically excluding countries merely because of their size or because academicians have not given them ample attention.[3] In the very least, this is sloppy scholarship. Is it not that the continued categorisations of 'relevant', 'irrelevant' or 'small' and 'weak' also feed into the same political discourse that puts a 'region' under the hegemony of a single nation? It is important to mention that the perception of South Asia cannot be constituted without showing the relationships, in all respects, that have existed among these weak and strong and relevant and irrelevant states and societies. The idea of South Asia, including its contemporary politics, has to be grounded in a history that has been interconnected, conversational, relatively bereft of enmities that nation states later brought along with them. These interconnections and conversations have involved everyone in this region. Hence, the issue of one nation/society being preferred over others will not do justice to the framing of an inclusive idea of South Asia. For instance, the religio-political relationship cannot be understood fully unless one is aware of the route taken by Hiuen Tsang to reach India through Afghanistan indicating that there was a rich Buddhist

---

[2] Arjun Guneratne and Anita M. Weiss, 2014, 'Introduction,' in *Pathways to Power: The Domestic Politics of South Asia*, edited by Arjun Guneratne and Anita M. Weiss, London, Rowman Littlefield, p. 4.

[3] I draw heavily from Enrique Dussel, Walter Mignolo and Anibal Quijano to make this point.

influence in parts of Afghanistan and the way, historically, politics undid that influence. When the Bhutanese photographer Pawo Choyning Dorji mapped and retraced this route in the recent past, it revealed many such aspects that would inform the complexity and the constantly transformed nature of the religio-political axis in the region. Similarly, Jayadeva Uyangoda[4] demonstrates the conversation across the region on the turf of religion and politics. In the 1930s and 1940s, a form of radical Buddhism emerged in Sri Lanka and the formation of these radical ideas had to do with the conversation that a group of monks had with scholars from India. A form of 'public and political Buddhism, a socially oriented strand of Buddhist interventionism' had developed during this period 'inspired by socialism and a vision of left-oriented political reconstruction'.[5] Rahul Sankrityayan mentored them when he went to Colombo to teach Sanskrit. When the monks went to Benares and Calcutta for higher education during the early 1930s, they encountered radical anti-colonial politics and 'were further exposed to radical anti-colonial politics as well as socialist politics of Shri Narendra Dev'.[6] This is a perfect example of one of the ways in which the formation of South Asian idea of religion and radicalism can be located. To talk about these interconnections is not merely a matter of kindling an academic interest in these themes. More importantly, it is also to demonstrate how intellectual history of the region can be written in a way that informs how the region was imagined under very specific conditions where seamless movement of ideas and people were not fettered by territorial boundaries. Hence, the region becomes relevant for us as a spatial delineation only for the practical purpose of beginning to think of an area where the connections across farcical borders of nation states can be explored. The intent, in this sense, is radically different from those bodies of scholarship that think of regions in terms of concrete political identities. We would only look at South Asia as a space where the human connections get curtailed by the intentions of nation states. South Asia as a simplistic geopolitical terminology should ideally be

---

[4] Jayadeva Uyangoda, 2018, 'Modern Buddhisms and Democracy: Diverse Encounters in India and Sri Lanka,' *Society and Culture in South Asia*, Vol. 4, No. 2, pp. 179–207.

[5] Uyangoda, 'Modern Buddhisms and Democracy', pp. 179–207.

[6] Uyangoda, 'Modern Buddhisms and Democracy', pp. 179–207.

avoided because more nuanced explorations might lead us to 'nations' and 'societies' beyond the eight that we presently think of as South Asia.

If we go back in history, there was a world when categories such as nation state-defined South Asia did not determine the nature of interactions and engagements among people across this huge landscape. Pilgrims travelled across the seas and mountains while artistic and music traditions travelled across to influence other places and so on. There are yet other worlds, where people dare to engage and interact without consideration of borders and boundaries erected by nation states. There is a distinct resonance of spirit, desire and an overwhelming urge among people to talk to each other, for instance, to share their everyday lives, struggles and imaginations. These worlds are reflected in the way people engaged in creative literature, social movements and the visual arts that helped converse across borders. There is a possibility to debunk and deny these existing borders, even as one mocks this idea of South Asia as rhetorical, dreamy and impractical. It seems impractical to generate a South Asian consciousness because often there is no clarity on the kind of consciousness that is implied by this idea. It is also because institutions would find it difficult to achieve this goal that ideally should evolve organically. Institutions can only facilitate this process if it is rooted in the deeper socio-economic and cultural grammar of societies. Hence, it would be a mistake to think of us as warriors or propagandists.

This is not a reductionist exercise in International Relations. It is much more than that, and in fact, is completely different from how the conventional International Relations scholarship imagines South Asia. As we see it, nation states are not the main actors in this framework of trying to develop an idea of South Asia. It appears so, simply because they exist in a concretised cartographic sense and also because this specific understanding has acquired significant power in determining the way popular politics might play out. Ideally, this imagination of South Asia should be more about people, about engaging with them, keeping the nation state and its politics of hegemony aside. So, if there are students of Pakistan who face visa issues while attempting to join South Asian University (SAU), it can only be seen as the creation of a nation state drama in a forum meant to perform something collective that goes beyond these borders. This shows how the logic of nation states has vitiated our minds as intellectuals as well as our inability to think in terms of any other idiom beyond that of surveillance. This is a situation that SAU faces each year with no concrete resolution in sight.

Conversely, however, when students from Bhutan were not applying in adequate numbers to SAU, the strategy that we employed was not to approach them with paid advertisements in conventional print or social media or seek the assistance of state agencies only. We knew from experience that this did not seem to work despite being followed up for a few years. Instead, we established a channel of conversations, dialogues and a mutual learning process not at the level of the university at first, but as an intellectual linkage by the Department of Sociology with younger colleagues affiliated with the Sherubste College of the Royal University of Bhutan. We reiterated to the colleagues in Bhutan consistently that SAU is also a Bhutanese university as much as it is of India, Afghanistan or Sri Lanka. Over months since 2016, we saw that the friendliness and self-reflexivity made them comfortable with this idea of a South Asian institution. They saw a possibility of conversation and the same was facilitated by our approach towards their students at the university who took away a message of dialogic possibilities unlike the historic subjection of their country as a dependent economy directly linked to India's strategic interests. It is important that an intellectual space needs to be defined in a particular way—it must convey a sense of openness, a possibility to be critical and each side needs to be ready to accept constructive criticisms.

The reading lists in courses that we reviewed hardly had any Bhutanese or South Asian material. A course on world political history talked only about the western history as if South Asia was not constitutive of that history, as if South Asian history was untouched by the historical developments such as world wars, cold war confrontations etc. The need to find an identity that some call regional consciousness is not the primary concern here. But it appears as a natural corollary when one transacts any discussion around why the knowledge produced in the region has been looked down upon and often routinely been discarded. It also happened historically because we have emotionally internalised, through a voluntary exercise, that the best possible knowledge can be had from the North only. This situation has reached such extremes that if one does not get admission to a decent university in USA, UK or Australia, one would at least try to get a degree from any other northern university rather than from a local one with a reasonable track record. This is more than democratisation of choices. It is the idea that superior knowledge inhabits particular sites, while most of the sites being considered in South Asia itself are potentially devoid of that knowledge. This trend continues when scholars build their own conceptualisations. So, if a course on agrarian relations, violence, inequality or even social theory is formulated, it hardly demonstrates the possible 'intelligibility' of the Southern Hemisphere. More than mere binaries, it is about exploring the possibilities of conversation with the world we inhabit. I cannot discount the fact, as cited earlier, that religion and politics were vibrant themes in South Asia. Hence any course on religion, faith, ritual or anything similar must take cognisance of that. Or, when agrarian relations in India are to be understood, the works of Swami Sahjanand Saraswati can be a great source to explore the peasant society. Some scholars have been trying to problematise this by critiquing the very idea of Europe as the centre, and the way the division of history has happened. For instance, Enrique Dussell[7] says,

> What calls attention here is that the Spirit of Europe (the German spirit) is the absolute Truth that determines or realizes itself through itself without owing anything to anyone. This thesis, which I will call the 'Euro-centric paradigm' (in opposition to the 'world paradigm'), is the one that has imposed itself not only in Europe and the United States, but also in the entire intellectual world of the world periphery. As we have said, the 'pseudo-scientific' division of history into Antiquity (as antecedent), the Medieval Age (preparatory epoch), and the Modern Age (Europe) is an ideological and deforming organization of history. Philosophy and ethics need to break with this reductive horizon in order to open themselves to the 'world,' 'planetary' sphere.

It is this very idea that Europe has been the centre of knowledge that makes South Asians relentlessly flock to the North. Some of the 'great' minds joined or started centres of South Asian learning. These centres in the West produced voluminous literature on South Asia and even now, much of the hegemonic knowledge comes from there. The problem does

---

[7] Enrique Dussel, 2003, *Beyond Philosophy: Ethics, History, Marxism, and Liberation Theology*, edited by Eduardo Mendieta, Maryland, Rowman and Littlefield, pp. 53–81.

not lie so much with the physical location of the scholarship, but with the way it tends to look at South Asia. Much of it creates an identity (that is South Asia), which communicates a gamut of entities embedded in one singular identity. But when it comes to epistemologically unravelling the multiple entities as the constituent of a singular identity, it fails to establish the necessary connections. Instead, it then becomes country specific and in most cases India dominant discourse.

In this context, it is also interesting to look at how terminologies are invented and what meanings they carry. Often, authors would talk about Pakistan, Bangladesh and India, but their geopolitical reference point is the 'Indian Subcontinent'.[8] In all probability, this might be because these nations 'came out' of 'India'. This is also evident when Oxford Dictionary defines 'Indian subcontinent' in the following words:

> The part of Asia south of the Himalayas which forms a peninsula extending into the Indian Ocean, between the Arabian Sea and the Bay of Bengal. Historically forming the whole territory of greater India, the region is now divided between India, Pakistan, and Bangladesh.[9]

South Asia as a geopolitical identity then is an extension of this by including Afghanistan, Maldives, Bhutan and Sri Lanka. Then, obviously, a question arises about the usage of categories—Indian subcontinent, which sounds so hegemonic, or South Asia.

The way South Asia as a terminology is often employed by scholars not only does injustice to many nations that constitute the category, but it also denies possibilities of conversation, which historically existed at different forms and levels and which can inform the present as well. As an example, if one talks of modernity and modernisms in South Asia and analyses them through the prism of works of art, then it would be only just to look at the conversation that might happen between the artists of India, Pakistan, Sri Lanka and Bangladesh, to understand and explain this. For instance, while formal archaeology and art history

---

[8] Menzie Chinn, November 1981, 'Indian Subcontinent: A Stunted Future?', *Harvard International Review*, Vol. 4, No. 3, pp. 15–17.

[9] https://en.oxforddictionaries.com/definition/us/Indian_subcontinent (accessed on 25 February 2019).

does not dwell on this in any significant detail, the uncanny stylistic resemblance of the frescoes in the fifth-century AD fortress, Sigiriya in Sri Lanka and the Ajanta cave paintings in Maharashtra, India is hard to miss. Though the first monumental structures in Ajanta date from second and first centuries BC, it was during the Gupta Period between fifth and sixth centuries AD that the more decorated caves came into existence. This is the same period as Sri Lanka's Sigiriya. One has to wonder if conversations and exchange of ideas did not take place across the oceans at this time as it did when it came to Sanskrit literary styles, rules of grammar, kinship terminology and ideas of faith.

Problematically, scholars have also employed the terms 'South Asia' and 'Indian subcontinent' interchangeably. The problem of this interchangeability is that 'South Asia' as a term is supposed to be more egalitarian in terms of relationships among nations whereas the 'Indian subcontinent' somehow provides centrality to one nation. For instance, Saurabh Dube in his essay on modernist art practices in South Asia says that he focuses 'on critical modernist moments, cutting across aesthetic forms in twentieth century South Asia.'[10] However, one does not find a healthy discussion on modernisms in South Asia in his discussion. It remains dominated by India. Modernisms in art have different trajectories in Sri Lanka and India or may be quite similar, or for that matter in Nepal and the other nations as well. The peculiarity of how modernism in Indian art evolved as opposed to its trajectory in the west is the main argument Geeta Kapur attempts to make in her collection of essays, *When was Modernism*.[11] Other modernisms in South Asia, though they had linkages with European modernism as a result of the colonial experience, nevertheless evolved their individual trajectories based on local conditions. Is there a possibility to generate a body of work where artists are conversing with each other? There is, and to some extent, the collaborative work facilitated by the South Asia Network for the Arts has shown us the possibilities of such conversations.[12] But in

[10] Saurabh Dube, 2018, 'Sobre las prácticas modernistas en el sur de Asia' ['On Modernist Practices in South Asia'], *Estudios de Asia y Africa*, Vol. 53, No. 1(165), pp. 199–224.

[11] Geeta Kapur, 2001, *When was Modernism: Essays on Contemporary Cultural Practice in India*, New Delhi, Tulika.

[12] See Chapter 21 in this collection for more information.

the long term, this kind of exercise needs a lot more work and it needs to evolve beyond the domineering shadow of India. Conversations among these societies, recognising common thematic engagements and building a critical knowledge base of a world that works as a system can allow us to understand and explain the politics of knowledge and cultural production in a much more nuanced manner.

One has not encountered any strong need to progress in this direction among intellectuals located in the western hemisphere. The reasons for this need to be discovered and analysed. While making this statement, it must not be construed as a rejection of the knowledge that is produced in an American or European University's South Asia Centre, but it is more about what constitutes that knowledge and what purpose it serves. First, a democratised sensibility that allows space for each and everyone with their own knowledge to join the table for a discussion without any pretension or hierarchy is the first step towards building up a body of knowledge on South Asia. Second, their engagement with the knowledge produced elsewhere on/of South Asia must follow as the next step of engagement. This is an intellectual project that essentially hinges on the rejection of the politics of nation states as well as the hegemony of privileged centres of knowledge. The solution to imagining a regional entity here is not through the imposition of different nations/societies/histories as matters of tokenism. It is more about the willingness to generate a conversation and the ability to get out of the narrowness that defines different societies or as entities that should be subsumed within the identity of one nation. So, if one talks about South Asia and talks about India as its representative, what it does is to portray the whole region from the perspective of one domineering power. This is also about the way relationships of the geopolitics and geo-knowledges have been explored by somebody like Walter Mignolo when he says, 'geo-politics of knowledge goes hand in hand with geo-politics of knowing. Who and when, why and where is knowledge generated (rather than produced, like cars or cell phones)? Asking these questions means to shift the attention from the enunciated to the enunciation.'[13] Hence, if

[13] Walter D. Mignolo, 2009, 'Epistemic Disobedience, Independent Thought and De-Colonial Freedom,' *Theory, Culture & Society*, Vol. 26, No. 7–8, pp. 1–23.

one builds bridges, they inevitably become bridges of solidarity of the oppressed and marginalised across borders. It might also allow one to dwell on how socioeconomic structures work across these borders and the different expressions that they produce.

Unfortunately, the politics of nation states embroiled in and emerging out of the politics of their respective ruling classes and their economic interests do not allow these breaches. Instead, they resort to measures such as strict and ridiculous visa regimes. Such a system sent back the daughter of Faiz Ahmed Faiz from a conference held in India merely due to her nationality.[14] Or the Indian government denies a visa to a scholar to attend a conference because his parents were born in Pakistan even before the Partition.[15] We have seen difficulties of trying to build collaborative research across South Asia and the difficulty in getting Pakistani scholars to conferences and meetings in India even when sponsored by SAU which is supposed to be an agency of all South Asian nation states. They do not get visas on either side of the India–Pakistan border. The nation state is inimical to the idea of any activity that does not get defined within its area of operation. It even wants to hold scholarship hostage to the agenda and anxieties of nation states, and unfortunately, many academics fall prey to this framework. A new vision that is located outside these narrow borders, which thrives on the poetic sensibilities of Nazrul, Faiz and Sahir[16] and in the historic people to people contacts beyond visa regimes, is required to understand and analyse South Asia. The narrow confines of much of the contemporary South Asian scholarship would only further the project of nation states,

---

[14] *The Citizen*, 13 May 2018, 'Muneeza Hashmi, Daughter of Faiz Ahmad Faiz, "Deported" From Delhi', available at https://www.thecitizen.in/index.php/en/NewsDetail/index/5/13790/Muneeza-Hashmi-Daughter-of-Faiz-Ahmad-Faiz-Deported-From-Delhi (accessed on 10 June 2018).

[15] An academic from Canada, Haroon Akram-Lodhi wrote to the Visa Office in Toronto on 28 October 2016 that he was told that because his father was born in Pakistan before partition he needed a clearance letter from the Ministries of Home and External Affairs to receive the visa. How does a state define a person of Pakistani origin? Commonsense says that it would be from the day when the new nation comes into existence and not decades before that. However, it did not seem to be the case. Definitions are made as per the convenience of the nation state and in such cases, rationality ceases to work.

[16] These poets produced works that would echo across borders.

and not allow one to see the extent of how similar discontents might lead to the emergence of social movements in India, Nepal as well as Sri Lanka or the conditions of decline of anti-systemic movements might be a common feature across borders.

The intellectual pursuit to undo the relationships of power among nations woven into the politics of nation states is also located within formal realms of institutions. It is, no doubt, difficult to imagine an institutional framework (which itself is located within its own geopolitical context) to transform this situation and build a possible world of South Asian knowledge. This would challenge certain hegemonies not only of statist politics but also of individual human tendencies and therefore will invite resistance of a complex kind. However, that is where the fun of imagining a new intellectual enterprise and public thought resides. For instance, one can begin with a basic framework of building an institution that gives importance to food regimes as significant ways of opening spaces of engagements. The geopolitics at the regional level also translates itself into some form of politics at local levels in the lives of people. One such expression of this geopolitics is the identification of nations with religion and attributing certain characteristics to the religion. The result becomes evident in the common notion of attributing specific food types with religion as well. So, in an institution that would aim to bring together people from across nations, such identifications have to be shunned and discouraged. The diversity of food is such that non-vegetarianism of Brahmins of Kashmir is different from that of Maithli Brahmins or Bengali Brahmins leave aside the fact that being Brahmins some even consume meat. Now, it will be destroying the possible use of food regimes as platforms for socio-economic, cultural and political engagement if I begin with the idea that if I serve non-vegetarian food such as basic chicken curry, it will fit the taste buds of all non-vegetarians of South Asia. In other words, the idea of constructing an ambience for conversation means that one needs to be sensitive to the differences in these subtleties.

Alongside this sensitivity, the idea to establish food regimes as open and liberal spaces would ensure that there is mutual respectability towards each other's lives (as food forms an intrinsic part of our lives). South Asians have to ultimately get out of their cocooned world of countrymen and countrywomen, experiment with their lives and learn to share and appreciate each other's lives across borders. Unless the communitarian life of South Asians is imagined along these lines, formal, informal and emotional interaction would stop, and as a result, sharing of knowledge and the building of discourses across borders would suffer. Nation states cannot ensure this. It can be ensured only through institutions, which can think of a project of nurturing social life that is located in a conversational existence, where borders become marginal. Such an approach will ensure that a new meaning to life is discovered and a new imagination of South Asia is created.

II

'Unofficial' Reimagining of South Asia

6

Beyond History, against the Present

Preliminary Thoughts on Reimagining 'South Asia'[1]

Sasanka Perera

Though we flippantly use the term South Asia and numerous cartographic renditions of this supposed reality exist, I am not too sure what it means when situated in the context of the region's past as well as its present. If I remember right, it is not by accident that a Maldivian diplomat observed in the 1980s that there should be South-South Asia to refer to the geo-cultural areas beyond southern India including Kerala, Tamil Nadu, Sri Lanka and the Maldives. He was attempting to make a distinction between these and the Hindi–Urdu–Nepali speaking northern part of the Indian subcontinent.

If we take South Asia for granted for the moment, there are a number of things we can agree on. The region has been in what might be called perpetual 'state of flux' from mythic and ancient times right up to the present moment.[2] I am not saying this in any negative sense, but to make the point that upheavals and the quotidian evolution of history have connected the destinies of the region in different ways, even though much of this memory might not be part of the region's

---

[1] Keynote address delivered at the conference, 'Connecting South Asia' organised by the Theertha International Artists' Collective and the Colombo Institute for the Advanced Study of Society and Culture at the Post Graduate Institute of Archeology, Colombo, 28 September 2012. It has since been published in *India + Sri Lanka—Sethu Samudram: Sethu Book Art Project*, Colombo and Bangalore: Theertha International Artists' Collective and 1 Shanti Road (2014). The author would like to thank the Theertha International Artists' Collective and 1 Shanti Road for granting permission to republish this chapter.

[2] Sasanka Perera, 2008, 'Preface', *South Asia Journal of Culture*, Colombo, Colombo Institute for the Advanced Study of Society and Culture.

collective conscience today. Beyond the overlapping histories, many of the countries in the region have similar or related experiences of culture, colonialism, the traumas of post-coloniality as well as the relative political chaos of modernity and malpractices of democracy and finally the consequences of 'constantly negotiating the global economic and cultural agendas within their own national perspectives'.[3] When Buddhism was at the height of its development, it crisscrossed what is known as South Asia today from Afghanistan to Sri Lanka, not to mention India itself and ventured beyond the region into the Far East. Though it transgressed borders many times in this reach, it did not encounter anything like today's militarised borders of nation states.

Even before these historically recorded events steeped well within mythic times, according to the narratives from the pages of *Ramayana*, King Rawan simply hopped on to his prehistoric aircraft, flew to Bharat and came back to Lanka forcibly bringing Sita with him. This mythical story is not very different from the kidnappings and forced disappearances in contemporary Sri Lankan politics. All Lord Rama had to do was to get the help of Lord Hanuman and cross the ocean with the aid of a bridge built through divine intervention, cross mighty mountains, all in a leap or two, and rescue the divine damsel in distress. Again, as mythological as all this might be, borders were crossed and recrossed in the realms of emotion, faith and perception without much of an issue, giving birth to ideas and beliefs that have survived the vagaries of time not just in our region, but even as far away as Bali, Thailand and Cambodia.

Since at least the sixteenth century, the poetry and music of Sufis in the region spread across the region and beyond, in the process paying no significant attention to existing borders and the influence of this cultural package could be felt and be seen in places known today as India, Pakistan, Bangladesh and Sri Lanka. But by now, the Sufi heritage despite its cross-cultural appeal and historical longevity is under attack in Pakistan and Bangladesh in the name of purity of religion and does not exist in Sri Lanka even as a distant memory. But it is still very much thriving in India as even a cursory visit to places like Nizamuddin Dargah in New Delhi as well as the popularity of Sufi music among audiences

---

[3] Perera, 2008, 'Preface,' *South Asia Journal of Culture*.

beyond the community itself would indicate. Since the 1930s and right up to the early 1970s Radio Ceylon's Hindi service, with its iconic programme, *Binaca Geetmala*, reached all the way from non-Hindi speaking Colombo to the Hindi-speaking heartland of North India to make its presence felt not simply on real-time via short-wave radio frequencies, but also through the later-day audio-cassette revolution.

Compared to these and countless other examples, the fluidity in the travel of ideas and manifestations of culture and practices in mythic and historic times is far less fluid in our own times, despite the massive changes in transportation and communication technology and rhetoric like 'knowledge hub' that one hears often in Sri Lanka from politicians while the intellectual space and the public sphere continue to shrink at an alarming pace. This has to do with the expansion and entrenchment of nation states in our region and the fundamental inability of our leaders to think beyond the limitations of the 'nation' despite its obvious dysfunctions. As many of us know by experience, we have also become imprisoned and restricted by an unhelpful and uncreative visa regime in this region.

In this context, South Asia is simply an abstract idea that has not been seriously explored intellectually though it has been used and abused politically. The fact that a landmass under this title exists in conventional maps even as some of its borders are contested is beside the point. For me, South Asia still needs to be imagined and rescued from the hallucinations of present-day divisive politics endemic in the region. So I will use the term South Asia today only as a vague geographic term that needs to be concretised in intellectual and political terms in times to come.

On the other hand, even though political structures such as South Asian Association for Regional Cooperation (SAARC) have emerged that often perform ritualised practices devoid of significant consequences, it is not easy to see 'regular and serious forums for South Asian scholarship to showcase our own research and our own thinking.'[4] Despite the passage of over half a century since the advent of official decolonisation, much of the readings and analyses of the

[4] Perera, 2008, 'Preface,' *South Asia Journal of Culture*.

core issues still emanate from Euro-American academia.[5] This is most obvious when seen from our deployment of 'conceptual formulations and theoretical approaches from the Euro-American zone' in 'exploring the region's social and cultural complexities often without much self-reflection'.[6] To be more precise, 'most things from cultural theorising to formulating development strategies percolate from these usual centres of knowledge often based on experiences exterior to our own, and these are later circulated everywhere via journals and books as authoritative texts that also come from the same centres'.[7] What is apparent is that 'provincialising Europe' in the sense once suggested by Dipesh Chakrabarty,[8] or to extend that logic to 'provincialising North America' as well has failed to receive traction in the academic and political discourses of our region beyond rhetoric and much noise.[9]

Ideally, we ought to have posed consistently the kind of fundamental questions that Chakrabarty raised in his book, which many others have elaborated since then:

> Can European thought be dislodged or decentred from the centre of historical practice in non-European places such as ours and what are the consequences we have to anticipate when cultural practices from our part of the world are translated into categories of social science which derive their own power from a completely different historical and political lineage?[10]

This, however, is neither a matter of promoting a naively simplistic and utterly parochial nativism or shunning the thinking from these dominant schools of thought and knowledge as a routine practice irrespective of their locations in Europe, North America or elsewhere beyond the region.[11]

---

5 Perera, 2008, 'Preface,' *South Asia Journal of Culture.*

6 Perera, 2008, 'Preface,' *South Asia Journal of Culture.*

7 Perera, 2008, 'Preface,' *South Asia Journal of Culture.*

8 Dipesh Chakrabarty, 2007, *Provincializing Europe: Postcolonial Thought and Historical Difference*, Princeton, Princeton University Press.

9 Perera, 2008, 'Preface,' *South Asia Journal of Culture.*

10 Perera, 2008, 'Preface,' *South Asia Journal of Culture.*

11 Perera, 2008, 'Preface,' *South Asia Journal of Culture.*

On the contrary, I am arguing for serious engagement with these issues within South Asia on a consistent, dynamic and larger scale. This is because 'South Asia has its own cultural dynamics, its own triumphs and failures or alternatives of democracy, their own versions of modernity, chaos and order sitting side by side.'[12] Do we always have to fly all the way to London, Berlin and New York to debate these issues?

It is in this context that I suggest that if we are keen to see the emergence of a dynamic cultural and intellectual environment in the region, delinked from the shackles of religion, ethnicity, caste, nationalism and parochial local politics and expansionist global agendas, we necessarily have to move beyond history but with memories of that history that are useful in our minds. And we clearly have to attempt this against and in spite of the multiple parochialisms, hierarchies and hegemonies of the present. If I am to place this within the Buddhist sensibilities I was brought up with that my generation has now conveniently forgotten, this outlines the necessity to be 'patisothagamin' or simply swim against the tide. The theme of my argument, 'beyond history and against the present' finds its genesis within this conglomeration of ideas.

How does one do this? Let me ponder over how we might reimagine South Asia which might help create a more robust intellectual climate on the one hand, and where derivations of culture might go beyond simple aesthetics of pleasure into discourses of social history, memory and active engagement and interrogation of politics, on the other. In this very preliminary exercise, I will focus on a handful of regional examples that I am familiar with.[13]

One project that immediately comes to mind because it consciously transgressed the contested militarised national borders between Pakistan and India at a time of extreme political anxiety is the public art collaboration, *Aar Paar* project. Despite heightened political anxieties, the project made aesthetic intrusions into selected public spaces in the two countries irrespective of the rhetoric of the two states and their various political bandwagons. The project was conceived and

[12] Perera, 2008, 'Preface,' *South Asia Journal of Culture*.

[13] The information on the *Aar Paar* and *Aham-Puram* projects are from a keynote address delivered by Anoli Perera in Bangalore in 2008.

coordinated by the Karachi-based artist Huma Muji and Mumbai-based artist Shilpa Gupta both of whom initially met in New Delhi in an art exchange programme in 1999. *Aar Paar*, literally means 'this side, that side' in Hindi as well as in Urdu. Interestingly, however, in both languages, it could also refer to a decisive battle. The project initiated a cross border conversation between two cities, Mumbai and Karachi that are both familiar and have also been made 'unfamiliar'. *Aar Paar* can denote a meaning of invisibility or the absence of tangible obstructions. Seen in this sense, cultural flows could flow across, as was attempted in this case, without the hurdles of borders.

The project was initially launched in 2000 and continued into 2002 as a second phase. It was formulated in the background of the Kargil War in 1999 and the communal violence in Gujarat in 2002. Artists from both countries were invited to contribute digitally created photographic or graphic artworks that could be exchanged via email between Karachi and Mumbai focusing on the theme 'search for peace and understanding'. They were then mass produced in each city using inexpensive offset printing technology. These prints were put up on walls alongside commercial advertisements, political posters and film posters, shop fronts and street corners. They were also distributed inserted within newspapers and some were given as handouts in public spaces. Altogether, there were 21 posters that were mass-printed and distributed.

The second project I want to briefly place in context is the *Aham-Puram* exhibition spearheaded by Theertha International Artists' Collective in Colombo through a long term collaboration with a group of artists based in Jaffna in northern Sri Lanka. Unlike *Aar Paar*, *Aham-Puram* did not cross borders of nation states digitally, but physically transgressed equally entrenched and ethnically and politically marked, defended and militarised local borders. *Aham-Puram* literally means 'insider/outsider' in Tamil, and is a concept borrowed from Tamil Sangam literature, particularly of the second-century AD. The exhibition was held in 2004 at the reconstructed public library of Jaffna whose imposing original structure was burned down by Sinhala hooligans in 1981 marking one of the most significant moments in the long-term mismanagement of interethnic relations in the country. The exhibition contained contemporary art from southern Sri Lanka and was conceived to document how southern Sri Lankan artists, most of whom were Sinhalas and Buddhists dealt with issues of conflict, violence, death, destruction and anxiety, thereby indicating similarities in suffering, anxieties and fears across ethnocultural and geopolitical borders. In addition, it was meant to open up possibilities of art-making that could transform the experiences of the north into new expressions capable of challenging the conventions and boundaries of art. Twenty-seven artists from the south participated in the exhibition that contained 72 artworks. It was a very ambitious and challenging project as it was not easy to transport 72 artworks through numerous Sri Lankan military and LTTE checkpoints in contested areas through an active war zone though a faulty and uncomfortable ceasefire was in place at the time.

On top of that, many of the artworks really did not seem like artworks at all to the average person including the military and LTTE sentries who were keen to inspect them. This was five years before the civil war finally ended; cooperation and logistical operations of this kind had not been attempted before in recent memory and, therefore, the event had no precedence as such.

What do these projects indicate when seen from the realm of possibilities within the larger space where we live and work and in our times? In both cases, contested national borders in the former and contested local borders in the latter were transgressed in order to ensure that ideas and manifestations of culture could flow across. In doing so, there was no dependence on or expectations from state structures. Rather, both efforts were undertaken despite and in spite of hurdles put in place by virulent forms of nationalism sponsored by nation states as well as other actors. What is important to me here is that small groups of citizens opted not to take 'NO' for an answer and attempted to explore a set of realities important to them and look for possible alternatives of discourse.

I am not advancing a simplistic idea that art or any other form of culture could transform politics as popular logic often presented by politically active artists themselves would articulate. In fact, I agree with Masahiro Ushiroshoji's caution against the naïve assumption that art alone can achieve an understanding of other cultures and values or in itself can heal disjuncture in relationships between societies and people.[14] Preziosi and Farago also argue for the rethinking of the power of the artist when they note, 'the agency assigned to the artist could vary according to who is speaking, to whom and to what purpose'.[15] Nevertheless, I strongly believe that art and other forms of culture as well as knowledge in the formal sense have a crucial role to play in the realm of politics, in the domain of discourse and within the vistas of our conscience if conceived seriously and produced squarely in the context of the spatial and temporal circumstances of the moment.

So the two examples I presented did not obviously transform the larger politics or the intellectual discourses in India, Pakistan and Sri Lanka. But in the processes through which they were conceived and implemented, through the tools that were formulated and the technologies that were adopted to overcome entrenched ground difficulties and attitudes, contested geographies were redrawn and reimagined and the flow of ideas across boundaries was made possible, at least momentarily. In what was literally and metaphorically a liminal moment, a few fragments of what we flippantly called South Asia was thought of differently. And what was imagined at that moment was far more palatable than numerous existing realities.

More importantly, these events indicate the extent of possibilities that exist if the region is to be reimagined. For me, they map out the landscapes of hope. Surely, we cannot expect such imagination from the political leaders of our region as well as from the nature of hegemonic politics that are presently in place in all the countries in the region.

I think this state of affairs nudges us in another somewhat connected direction. That is, to think about how locality, place and the nation are located and understood in the production of knowledge as well as culture. Though the examples I referred to earlier found as their point of departure political specificities of three countries, those specificities are not strictly local in the sense that they are not confined merely to the peculiarities of places narrowly defined. It is in

[14] Quoted in Caroline Turner, 2005, *Art and Social Change*, Canberra, Pandanus Books, p. 5.

[15] Donald Preziosi and Claire Farago, 2012, *Art is Not What You Think It Is*, Chichester, Blackwell Publishing.

this context that Rustom Bharucha observes in his book, *The Politics of Cultural Practice*,

> while India is the 'lens' through which I see the world, it is also the stimulus that brings together any number of sites that are embedded in an intricate network of social, historical, political, and economic contexts at once localized and mediated by global and national agencies.[16]

And he further notes that these sites are not 'predetermined cultural realities but constructions that are held together not so much by what is "given" in any culture, but by what is "invented" through their negotiations of specific interventions, assaults, inputs, and collaborations'.[17]

When perceived from the perspective of these sensibilities, though the civil war in Sri Lanka primarily emerged as a result of the country's inability to manage its interethnic relations, its subsequent militarisation and the devastating end had much to do with: (*a*) India's monumentally visionless projection of power across national borders, (*b*) China's crude interest in acquiring military and political assets far beyond its borders irrespective of local consequences, (*c*) global trade in arms that had no reference to ethics and (*d*) the entire post-9/11 discourse against global terror as scripted, narrated and acted out by the United States' and the European Union's political interests.

On the other hand, the political wilderness in the hegemonic thinking of India–Pakistan relations that often seems impossible to overcome stems from the fundamental inability of both the countries to grow out of the pains of the partition. But isn't that inability as local as it may be, also fuelled by global power structures from the time of the cold war to the much more chaotic present whose foreign policy agendas were driven to find allies and enemies in different confrontations both military and ideological?

In this overall context, Nikos Papastergiadis observes in his book *Spatial Politics: Art, Place and the Everyday*, that 'artists have always had a strong interest in representing the experience of being in a specific place and responding to current political issues' thereby self-consciously

---

[16] Rustom Bharucha, 2001, *The Politics of Cultural Practice*, New Delhi, Oxford University Press, p. 3.

[17] Bharucha, *The Politics of Cultural Practice*, p. 3.

referencing the local.[18] Though difficult to generalise beyond a point, this is what the so-called political artists including the individuals involved in the examples I have provided had aimed to do.

Nevertheless, Papastergiadis notes further, that 'the idea of representing a local place or reacting to political issues can no longer occur in isolation from global concerns' while 'they [meaning the artists] are often very protective and committed to these places they are also deeply aware of their links to global debates and part of international dialogues on the meaning of their practice and its relevance to others'.[19] So it is no accident that many of the artists involved in both art events referred to earlier were members of globally linked networks that ensured the flow of not only ideological tenets in aesthetics and politics but also structures of knowledge on methodological skills, technologies and material.

Seen in this sense, consciously or unconsciously, these kinds of events that might take as their point of departure something seen and experienced as local can only be understood more fully within a global or regional setting, thereby fundamentally destabilising what we simplistically think is local. For me, these kinds of moments are road signs that might show us how our region might be reimagined and where we might be able to take it.

This brings me to the last point I want to make, which has to do with the nature of formal knowledge we produce in our academic institutions and their references to the lived experiences in our region. I find an unhealthy disjuncture between the two. I am not denying the fact that the so-called local research, some of which is somewhat serious but much of which are simple descriptions of events that are not published and redistributed in our region. My concern has to do with inadequate theorisation and conceptualisation based on local and regional experiences that may allow us space to interrogate everything from the dynamics of contemporary international relations to identity politics. Whenever I have said this in the past, a number of colleagues

---

[18] Nikos Papastergiadis, 2006, *Spatial Politics: Art, Place and the Everyday*, London, Rivers Oram Press, p. 3.

[19] Papastergiadis, *Spatial Politics*, pp. 3–4.

accused me of harking back to a nativism of a bygone era. This was not my intention then and it is certainly not my intention now.

Though I find Bharata Muni's *Natya Shastra* and Kautilya's *Arthashastra* fascinating as texts and sometimes even useful in contemporary but limited aesthetic and political contexts, history and the past cannot be seamlessly re-established in the present. However, is it not possible to think creatively in sociology, international relations and political science, just to take three disciplines I have thought about in this context in recent times? Is it not possible for us to move away from the hegemonic preoccupation with post-Bismarck diplomacy and predictable conflict resolution theory in international relations thinking in the region? Can't we revisit our overdependence on Marx and Foucault as well as an almost pathological obsession with caste, class and now gender in sociology and social anthropology? Is it impossible to find new objects to interrogate which might allow us to rethink our theory as well as the nature of research and knowledge themselves?

In this context, I have often wondered why visual culture and particularly painting, sculpture and installation in our region have not moved beyond art history into areas such as international relations and sociology. To explore this context, let us for a moment consider the politics of art as a wider intellectual discourse. All of us I am sure are quite conversant with the fact that in terms of most conventional systems of reckoning, the correlation or the critical relationship between art and politics is not always clear; often it could be tenuous.

At the same time, simply because sociopolitical calamities prevail at a particular time and place that alone does not necessarily mark the emergence of politically expressive art or works that present some form of critical engagement. In fact, precisely due to such calamities and the diminished sense of safety such times might usher in, art could become much more apolitical or even aesthetically sedate. Susan Landauer notes that periods of cultural and political ferment do not necessarily lead to the production of art 'affectively addressing that ferment'.[20] It is in this

[20] Susan Landauer, 2006, 'Countering Cultures: The California Context,' in *Art of Engagement: Visual Politics in California and Beyond*, edited by Peter Selz, Berkeley, University of California Press, p. 1.

context that she refers to the lack of politically engaged art among the avant-garde in New York in the 1960s when multiple political crises were impacting not only the United States but the world in general.[21] It is their lacklustre response to the Vietnam War that moved Susan Sontag to describe their approach as an 'aesthetic of silence'.[22]

These kinds of restrictions have been evident not only in the United States that Landauer refers to but also in many other parts of the world including in our own region. It is in this context that the work of many contemporary artists in the region have often been labelled as not authentic, anti-national, pro-western and so on within a restricted discourse of nationalism and authenticity. Nevertheless, many well-known contemporary artists in the region have produced work with a certain degree of criticality even if some of them may not consider themselves to be political artists as such. Sheeba Chachi of India, Naiza Khan and Asma Mundarawala of Pakistan, Begum Lipi Thayeb of Bangladesh, Sujan Chitrakar and Asmeena Ranjit of Nepal and Jagath Weerasinghe, Pradeep Chandrasiri and Chandragupta Tenuwara of Sri Lanka are some of these among many. Caroline Turner's 2005 book, *Art and Social Change*, paints an extended canvas of this very interesting scenario throughout the wider Asia-Pacific region.

The point I want to make is that art of this kind invariably goes much beyond what is conventionally thought of as art and this kind of work makes better sense when located in the specificities of their production rather than by merely focusing within the frame. It is in such a context that Peter Selz observed when referring to German impressionist painting, the need to focus on ideological currents of the time rather than a mere contextualisation within a discourse of formalism when attempting to situate art within the larger context of evolving politics.[23] This consideration impacts art everywhere at all times.

If we accept the reality of this context and the discursive possibilities it offers, is it not possible that *Aar Paar* and *Aham-Puram* projects and

---

[21] Susan Landauer, p. 1.

[22] Quoted in Susan Landauer, p. 1.

[23] Peter Selz, 2006, *Art of Engagement: Visual Politics in California and Beyond*, Berkeley, University of California Press, p. 25.

others like that could allow us to envision how diplomacy in our time and our region might be refashioned? Is it not possible that the same projects and their contexts might provide us insights on how theories and methodologies in conflict resolution and transformation might be rethought and localised? Why is it that sociology in our times is so manifestly fearful of research categories such as visual culture which by and large remains with practitioners, in commerce, in the discourses of art historians or simply as a means for aesthetic pleasure?

Cannot contemporary art offer avenues towards comprehending violence, nationalism and the politics of memory in our times as a handful of sociologists, particularly in India have attempted to do? It seems to me that the problem lies within the sedate and almost regressive structures and hierarchies of our academic institutions within which new methodologies and areas for research as well as theorisation is actively discouraged; this is also the reason why the domains and methodologies of research and writing considered sacrosanct by the old guard and their contemporary followers are so religiously reified and protected.

To be quite frank, I don't think mainstream social sciences in our region have even thought of exploring what art actually seems like in contemporary contexts. It seems to me that the title of Donald Preziosi's and Claire Farago's recent book, *Art is Not What You Think It Is* (2012), could work as a provocation to the regional social science enterprise to critically reassess their research objects. They also suggest something interesting that might be quite useful as an idea if practitioners of social sciences in our region opt to revisit what art is, what it does and what it could do in our localities. According to them, the art of the future should be imagined as 'embodied knowledge practice that is flexible and susceptible to further re-articulation and redefinition.'[24] But they are realistic enough in accepting that

> articulating art-making practices as embodied forms of cognition will not in itself solve the dilemmas of the current commodified art system. But such a re-conceptualization of what art does and *what that doing itself does*, offers a responsible way forward on many fronts.[25]

---

[24] Preziosi and Farago, *Art is Not What You Think It Is*, p. 160.

[25] Preziosi and Farago, *Art is Not What You Think It Is*, pp. 160–161.

This is part of the reality within which we live and work today in someplace vaguely and flippantly called South Asia. For me, there is much in our circumstances that needs to radically change. This is what some of us are trying to do in an entity called South Asian University against many odds. Now, after about one year, surviving multiple crises and many battles that typify the retardation of higher education in our part of the world, we think it is possible for us to introduce interdisciplinary courses in the departments of International Relations and Sociology on such 'weird' themes such as the social history of jazz and the politics of food with a focus on our region and beyond. This is mostly because there is no old guard as such and no burdensome institutional traditions of regression within the Faculty of Social Sciences even though beyond it, the spectre of conventionality looms high like a familiar and omnipotent but inconsequential poltergeist.

When we think of the region, there are moments in our collective histories that might give us ideas in the present; but clearly, we have to move beyond history. The present, on the other hand, is an unending source of anxiety though not necessarily without hope, as our experience at South Asia University would indicate. But it should be equally clear that we cannot take the present for granted but often need to move against its hegemonies. So for me, the path towards reimagining our region and its intellectual traditions is necessarily beyond history and against the present.

7

An Emotive-Intellectual Inclination to another South Asia!

Dev Nath Pathak

An unverifiable story about George Grierson's quest for languages in colonial India (a subcontinent which was more than contemporary geopolitical India) is pertinent to commence this chapter. As a meticulous surveyor, Grierson had made a list of languages in India and he was going around, recording responses and documenting details about these. In due course, he came upon a language in his list, named 'junglee', literally meaning, the wild. On seeing this, his search for the geographical and demographic location of the language began. He went from one town to another, from one village to another, from one kasbah (a unit of residential location in vernacular) to another, from one sadar (a unit of administrative division) to another, asking whether anybody had heard about the language. Everywhere he got the same answer: 'O yes, we know, but it is not spoken among us, it is spoken by folks in another village, another town, another kasbah, another sadar!'

Needless to say, the story is pregnant with possibilities and invites all sorts of intellectual mischief in order to serve epistemic-babies. Just like 'junglee', perhaps it is difficult to physically locate the region popularly known as South Asia. It is everywhere and yet it is nowhere. Much like an emotionally charged episteme, it is in people's love, hatred, fear, assurance, distance and proximity. It is here and now, it was there and then and it would be near and far forever. Truly, this is how it seems to be, since, it precludes foreclosures and disables certainty. No, this is neither for a poetic swag nor for a postmodern tryst. Far from that, it is about the region and its bewildering mix of people, issues, culture and politics. Second, as the unverifiable story of Grierson mentioned earlier suggests, just like 'junglee', South Asia too deserves a saviour prefix, 'another'. The respondents of Grierson could have easily killed the search of a diehard linguist-surveyor by answering: no, it is not spoken anywhere. Instead, the unequivocal answer, across and afar, was in support of the existence of the somewhat non-existent junglee.

The saviour prefix, another, kept the quest alive and the surveyor optimistic. Such is the power of a simple and innocuous adjective! Another! Intellectually instigating, politically promising, culturally confusing and ideologically loaded. This is so in everyday life of a phenomenologist's framework of the mundane as well as in the spectacles of real politics. Even though we don't know the exact whereabouts of another 'village', 'town', 'kasbah', 'sadar', we don't give up. With such uncertainty we have the hope of finding this, another, some day, some place, with some people. As is with 'junglee', arguably, so is with South Asia.

The prefix 'another' with South Asia is indeed not too enigmatic.[1] Nor is it a mere semantic usage in imagining the region. It is a 'loaded' metaphor, a heuristic device, employed with convenient eclecticism in the discursive trope. And the 'load' of 'another' solicits due unravelling, through glaring gaps and jump cuts in order to be respectful to the constraint of space. One of the most abiding features of the 'loaded another' is the curious dynamics of darkness and light, ignorance and knowledge, certainty and uncertainty. As to how it pertains to 'another', and more importantly, its association with South Asia, will surface soon. Before that it is necessary to make the metaphor less obtuse through a thought-provoking parable, which the grand folklorist A.K. Ramanujan etched, in printed posterity for our easy reference:

> ...one dark night an old woman was searching intently for something in the street. A passerby asked her, 'Have you lost something?'
>
> She said, 'Yes, I've lost some keys. I've been looking for them all evening.'

[1] Dev Nath Pathak, ed., 2018, *Another South Asia!* Delhi, Primus.

> 'Where did you lose them?'
> 'I don't know. Maybe inside the house.'
> 'Then, why are you looking for them here?'
> 'because it's dark in there. I don't have oil in my lamps. I can see much better here under the street lights,' she said.[2]

The parable aptly underlines the necessity of shifting these kinds of exploratory quests to hitherto peripheral domains. This calls for a shift from the intellectually closeted dark chambers of discourse to the various well-lit avenues replete with curious tidbits, knick-knacks and objects of enquiries. This is what signifies another, in short. 'Another' as a prefix of South Asia alludes to imagining the region 'differently' with materials, issues and epistemic units that are strewn in the fecund sociocultural and political field of the region. And this process of imagining entails acknowledging the delimiting effects of the conventional deliberations, departing from the potential discomfitures as well as 'harvesting new images.'[3]

Cauldron of Confusion

There is another reason why the prefix 'another' is crucial insofar as South Asia is concerned. This is related to the disciplinary boundaries which, allegedly, impede the novel processes of comprehending a region. These disciplinary boundaries and illogically fortified scope of some of the disciplines saddled with the objective of understanding the region could be in tune with the demands of nation states. While common sense is fraught with confusion, the illegitimacy of clarity in the academic discourse is not conducive to understand the region either. Let's take the example of the two disciplines, international relations and the Siamese twins, sociology and social anthropology.

---

2 A.K. Ramanujan, 1999, 'Who Needs Folklore,' in *The Collected Essays of A.K. Ramanujan*, edited by Vinay Dharwadker, Delhi, Oxford University Press, p. 533. This motif led me to start an enquiry into the dark chambers of Maithili folklore elsewhere, in Dev Nath Pathak, 2018, *Living and Dying: Meanings in Maithili Folklore,* Delhi, Primus.

3 This is formulation by Imtiaz Ahmed, an unusual scholar of International Relations from Bangladesh, in Pathak, *Another South Asia!*.

A provocative proposition could be healthy for an 'appetising' beginning. International relations scholarship has not been successful to wriggle out of the conventional modes and hence has not developed a good sense of 'another' about South Asia. The same could be proposed for sociology and social anthropology too. Despite the variable subject areas, the two are too nationalist to give birth to serious engagement with the region, let alone any 'anti-national' thoughts. And this is what constitutes the mainstay in the following part.

The disciplinary self-reflexivity in International Relations (IR) is fairly new and only partially successful despite some of the pursuits in this direction. It is not rare to hear that IR in India, 'has not been particularly self-reflective over the years'.[4] IR may have played more with words than in deed, and hence, 'war is its traditional forte'.[5] This is in the wake of the becoming, or rather unbecoming, of a discipline in its historical trajectory, 'The field began as a peace-oriented discipline in the years immediately following World War I. It then shifted in the main towards a conflict-and-threat emphasis in the interwar years as aggression inched forward in Europe and Asia'.[6] There has been a 'spectacular disciplinary failure' on many counts. And the failing—according to many conscientious IR scholars including Sylvester—augurs well for disciplinary possibilities. The latter solicits IR to shun its safe, comfortable and narrow frames of analyses. It requires the scholars to explore, as Sylvester aptly titles the work, 'International Relations where We Least Expect It'. Also, it perhaps demands from IR scholars to engage with various disciplines of social sciences and attempt to enculture the in general terribly acultural studies in IR.[7] To be more precise, 'the return of culture and identity in IR theory' demands cross-disciplinary (social

---

[4] Kanti Bajpai, 2009, 'International Studies in India: Bringing Theory (Back) Home', in *International Relations in India: Bringing Theory Back Home*, edited by Kanti Bajpai and Siddharth Mallavarapu, Delhi, Orient Blackswan, pp. 18–19.

[5] Christine Sylvester, 2009, *Art/Museums: International Relations Where We Least Expect It*, London, Paradigm Publisher, p. 1.

[6] Sylvester, *Art/Museums*, pp. 4–5.

[7] Yosef Lapid and Friedrich Kratochwill, eds., 1996, *The Return of Culture and Identity in IR Theory*, London, Lynne Rienner Publishers.

anthropological in precise) approaches in IR. Therefore, Navnita Behera was correct when she noted,

> The epistemic foundations of IR in South Asia are on a weak footing as theoretical work remains a much 'dreaded and despised' enterprise across the region. This is partly due to the persisting ethnocentrism or Americanocentrism of Western theories that often leads to alienation when its tools prove to be ineffective in understanding the ground realities that are rooted in a very different historical, social and cultural milieu.[8]

This has promoted a set of grotesque practices in IR in India leading to the intellectualised obscurity of IR. As a student of IR suggested, 'either IR studies are too simple to be intellectually, theoretically and philosophically exciting, or they are excessively intellectualised, though merely phony, to become part of the practices. Not a single university in South Asia has been able to transform the thoughts and practices in IR'.[9] This seems a viable allegation in the face of abysmally nil innovation in course-designs, pedagogic practices and encouragement for novel research themes. A random survey of the courses in IR offered across the region could perhaps vindicate the allegation. In this wake, it seems likely to believe, as a student provocatively argued, 'IR scholarship, teaching, and researches are merely about gaffing intelligently, without any references to cultural life of the objects of studies'.

Moreover, the theoretical poverty of IR in India is a shared malaise in the region and it is not only due to the geopolitical conditioning of the discipline but also due to the overlapping surrender to the predominant methodological (precisely, epistemological) (neo)realism, positivism and to top it all scientism. Episteme, thus, is a clinical and indubitable category in the traditional IR in the region. This, however, amounts to a series of '"silences" of South Asian IR',[10] conducive for the nationalist framework of politics as well as scholarship.

---

[8] Navnita Chadha Behera, ed., 2008, *International Relations in South Asia: Search for an Alternative Paradigm*, New Delhi, SAGE Publications, p. 14.

[9] The name of the student is not revealed on the request for anonymity. I am dwelling upon my communication with a few IR research students at South Asian University and Jawaharlal Nehru University.

[10] Behera, *International Relations in South Asia*, pp. 14–24.

While the case of IR in South Asia is unpleasantly peculiar, the case of sociology and social anthropology is seemingly complex too. Unlike IR, there has been a self-reflective tendency in sociology, perhaps a disciplinary predisposition. It has been so prominent that one could sarcastically suggest that sociology trains in a narcissistic self-criticism. Paradoxically though, despite the heightened sense of self-reflexivity, sociologists have not been able to overcome the delimiting nationalistic framework in which they blissfully operate. A cursory glance at the history of sociology and social anthropology in the region may lead to the comprehension of disciplinary distinctions along national lines. There surfaces a sense that sociology in a particular national context is an isolated disciplinary island. For example, sociology and social anthropology in India do not seem to engage with their counterparts in Pakistan, Bangladesh, Nepal etc. Sociology in Afghanistan or Maldives or Bhutan, no matter in what shape, would never figure in the history of sociology in Bangladesh or India. This is despite that 'reflexivity' has been a buzzword in the disciplinary framework of sociology and social anthropology across the globe. And indeed 'reflexive sociology', translating into 'Sociology of Sociology',[11] has been central in India for quite some time. It is safe to suggest that sociology of sociology in India began with the debates on Sociology of India by the French sociologist Louis Dumont. Many waters have flown ever since and the debates have heralded the issues of indigenous, problems of epistemological nationalism, acknowledgement of the crisis in the practices of sociology in India and the recent revisiting of the idea of pluralism. But unfortunately, in the Indian context, it seems self-reflexivity of sociology has been reduced to crisis-mongering,[12] without any vision, and least of the deeds, towards making transformations in teaching programmes, course-content, pedagogic practices and exploration of uncharted areas of research.

---

[11] Alwin Gouldner, 1970, *The Coming Crisis of Western Sociology*, New York, Basic Books.

[12] To follow this line, see for example, V. Das, 1993, 'Sociological Research in India—The State of Crisis', *Economic and Political Weekly*, Vol. 28, No. 23, pp. 1159–1161; S. Deshpande, 1994, 'Crisis in Sociology: A Tired Discipline', *Economic and Political Weekly*, Vol. 29, No. 10, pp. 575–576; A.R. Vasavi, 2011, 'Pluralising the Sociology of India', *Contributions to Indian Sociology*, Vol. 45, No. 3, pp. 399–426.

In this wake, it shall be posited that sociology and anthropology in India seldom undertook a regional turn.[13] An exceptional deliberation published in *Sociological Bulletin*, an outcome of a South Asia Workshop titled, 'The State of Sociology: Issues of Relevance and Rigor'[14] under the aegis of Indian Sociological Society, made a modest attempt to put together narratives of disciplinary practices from various parts of the region. A similar endeavour, namely International Sociological Association Conference of South Asia titled 'Sociology in South Asia: Heritage and Challenges', putting together a small congregation, was held on 25–27 March in 1997 in Mumbai (India).[15] However, such initiatives, few and far between, remained merely a congregation of various narratives conditioned by the national contexts. One of the reasons, among several others, behind the lack of encouragement for sociological engagement with the region, could be the binary opposite underpinning the discursive frameworks. The binaries are of local and global, without heeding the trans-local, the regional. Furthermore, the binaries are of national and international, without heeding transnational, the South Asian. This surfaces bluntly, for example, in a sociologist such as T.K. Oommen's advocacy for 'internationalisation of Sociology'.[16] While it reckons with the delimiting impact of the national-rootedness of the discipline and appeals for creating a non-western notion of internationalisation, it seldom engages with the regional. Oommen, joining the ilk of nationalist sociologists, only eclectically uses instances from various nation states in the region and hardly delves into the intricate details of the 'region' or regional sociology.

It is in this context, fraught with paradoxes of the two disciplines, namely IR and sociology and social anthropology, it is imperative to

---

[13] Our concerted effort towards this led to an initial outcome, see Ravi Kumar, Dev Nath Pathak and Sasanka Perera, eds., 2018, *Sociology and Social Anthropology in South Asia: Histories and Practices*, Delhi, Orient Blackswan.

[14] The workshop was held on the special issue of the journal *Sociological Bulletin* (2005, Vol. 54, No. 3) is available at http://www.jstor.org/stable/23620630?seq=1#page_scan_tab_contents (accessed on 9 August 2018).

[15] See http://www.isa-sociology.org/colmemb/national-associations/en/meetings/reports/SouthAsia.html (accessed on 9 August 2018).

[16] T.K. Oomen, 1991, 'Internationalization of Sociology: A View From Developing Countries', *Current Sociology*, Vol. 39, No. 1, pp. 67–84.

critically depart from the beaten tracks. In other words, if we ought to be thinking regionally within these disciplines, we need to make 'another' our creative muse. The reason why 'another' is crucial for the reconfiguration of the idea of South Asia is the abundance of notions to which this chapter briefly alluded to earlier. This abundance is played out on the predominant trope of discussion on South Asia in IR scholarship. And, needless to say, it seems to be heavily determined by the pivot of SAARC and thereof by the scheme of nation state. Hence the exploration of 'bi-lateral relation' is in the centre, along which issues of trade, security and development are explored.[17] Needless to say, the thematic gloss of culture and civilisation also makes 'cameo-entry', perhaps akin to the pop-cinematic item number, in this trope. But then, it allegedly suffers from various levels of intellectual poverty. The utter paucity of conceptual depth and sheer lack of imagination, probably, are the key traits of this trope, which perpetuates the logic of SAARC and adds very little to the idea of South Asia.

'Another': In Defence of Utopia(s)

The prefix 'another' is a pertinent metaphor, a heuristic device in Weberian sense, to facilitate constructive transcending of the vexed notions attached with the term South Asia. The prerequisite for the verb 'transcending' is, among other things, a noun 'transcending'. Utopia in a broader sense, as a sociologist of knowledge, Karl Mannheim elucidated, is such a 'reality-transcending' device. In the wake of the reduction of social sciences, or for that matter sciences in general, into knowledge enterprise geared towards 'solution of the immediate, technical problems of social life', the dominant questions are: 'How can I solve this concrete individual problem … I need not worry about the whole, the whole will take care of itself'.[18] This is the scheme of social sciences in which a sceptical-relativist point of view renders

[17] A typical example of this kind of works is a volume, S.D. Muni, ed., 2010, *The Emerging Dimensions of SAARC*, Delhi, Foundation Books.

[18] Karl Mannheim, 1966, *Ideology and Utopia: An Introduction to the Sociology of Knowledge*, London, Routledge and Kegan Paul Ltd., p. 229.

history into undifferentiated and more bluntly into an irrelevant field of enquiry by banishing ideologies and utopias. This befits the 'search for eternally valid generalizations' and conjures the 'dominant type of mentality' 'congruent with the reality of capitalist society'. Mannheim is not entirely pessimistic and hence anticipates the intellectuals to perform an important role: 'spiritualize the present' 'through romantic reconstruction'.

This fundamental awareness leads us to fathom the relation of South Asia and utopias. Speaking of the significance of utopias, in the realm of history and identity politics, historian Romila Thapar notes,

> All of us in South Asia, not to mention other ex-colonies, have faced the same questions of how to define ourselves as citizens of a new nation and of course, the question of identity or identities. We in India thought the answer was simple—it was the single identity of being Indian. But the reality on the ground has turned it into a complex question without a simple answer because even a single identity can subsume others. The utopias that we wished for have retreated in the face of identities in conflict.[19]

And one of such endangered, perhaps extinct, utopias related to South Asia, is that it alludes to, what Thapar underlines as mixed cultures. Among several forces acting against the utopian notions in the history of colonial and post-colonial South Asia seems to be nationalism and its various institutional avatars. And hence, it is enjoined upon the scholars, activists, artists, performer, cultural critics and ordinary folks with fluid faiths, to always seek for what is also known as 'Southasian Sensibility'. The latter was a yield of a 'practical vision of regionalism', which Dixit articulated in the following words, '"being Southasian" is an essential part of the multiple and cross-cutting identities the people of this region enjoy, from the local to the provincial, national and Subcontinental'.[20]

South Asia, with due respect for 'another', ought to be transcendental of the modern sense of territoriality and the official notion of

---

[19] Romila Thapar, 2014, *The Past as Present: Forging Contemporary Identities through History*, Delhi, Aleph, p. 42.

[20] Kanak Mani Dixit, 2012, *The South Asian Sensibility: A Himal Reader*, New Delhi, SAGE Publications, p. xi.

regionalism. The coveted utopia thus could enable us to see 'Southasia' as a penumbra of cultures from Balochistan and Afghanistan eastward and southward to Tibet, Burma, Sri Lanka and the Maldives. This sits well with a proposition by the historian duo, Ayesha Jalal and Sugata Bose, emerging from an intensive and nuanced engagement with rich archival details of the region. With such historical accounts about the politico-cultural possibilities, one tends to dream that borders may be made irrelevant in South Asia. Even though a nation acquires the imagery of a mother[21] (divine or mundane), putting aside the problematic of cultural-nationalist engendering, one tends to see 'visions of nation' in plural. And if we have the liberty to do anthropological mischief, we can posit that mothers never stop their children to feel emotionally inclined to mother's sister, colloquially *Maa-si/Mausi* (literally, like mother). One tends to read hope amid nationalist ranting, again with a sanguine historian like Sugata Bose, that motherhood of a nation is not detrimental to the innate wanderlust and imbibed emotional inclinations of children. Therefore, children of the mother(land) can comfortably admit the presence of emotional entanglement with lands from near and far, real and surreal, crossing of borders in mind and space and of things. The utopianism of this proposition is well neigh supported by the past as well as the present. However, this is not to be ignorant of the adverse effects of differences and vested interest in a 'political revivalist' unity. There is a utopia of 'Akhand Bharat' that threatens, rather than invites, for a unification of national territories. A particular variety of conservative politics in India has nursed an idea of a unified India, in the spirit of empire building, inclusive of Pakistan and Bangladesh. One ought to be aware of the viciousness of such proposed unification as much as of the various lines along which nations are divided. Such notions premise upon the ability of military aggressions into national territories for more militant reaffirmation of nationality, again with a 'be-witching' type of motherhood created out of a nation. Amid rivalling political utopias, a better one is of another South Asia, which aids in departing from monoliths and allows a

[21] Sugata Bose, 2017, *The Nation as Mother and Other Visions of Nationhood*, Delhi, Penguin.

creative-constructive play with history. It revolves around peoples of the region. And hence,

> Instead of pointing nuclear-tipped missiles at each other, the peoples of the subcontinent may be able to indulge their shared passion for food and film, music and literature as well as the game of cricket, if they have a better understanding of their common history.[22]

Lastly, it is imperative to mention a word of caution while seeking to defend 'another' as a signifier for utopias. The usage of 'another' has figured elsewhere in discussing 'Asia', 'through its conflicting modernities, wars, and a spectrum of differences, that nonetheless coexist with legacies of kinship and intimacy that are becoming increasingly harder to define in the age of globalization'.[23] This implies that 'another' does not signify a utopian hagiography of the continent. And hence, Bharucha seeks to depart from any atavistic utopia, underneath the platitudes of 'New Asia' or 'One Asia'. This is the scheme in which an insightful and rapturous reading of the proposition of Rabindranath Tagore and Okakura Tenshin unfolds in Bharucha's all-time relevant book fittingly titled 'Another Asia'.

The caution against utopianism is well placed in the given situation where the utopia of 'Akhand Bharat' (mentioned earlier) seems to take centre stage. Also, this is a meaningful caution in the wake of a voluminous hagiography of the region coming from many glib-talkers (mentioned earlier). More importantly, it is important for the reasons that Mannheim had suggested: a utopia could become a dominant ideology over time. Ideology, being an epistemic tool to maintain the status quo thus goes against the character of a utopia that is an epistemic tool to burst the status quo asunder.

---

22 Sugata Bose and Ayesha Jalal, 2011, *Modern South Asia: History, Culture, Political Economy*, New York, Routledge, p. 210.

23 Rustom Bharucha, 2009, *Another Asia: Rabindranath Tagore and Okakura Tenshin*, Delhi, Oxford University Press, p. xxii.

8

Localising South Asia, Theoretically

Dev Nath Pathak

We are too besotted with the category of the global, as though it were a spectacle of the milieu. It determines the way we make sense of the dynamics of the local. It yields, on one level, an atomised microscopic local, and on the other, a globally mediated local. At the microscopic level, an atomised version of local, pertaining to a particular cultural thread in isolation, subscribes to the logic of cultural relativism, a slippery passage from where a return to general discourse is difficult. On the other hand, globally mediated local subscribes to the idea of the hybridity of cultural forms in the pale of transnational flows and obscures the idea of any cultural specificity of the local. In a varied manner, the duality of sense, vis-à-vis either atomised microscopic local or globally mediated local, pertains to the idea of provincial globalisation.[1] Amidst the thickness of debate on globalisation, which borders theoretical obtuseness, there surfaces a sense of globalisation as a bipartite phenomenon, with one aspect promoting local, while the other thrusting towards the global. Hence Zygmunt Bauman operated with an alternative term 'glocalization'; and Ritzer went further on into the intricacies of the glocal to suggest of a complementary term 'grobalization'. The idea is to steer clear of the theoretical obtuseness and unearth something simpler about local. Hence, it is useful to look at the dynamics of the local. Despite its transnational circulation of cultural forms, the local unfolds an opportunity to transcend the theoretical limitations of globalisation and its various obscure cognates,

[1] Zygmunt Bauman, 1998, 'On Glocalization: Or Globalization for some and Localization for Some Others', *Thesis Eleven*, Vol. 54, No. 1, pp. 37–49; George Ritzer, 2003, 'Rethinking Globalization: Glocalization/Grobalization and Something/Nothing', *Sociological Theory*, Vol. 21, No. 3, pp. 193–209.

glocalisation or even grobalisation. It is, therefore, imperative to ask as to what sense of local stems from the realm of culture, popular and contemporary, in the region of South Asia.

Imagining Community Differently

In academic socialisation we are burdened with over-deterministic readings of Benedict Anderson and Arjun Appadurai, and hence, it seems we are too literally an imagined community governed by a strong mediascape and a conditional ideoscape.[2] And hence our sense of cinema, music, art and aesthetics, is ruled by the popular ideas about the region. The local, thereby, is configured in the matrix of global as relational and contextual, but mediated by global-deterritorialised mass media. While there is no denial of the deterritorialisation thesis, there is a problem in this formulation pertaining to the fact that it persists with the idea of imagination through modular modernity of Benedict Anderson. The flip side of this reasoning is quite vociferous too. By the way of reflecting upon the idea of South Asia, in terms of international relations and diplomacy, there has been a tendency to perceive only the features of modern nation states. Even if this stance appeals for a re-envisioning of South Asia and it does so with reference to conflict-torn countries of the region, it demands to seek beyond 'monological imagination'; ironically enough, it perpetuates the peculiar picture of South Asia as a conglomerate of upset nation-states.[3] In a pithy critique of the dominant way of imagining and discussing South Asia, Ashis Nandy calls it acultural, emotionally empty, territorial concept. This is usage in compromise, a neutral terrain, which serves the need of the countries of South Asia to distance them from anything of past and yet stay in a relationship. The countries of South Asia, as part of South Asian Association for Regional Cooperation (SAARC),

---

2 Arjun Appadurai, 1997, *Modernity at Large: Cultural Dimensions of Globalization*, Delhi, Oxford University Press; Benedict Anderson, 1991, *Imagined Communities: Reflections on the Origin and Spread of Nationalism*, London, Verso.

3 Sankaran Krishna, 1999, *Postcolonial Insecurities: India, Sri Lanka and the Question of Nationhood*, London, University of Minnesota Press.

reinvent the relationship by rubbing off all the available resources of the relationship. However, the meaning of the usage lies in its past which, through the forces of Indic civilisation, enabled the poets and thinkers to connect cultural dimensions beyond boundaries. Hence, 'the works of Jibananda Das, arguably independent India's greatest poet, invokes Bengal that is primarily Bangladesh'.[4] In the same breath, the organisational expression of the region of South Asia, SAARC, is far from being people's association; and hence it fails to capture the cultural component of the region despite the ill-structured approaches towards the culture of the region.[5] However, the only sign of hope for the realisation of South Asia is at the level where appear the smugglers who operate in a free-trade zone and where popular Bombay cinema and TV soap operas are a source of connectivity for the people.

In this light, it is imperative to reimagine South Asia, and its local manifestations, through a cultural matrix without falling prey to the state or at times, corporate sponsored delimited notions. But in the meanwhile, there is a need to take into account certain intricacies. In the age of 'narcissistic celebration of distinction', whereby everything is subject to individual rights and patenting law, it is imperative to note the circulation of sociocultural forms of art beyond the restriction of authorship and copyright. The geopolitical boundaries and internal disputes or treaties of friendship among states in the region do not inhibit the free flow of these cultural forms. To the extent of a hyperbolic assumption, law of the land or the legal accord between the nations too fails to regulate the circulation and consumption of the cultural forms. The contemporary discourse on globalisation and circulation of cultural forms, art and cinema, for example, sheds light on the complexity of this issue.

It is significant to recount a few slices of cultural reconfiguration of the region. The songs from Bollywood (specifically popular Hindi cinema) reproduced into instrumental numbers and played on board a Sri Lankan airlines flight, do not surprise a flyer from South Asia. It was, as though, as original as 'the original' song and music. A popular song

[4] Ashis Nandy, 2005, 'The Idea of South Asia: A Personal Note on Post-Bandung Blues,' *Inter-Asia Cultural Studies*, Vol. 6, No. 4, pp. 541–545.

[5] Dev Nath Pathak, 2018, *Another South Asia!*, Delhi, Primus.

from Hindi cinema rambling from the music player in a ferry hovering at a jetty at Male or cruising between islands in the Indian Ocean is a routine matter of everyday life in the Maldives. Also the musical note from an old Hindi film song, on which an old Sinhala song or an old Dhivehi song is based, echoes that the idea of authorship is not the determinant factor in the popular cultural (re)productions, which could be partly mechanical reproduction of artwork. Nobody asks who the singer is or who the author is or where does the song belong to originally. The question of authenticity is only an academic/official anxiety and not a detriment in the circulation and consumption of the reproduced forms. It sounds nice and hence everybody laps it. A Dhivehi youth says he hates to watch Dhivehi cinema; for, they are bad clones of Hindi cinema; hence, it is better to watch Hindi cinema. Youth in Lahore express more liking for the cinema smuggled from across the borders. The social landscape of Nepal hitherto expresses the romance with Hindi cinema, despite occasional discomfort on the issue of some Bollywood actor passing an undesirable comment about the Nepali in Bombay.[6] In a nutshell, it underscores the circulation of Hindi cinematic content and engagement of people in the region with the same, irrespective of territorial barriers, legal regulation of ban or anti-piracy.

The pundits of culture might despise it; the political boundaries may not find it suitable for the ideology of territory and nationality; the political economists might perceive a danger to the normative economic structure behind it; the academics may conceive host of conceptual jargons to describe it. However, the phenomenon itself remains as simple as people's openness to the forms of popular art. It is thus imperative to understand South Asia afresh with due attention to the locality.

In a nutshell, the possibility of reimagining dwells upon the ability to depart from the dominant leitmotifs. Elsewhere, Shakuntala Banaji[7] noted that the history of the region comes to be read mainly

[6] http://www.humanrights.de/doc_en/archiv/n/nepal/news/271200_4killed_Hrithik_protest.htm (accessed on 17 October 2018).

[7] Shakuntala Banaji, ed., 2010, *South Asian Media Cultures: Audience, Representations, Contexts*, London, Anthem Press.

and even solely within the sporadic, ideologically dangerous and/or simplistic frame of such internationally sensational events and the media discourses that surround them. One manifestation of this trend, both in journalism and in academic writing relating to South Asian media and politics, is the tendency to emphasise religious differences, conflicts and borders rather than both positive and negative civic solidarities and shared cultural trends. Second, large areas and aspects of media production, interpretation and use are discussed via highly simplistic frames of reference. Others are misrepresented (deliberately or unconsciously), suppressed or ignored. In the popular picture of strife-torn South Asia, afflicted by political violence and divided along the lines of caste, class, ethnicity, gender etc., what is lost is the shared history of culture and media in South Asia. The key casualty in the dominance of mediated reality of South Asia is the socially mediated cultural dynamics in the transnational context. The most tempting themes, of violence and discrimination of various sorts, are indeed relevant and pertinent in connecting the region of South Asia. Cultural expressions are fraught with these motives too. However, these cultural expressions are also a testimonial to local-to-local exchanges, the dynamic nature of the local, in the backdrop of historical political regime changes and the political economy of the industry.

Given this complexity of the case of South Asia, this chapter henceforth unravels the deliberation, instrumental in understanding the characteristics of mobility of cultural contents. The discursive construction of the meanings of artwork and cinema in the age of globalisation involves two poles between which it vacillates. These are the poles of mass-cult and global cult.[8] One is the older pole that garnered high voltage deliberation upon the mass character of the cinema and the other tends to leap up to the global marks to vindicate the progressive strides of cinema. It is not impossible to unearth similar poles and vacillation in the discourses on art. Complexity in the discourse, due to the presence of inarticulate class position, occurs. That our discourses

---

[8] Arvind Rajagopal, 2011, 'Afterwords: Fast-forward into the Future, Haunted by the Past: Bollywood Today,' in *Global Bollywood*, edited by Anandam P. Kavoori and Aswin Punathambekar, Delhi, Oxford University Press, pp. 300–306.

are not merely to look for the characteristics of masses in the art, craft, cinema and music from the region, it is also to vindicate its global value by perpetuating the ideology of a particular class, comes to critical comprehension. By manoeuvring between the two poles, with due respect to the third dispositional pole, a significant meaning is created discursively which establishes a maxim of our age. That art of South Asia is global despite the mass and class involved therein.

Local in the Wake of Global

The recent talk on the art of the region, in the context of the global dispositions of artwork, critically underlines the flimsiness of art as a metonym for a nation. Departing from the relics of nationalism and ideology of the ruling class, it is argued, that the artworks, on the other hand, are reaping the benefits of 'cultural hybridisation'. To quote Webb,

> Even artists who are not overtly political or clearly identified with an indigenous or other local community are not necessarily coopted by other political imperatives: the alternatives to nationalist productions are not only localism or globalism. Despite the formidable effect of globalization on the lives of everyone, there can be no such thing as truly global arts culture, and hence no general homogenization of image or practice, because identity and cultural attachment—which are expressed through art—rely on emotional and traditional resonances.[9]

The complexity of the engagement and production of art in the contemporary art world, which is characterised by 'post-national, non-global' art forms and processes, it is imperative to look beyond the simplistic binaries of national–global and traditional–modern. But then, the dominant notion of 'cultural hybridisation' that appears nearly as a taken-for-granted idea in contemporary analyses, invites a critical engagement too. It is this anxiety that finds an echo, while looking at the postcolonial experiences of the third world. Geeta

[9] Jenn Webb, 2005, 'Art in a Globalised State,' in *Art and Social Change*, edited by Caroline Turner, Canberra, Pandanus Books, Research School of Pacific and Asian Studies and The Australian National University, p. 35.

Kapur proposes a liberal resolve as she argues, 'To put it in more ideological terms, we must look not for hybrid solutions to the tradition/modernity dichotomy but for a dialectic'.[10] Furthermore, the resolve posits to disclose the heterodox (countercultural) elements of the national culture in the artistic creations by factoring in visual inputs of the popular, the marginalised cultures of tribal communities, of minorities and Dalits, of women. Invariably in a similar vein appears a historical trajectory on the art scene in Sri Lanka. Beyond the binaries of tradition and modernity, Jagath Weerasinghe noted a veritable invasion of 'small town Sri Lanka' into 'Colombo's metropolitan art world'. In the decade of 1990s, the artists from the repressed groups in their artworks have 'transformed the frustration, despair and alienation ensuing from sociopolitical devastation and urban delusions and chimeras into methods to become accepted and acknowledged in society'.[11]

However, in the meantime, social anthropological opening for the consideration of artworks in conjunction with the societal, cultural and politico-economic influences paves way for what is aptly termed 'theorising the local'.[12] The category of 'local' however warrants a critical deliberation, to which I will return later. It is important to note that the preoccupation with a plain notion of 'local', stemming from the congenital orientation of social anthropology towards the 'primitive' and thereof 'other' in an evolutionary scheme, has undergone a qualitative change. As a recent proposition suggests, 'An Anthropological approach places art in its social context. The relativism of anthropological theory broadens the definition and concept of art by elucidating its contexts—whether local or global'[13].

---

[10] Geeta Kapur, 2005, 'Dismantled Norms: Apropos other Avantgardes,' in *Art and Social Change*, edited by Caroline Turner, Canberra, Pandanus Books, Research School of Pacific and Asian Studies and The Australian National University, pp. 46–100.

[11] Jagath Weerasinghe, 2005, 'Contemporary Art in Sri Lanka', in *Art and Social Change*, edited by Caroline Turner, Canberra, Pandanus Books, Research School of Pacific and Asian Studies and The Australian National University, pp. 180–195.

[12] Richard K. Wolf, ed., 2010, *Theorizing the Local: Music, Practice and Experience in South Asia and Beyond*, New York, Oxford University Press.

[13] Howard Morphy and Morgan Perkins, eds., 2006, *The Anthropology of Art: A Reader*, Oxford, Blackwell Publishing, p. 21.

In order to make sense of the 'aestheticised object separated from the rest of life', as popular in the discourse on art, the anthropological discourse in contemporary times is geared to place artwork in the matrix of everyday life. Of course, it entails a departure from the early occupations of social anthropology as well as from the early theoretical paradigms, of primarily functionalism and structural functionalism. In a manner to derive a lineage of inspiration, due to the American Anthropology as informed by the works of Franz Boas and his students Kroeber, Sapir and Benedict, the anthropological approach to art underlines the agency of the local. It is thus convincing that in the maze of the spectacular nomenclatures like 'world music' and 'world art', agency to the indigenous people is denied.

> The local is not nested in the global (or displaced by it), but rather articulates with it. We would expect a future anthropology of art to contribute to a more subtle and nuanced understanding of the relationship between local and the global, and to situate the social and cultural production of art in space and time in a way that reveals the reasons for its irrepressible diversity and inventiveness. This requires a sophisticated understanding of local contexts of production—not frozen in pre-colonial time/space, but dynamic and productive.[14]

It is in this sense that the appeal for 'theorising the local' attracts our attention. Amidst the 'spectacular aspects of cultural circulation' charged with the grandiose of terminological prefixes and suffixes such as 'world' or 'global' the local assumes a secondary status. Wolf argues, 'in the "global hierarchy of values" only the best stuff, from an international market perspective, comes to represent a country like India or Ireland, or vast region like Africa'.[15] In this scheme, India in an architectural sense would monumentally mean Taj Mahal and anything ordinary would mean non-entity. The classical music and folk music would be cited as the real music and popular music from Hindi cinema would generate instant scepticism. The inherent logic in the hierarchy of values is expressive of the sale value of 'globally

---

[14] Morphy and Perkins, *The Anthropology of Art: A Reader.*

[15] Wolf, *Theorizing the Local*, p. 5.

mediated local'. The global market acknowledges and accepts what is palatable for global consumers. It is not the music per se, it is the form of music that matters. In this scheme, music that transcends locality is more interesting and lucrative than the so-called traditional music of a particular place. This tendency is what some scholars have termed 'single anthropological globalism'. What would be, then, the nature and scope of the act of 'theorising the local', when the category of local is but a construct of the global? Wolf suggests that it would imply 'paying attention to forms of knowledge implicit in performing and experiencing music', 'questioning the processes that have led to the creation of grand intellectual and institutional schemes' and 'thinking through ethnographic material'. In implication, it would also amount to fathom an intricate dynamics between context, emotion and cultural forms. As American anthropologist Franz Boas suggested in the first quarter of the twentieth century,

> The emotions may not be stimulated by the form alone but by the close associations that exist between *form and ideas* held by the people. When forms convey meaning, because they recall past experiences or because they act as symbols, a new element is added to enjoyment. The form and its meaning combine to elevate the mind above the indifferent emotional state of everyday life.[16]

While theorising the local with an eye at the ethnographic details the contemporary scholarship ought to be ready to use a broader framework to juxtapose the historical and mythological present and past, institutional–structural arrangement and individual–agential endeavours on the anvil of analysis. The question of 'local' in a dialectical play with global would then make more sense beyond a potential reification of the term. And yet, in the discursive realm of art, there is conspicuous absence of the deliberation upon the local-to-local dynamics, interregional (local) dialectic that could help build an idea about art and aesthetics in South Asia in the wake of globalisation, barring a few exceptions. It is interesting to note that the contemporary visual artists of South Asia have begun to forge relationship by exhibiting

---

[16] Quoted in Morphy and Perkins, *The Anthropology of Art: A Reader*, p. 12.

their works in collaboration. Example of the exhibition mounted by artists of India and Pakistan, titled *Aar-Paar*, literally meaning 'this side-that side' is well known.[17]

Conclusion

The phenomenon of dynamic local is complex indeed. Precisely when it is looked at through the contemporary popular culture rather than from the components of Indic civilisation. It is doubly complex because the dynamics involve not only the mobility of one local towards the other. There is indeed multilateral mobility, which this chapter has not dealt with. However, mobility of the content of popular Hindi cinema, as an elementary case of the dynamic local in South Asia, provides a pretext to renew intellectual moorings in the imagination of the region. The dynamics of local could arguably have posterity; perhaps, from time immemorial in the history of human civilisation there have been civilisational fusions. But then, beyond this conventional frame, there is a need to locate the imagination of the region at the level of ordinary people's culture. The circulation of cultural content and repackaging of the same in different locations of South Asia without much regard for the question of origin and authenticity presents only a little slice of the dynamics of local. But then, it gives us a reason to transcend not only the binaries of tradition and modernity but also offers a fashionable solution, namely hybridity.

[17] See http://groundviews.org/2012/10/03/long-read-beyond-history-against-the-present-preliminary-thoughts-on-re-imagining-south-asia/ (accessed on 21 October 2018).

9

'South Asia' as an Idea and a Problem of Modernity[1]

Sasanka Perera

My engagement with the question of modernity in South Asia would be in the form of an anxiety-ridden and curious wanderer meandering through the intellectual and cultural terrains of this region. I will begin with some questions for revisiting modernity along with the idea of South Asia. I choose to specifically dwell upon the idea of South Asia for various intellectual imperatives. For one, the question of modernity has been seemingly discussed within the confines of sovereign territories of nation states as if it recognises the national borders. My sense is, it is heuristically important to locate modernity in a kind of regional framework by stressing upon its relation with the idea of South Asia. Second, continuing with the first imperative is the realisation that deliberations on modernity, its characteristics in historical and sociological purview, seem to be a dominant muse on theoretical turfs alone. This is the time when we should look much beyond this, towards instances of more organic connections among local contexts within the region of South Asia in order to propose ways forward in theoretical deliberations on modernity. At this point, however, I am not too keen to speak about modernity as such or its various appearances in the region. My interest is to outline a few issues of one specific construct of modernity in our region. And that is South Asia itself.

---

[1] This chapter is a marginally edited version of the plenary lecture delivered at the conference, 'Modern Matters: Negotiating the Future in Everyday Life in South Asia,' Lund University, Thursday, 22 September 2016. Much of the first part of this text has since been published in the essay, 'Reimagining and Re-narrating South Asia: Artists' Travel and the Practice of Visual Art as a New Experiential Cartography' in Dev Nath Pathak, ed., *Another South Asia!* New Delhi, Primus Books, 2018. The author would like to thank Primus Books for their consent to republish this chapter.

South Asia is often seen as a concrete reality imagined primarily in geophysical or cartographic terms. This is more clearly visible in contemporary political science and international relations scholarship, even though other disciplines such as sociology also do not do any better. I think this is mostly due to our inability to transgress what might be called 'nationalised' domains of knowledge production that hinder the possibility of comprehending the region across both disciplinary and national borders in sociocultural and emotional terms. In this general context, I will briefly look at the region as an incomplete idea and the problem of modernity that still needs to be explored and worked out. For me, South Asia is not a given. At best, it is a work in progress and thus a challenge to those notions of modernity that allude to the rigidity and finitude of its constructs. In saying so, I am reminded of the Zygmunt Bauman's detailed discussion on the ambivalence of modernity, ambivalence between familiar, indubitable and the classified, and everything that seems odd in the conventional framework of modernity. One need not subscribe to the scheme of post-modernity to reckon with the ambivalent character of modernity, particularly in the context of South Asia.

I will revisit recent debates on what South Asia means both as a product of modernity and as a specific kind of lived reality, a process in perpetuity. Later, as another incomplete effort, I will also briefly place in context how academic rituals of knowledge production look at South Asia and pose the question if it might be possible to reimagine the region through more nuanced forms of cultural and intellectual knowledge production. My immediate interest comes from a specific location. That is my institutional location at South Asian University established by South Asian Association for Regional Cooperation (SAARC) where I often hear official platitudes of regional cooperation, South Asian consciousness and so on, without much to see on the ground. So I am often caught between South Asia of official imagination and rhetoric, South Asia as it exists on the ground and South Asia as it could exist according to the fantasies entertained by some of us—not only as a place but also as a framework for research.

In this context, though we seem to take South Asia for granted and as a given, I am not sure if things are this simple. Let me share with you some of my anxieties. My concern is, when all of us take South Asia for granted, as does SAARC, do we get a fuller and a nuanced perception of the region? Or in other words, does South Asia as a modern finished entity communicate all of its latent as well as manifested unfinished nature? Is our knowledge of the Maldives for instance, comparable to that of India? Or, to take a less extreme example, do we know at least as much about the Maldives as we do about Sri Lanka? Or, do our perception, understanding and knowledge of the region remain merely at the level of rhetoric, in the safe and comfortable framework of modernity where things are classified and differences are erased beyond redemption? Does this even matter in the real world? Let me outline some of the key issues of South Asia as a product of modernity and explore if academic and cultural practices have a better chance of imagining South Asia differently or more fully?

Comprehending South Asia

Imtiaz Ahmed's simple suggestion that 'the idea of South Asia is both new and old'[2] makes perfect epistemological sense as it places in context historical and contemporary enigmas associated with the region and the concept. What he means by this is that the terminology of 'South Asia' is new. Compared to this, however, if the term also includes 'the people and the things that make up the region', then it is a fairly old idea, based on 'civilizational and historical' imperatives.[3] In the same context, as suggested by Nandy, 'the idea of South Asia is partly artificial' as are 'its nation states' while it is also 'partly an imposed one'.[4] Both Ahmed and Nandy seem to be in unison in suggesting that South Asia has more layers within its structure of meaning than the dominant value-system and cognitive apparatus of modernity would allow us to perceive.

---

[2] Imtiaz Ahmed, 2012, 'Regionalism in South Asia', in, *International Journal of South Asian Studies*, Vol. 5, No. 1, January–June, p. 1.

[3] Ahmed, 'Regionalism in South Asia', p. 1.

[4] Ashis Nandy, 2005, 'The Idea of South Asia: A Personal Note on Post-Bandung Blues,' in *Inter-Asia Cultural Studies*, Vol. 6, No. 4, p. 541.

The coinage, 'South Asia', is often attributed to the US State Department and was the result of post-World War II and Cold War era political compulsions primarily as understood by the United States. Like many other contemporary ideas and categories in the region that came to us via the discursive practices of modernity, it is an importation that has been politically adopted by the eight nation states which currently constitute SAARC without significantly exploring its nuances. At the level of SAARC and in the official perception of the nation states that constitute SAARC, South Asia merely remains a political and cartographic category. At the level of quotidian practice, it is a flippantly used concept. The terminology itself was used more often in foreign policy and security studies circles in the United States and Europe until 1985 when SAARC was established. The division of the world into convenient areas of study, which includes South Asia, occurred soon after the end of World War II and the clear emergence of the United States as a superpower. In this context, it became imperative that the world was more clearly dissected, studied and situated which went beyond the older areas of study made necessary as a result of colonial expansion. More specifically, this required the production of knowledge about areas of the world of which American policymakers knew very little.[5] This was not a simple intellectual curiosity. More importantly, it was a political imperative that also fed into the schemes of global security, intelligence and politics of carving out spheres of influence in the emerging Cold War. It is in this context that the interest in the idea and category of 'South Asia' made political sense to the United States Department of State. In these larger intersections of meanings, politics and sensibilities, the study of specific world areas including South Asia expanded rapidly in the US university systems with the establishment of centres of expertise with funding from the National Defence Education Act of 1958.[6] This also shows the security prerogative in understanding these kinds of global areas as specific political 'curiosities' rather than cultural areas or interconnected

[5] Arjun Guneratne and Anita Weiss, eds., 2014, *Pathways to Power: The Domestic Politics of South Asia*. Lanham, Rowman & Littlefield, p. 4.

[6] Guneratne and Weiss, *Pathways to Power*, p. 4.

social systems through which ideas, objects and people flowed over a considerably long historical period, much before the advent of European colonialism and the nation states which currently inhabit the region.

In this sense, South Asia as a specific category and label was invented in North America, fine-tuned in Western Europe and was finally imported to the region. And by and large as a consequence of these dynamics, the people in this region are mere inheritors and followers in this scheme of things rather than creative re-inventors. One of the basic problems with 'South Asia' being invented in this manner and as it exists at the rhetorical-epistemological plain today, is its apparent levelling of culture, politics and social variations across the region, making invisible its complexities and inherent anxieties. Is this an inevitable consequence, though a necessary evil, in the scheme of modernity? At this conjuncture, let me make two basic propositions, underlining the possibility of rethinking South Asia beyond the strict pale of modernity:

1. These issues in the recent construction and meaning in the category of South Asia do not mean that an imagination of the region did not exist in different ways in the pre-colonial past or does not exist today at the level of different kinds of practices undertaken by people. But much of this exists beyond the flippant deployment of the idea of South Asia.

2. In this general context, it is also clear that the realisation of SAARC as a truly responsive and relatively an internally egalitarian regional organisation has not borne fruit in any significant fashion mostly due to the hegemony of statecraft of nation states within SAARC generally practiced with an obsessive focus on the nation.

Let me now focus on South Asia as an area, an idea and a problem. In their new book, *Pathways to Power: The Domestic Politics of South Asia*, Arjun Guneratne and Anita M. Weiss, note that as an area for study, compared to many world regions such as Southeast Asia carved out for study that lack a sense of organic unity, the logic of selecting South Asia as a group of states that should be collectively explored is easier to fathom.[7] As they point out, most of these countries share 'cultural affinities deriving from a common past as well as the legacy of the British Indian empire' which established within the nation states that emerged after official decolonisation 'similar frameworks of constitutional governance, public administration, military organization, systems of law not least, a common elite language of English.'[8] However, cultural affinities from a somewhat connected past are mostly underrepresented in the rhetoric of regional and national politics today.

Despite incessant meetings, cultural events and conferences, where the notion of South Asia seems to be taken for granted, what it actually means is not always clear. Also, South Asia as a coherent geopolitical entity with a sense of collective cultural belonging is even more difficult to imagine and even more difficult to achieve in the context of contemporary politics of nation states. Providing a partial answer to this state of affairs, Ashis Nandy has described South Asia as the only region in the world where most states prefer to define themselves, 'not by what they are, but by what they are not.'[9] According to him, 'Pakistan, Sri Lanka and Nepal try desperately not to be India' while Bangladesh 'has taken up the more onerous responsibility of avoiding being both India and Pakistan.'[10]

Despite Nandy's exaggeration of regional politics, it seems to me that at some level, he is referring to these countries' established practice of being the antagonistic 'other' of each, based on the manner in which contemporary political compulsions of nation states unfold locally, rather than with reference to some of the shared cultural practices that no longer take the centre stage in regional or national–local politics. More insidiously, these practices and histories are no longer within recallable collective memory for most people as well. Ahmed has noted that 'regionalism in South Asia is as much an effort as it is an idea.'[11] Very clearly, that effort is still by and large an abstract notion that needs

---

[7] Guneratne and Weiss, *Pathways to Power*, p. 4.

[8] Guneratne and Weiss, *Pathways to Power*, pp. 4–5.

[9] Ashis Nandy, 2005, 'The Idea of South Asia: A Personal Note on Post-Bandung Blues,' in *Inter-Asia Cultural Studies*, Vol. 6, No. 4, p. 541.

[10] Nandy, 'The Idea of South Asia,' p. 541.

[11] Ahmed, 'Regionalism in South Asia,'

to evolve beyond mere abstraction and travel to the streets and the consciousness of the region's people. On the other hand, as argued by Nandy, the concept of South Asia at certain levels can be seen as an 'acultural, emotionally empty, territorial concept'.[12]

Hindustan, Al Hind, Bharatvarsha and South Asia?

In a sense, both Ahmed's and Nandy's ideas are very similar. Both are talking about an idea that needs realisation in contemporary times. However, while Ahmed offers some hope,

Nandy offers none or very little. His antipathy towards the concept comes from his disagreement with the terminology of South Asia, which he considers to be ahistorical. Even though he accepts that it is a 'compromise' and a 'neutral term', he is unhappy with this 'improvisation', which he only deploys 'in deference to my friends and colleagues from the rest of the region'.[13]

This disagreement needs some reflection as it has much to do with comprehending the kind of regionalism that could emerge or might not in South Asia by focusing on how history is read in the present. Nandy suggests that the term South Asia acquired public status in the region in the 1980s 'because the medieval name of the region, Hindustan or Al Hind, and its ancient name, Bharatvarsha or its lesser known variation, Jambudvip—had become ideologically tainted' due to the association of these terms with the nation state of India.[14]

It is correct that terms such as Hindustan, Al Hind, Bharatvarsha and Jambudvip often referred to an extended area in the medieval and ancient past much beyond the borders of present-day India, the nation state. This area included much of contemporary subcontinental South Asia in geographic and civilisational terms. But unlike what is expected today as a pronounced regionalism by proponents of the idea of South Asia, these earlier notions were vague, liminal and too flexible at best though they consisted of lived-realities encountered in travels,

[12] Nandy, 'The Idea of South Asia', p. 542.

[13] Nandy, 'The Idea of South Asia', p. 542.

[14] Nandy, 'The Idea of South Asia', p. 542.

circulation of ideas, myths and so on. In other words, these ancient experiences were proximate at some levels and distant at others.

On the other hand, one has to wonder whether present-day nation states such as Sri Lanka and the Maldives, separated from the mainland by the ocean, were part of the extended reality and imagination represented by Hindustan, Al Hind, Bharatvarsha and Jambudvip compared to subcontinental mainland. More broadly, I have in mind the areas which include southern states of India in addition to the Maldives and Sri Lanka. It is this cultural area which a Maldivian diplomat once referred to as Southern South Asia.

Sri Lanka for instance, shared many cultural and religious practices, kinship systems, languages, language scripts, monarchic practices and very proximate and sometimes extremely hostile political relations with kingdoms in the mainland as local inscriptions as well as historical chronicles such as *Deepwamsa* (compiled in the fourth century) and *Mahawamasa* (compiled in the fifth century) written in Pali attest. The lesser known of the older terms for the region, Jambudvip was well-known in Sri Lanka by its Sinhala term Dambadiva that remains in use even today in much the same way it was understood in the ancient Pali chronicles of the country. But today, it is used in Sri Lanka in reference to India only when it comes to the discourses of Buddhist pilgrimage.

This relationship is also evident from details embedded in the Sinhala dance routine known as 'Wadiga Patuna'. This is part of the healing ritual, 'sooniyam', depicting through comic sequences, the entry of Brahmans to Lanka from 'India' (or to use the older forms, from Hindustan, Al Hind or Jambudvip). According to myths associated with the dance and the ritual, the Brahmans came to Sri Lanka from 'India' to heal the sickness the local king was suffering from. There was no local expertise to address this condition. As the Brahmans enter Lanka, the language initially used by them is a mixture of Sanskrit, Tamil and Sinhala that clearly marks out their difference, unfamiliarity with local conditions and above all, their 'foreignness'.

Their foreignness and distance from the local cultural terrain are further emphasised by their costumes and long beards that portray aspects of Sinhalas' imagination of Brahmans. Significantly, the Brahmans were not recognised or understood by the local ritual experts, and by extension the people as well. But towards the end of the ritual, mutual understanding becomes possible as the language transforms into 'Sinhala' while Sanskrit and Tamil elements disappear. On the one hand, it is possible to argue this is a representation of the assimilation or Sinhalisation of migratory Brahman communities. On the other hand, it is also indicative of the distance and relative unfamiliarity of specificities of the cultural world beyond the island's oceanic boundaries away from certain layers of familiarity. And it took considerable effort and time to acquire familiarity of this cultural world beyond the ocean, if and when necessary.

In terms of this understating, Jambudvip was both familiar at some levels and very unfamiliar at other levels. It was emotionally proximate in some respects but physically and politically distant in other ways. It was familiar as a place associated with the life of Buddha and other cultural practices as well as a source for specific materials and expertise such as ritual specialisation as evident in many ritual texts and Sinhala myths. But it was also a place in the distance that one could reach only after crossing the 'seven seas' (*sat samuduru*). Besides, it was a source of invasion and catastrophe, a source from where political instability and historical ruptures reached across the ocean.

In this specific context, there are no historical references in Sri Lanka that allow for an argument for a consciousness of the region in its pre-colonial and ancient manifestations as a specific cultural and emotional zone. It also does not appear that the ancient terminology at least in the Lankan context provided a sensibility for an overarching regional identity despite very obvious instances of cultural and mythical familiarity one can cull out from literary and ritual sources. Given this historical reality, it is not possible to make a claim for Hindustan, Al Hind, Bharatvarsha as a possible gloss for South Asia in contemporary Sri Lankan political contexts though Jambudvip might touch a more sympathetic chord due to its Buddhisisation in the Sri Lankan context within practices of pilgrimage. But then, that would only refer to a Buddhist world closely and emotionally linked to the life of the Buddha.

In the discussions of the historical context, an issue that is generally not addressed in these discourses is the fact that such terminology was given by the literate and often Brahmanical segments of society in literary sources. Was the textual significance that these terms created similarly evident in the non-textual references and practices? For instance, when Hindu pilgrims travelled to their sacred places as did Buddhists, they navigated across a 'sacred geography' within which everything happened to be 'part of a living, storied, and intricately connected landscape'.[15] In their travels, they dealt with what Diana Eck has called a 'polycentric' landscape where each site had its own significance.[16] The wanderings of these pilgrims painted on the ground a very different and nuanced cartography as well as an experience of an extended place. But was it understood in these routine practices as Hindustan, Bharatvarsha and so on? Or were they perceived merely in experiential terms?

More importantly, however, the older broader civilisational aspects of terminologies such as Hindustan—irrespective of their limitations in contemporary use—have been appropriated by the Indian nation state for its own limited purposes that have brought these terms into 'constant tension with the Indian nation-state'.[17] And today, these terms have also been appropriated by non-state entities within India for their own parochial political use as well, which further complicates their use for any collective entity beyond the borders of present-day India.

This also means a further distancing of such terminology across the region's emotional makeup. In this specific historical and political conjuncture, South Asia remains the only neutral political terminology throughout the region despite Nandy's characterisation of it as an 'acultural, emotionally empty, territorial concept'.[18] It seems to me this apparent emotional emptiness and lack of a sense of history in the concept needs to be addressed by precisely infusing into it what is missing. But such a consciousness cannot come from SAARC. It also can hardly be expected from agents of South Asia's disparate state bureaucracies. Besides, in terms of global politics as well as the way in which regional politics routinely play out within the region in SAARC

---

[15] Diana L. Eck, 2012, *India: A Sacred Landscape*, New York, Harmony Books, p. 2.

[16] Eck, *India*.

[17] Nandy, 'The Idea of South Asia', p. 543.

[18] Nandy, 'The Idea of South Asia', p. 542.

as well as beyond it, the centrality of India overshadows much of the remainder of the region. This is not a simple matter of recognising India's economic or political power. That would be obvious. But that centrality needs to be tempered with a nuanced sensibility towards the region in terms of culture, politics as well as knowledge if the region is to be imagined differently than it is today. The question is whether this is possible. In this sense, it is clear that despite thirty plus years of SAARC and the numerous efforts of sensible proponents of the idea of South Asia, the consciousness of South Asia that necessarily has to come from the wider recognition of its regionalism by the region's people, is yet to be collectively defined and embraced by the wider regional polity.[19]

I think what I have said so far should make it very clear why I prefer to see 'South Asia' as an incomplete idea or as a problem we have inherited from the way modernity has manifested in our region and from the ways in which the nation states in the region have interacted with each other, rather than as a concrete and coherent reality. But I am not sure if this incomplete picture of the region with its inherent contradictions and uneven play of politics and the difficulties these situations throw out are taken into account whenever South Asia is invoked in both political and academic rituals of our time.

South Asia and Academia

From this obvious position, let me pose one rhetorical question: Since South Asia's nation states as well as its main regional forum SAARC cannot work out a rational regional sensibility that would allow us to comprehend the region more fully, who could? Before my sense of romance and idealism on these matters began to falter, I used to believe that this is something academia might be able to do by devising regional frameworks for research and knowledge, which might allow us to trespass across both disciplinary and national borders. But now, it appears more clearly that nationalised systems of knowledge

[19] Nandy, 'The Idea of South Asia', p. 542.

production as well as global real politics have not allowed us to do so. I want to briefly explore this by looking at the structure of two academic platforms as simple illustrations. One is the conference 'Modern Matters: Negotiating the Future in Everyday Life in South Asia' held at Lund University on 22 September 2016. I take this as a typical South Asia conference. And the other is the excellent book series known as *South Asia Across Disciplines* published jointly by the University of California Press, University of Chicago Press and the Columbia University Press. For me, the question is: Are these forums able to perceive South Asia in a more nuanced and comprehensive fashion than how SAARC or state entities perceive it?

Let's look at the conference first. South Asia Swedish Network has been hosting important academic events for a considerable period of time. 'Modern Matters: Negotiating the Future in Everyday Life in South Asia' is one such event. How does South Asia manifest in the conference in a concrete sense? I counted 57 entries in a cursory exploration of the initial submissions. Of these, 46 focussed on India, two on Nepal, one on Bangladesh, one on Afghanistan, one focused on the Pakistan–Afghanistan border zone, one on Sweden and India, four suggested their interest was on South Asia though I was not sure of the actual focus and I simply could not fathom the focus of one more paper on the basis of the title. The actual numbers are not important here. What is important is the pattern of research and the cartography of South Asia these presentations formulate in terms of the knowledge they produce. Clearly, there is an overwhelming emphasis on exploring the present as well as the past of India.

One could see a similar uneven focus in *South Asia across Disciplines* as well. Without a doubt, it is a significant initiative. And it is even more significant now because, thanks to the collaboration between the three original US-based publishers and Primus Books in Delhi, those of us in the region can also aspire to buy these texts and read them at leisure. The stated aim of the series is to publish 'work that aims to raise innovative questions in the field', which 'include the relationship between South Asian studies and the disciplines; the conversation between past and present in South Asia; the history and nature of modernity, especially in relation to cultural change, political transformation, secularism and religion, and globalization'.[20] From what I have read, the hopes of innovative approaches and the opening up of new archives seem to have been achieved. And intellectually, this makes perfect sense. But ideologically for someone like me, still harbouring hopes for a fuller understanding of South Asia, the knowledge the series has so far generated on South Asia in so far as sources and focus are concerned, is clearly uneven. For instance, from about 32 published and forthcoming books, 20 focus on India, one on Nepal and India, one on West Asia and India, one on Bangladesh, one on Pakistan, one on Nepal, one on Sri Lanka, one on Southeast Asia, one on the Tibetan and the Himalayan region, while four have South Asia as their focus on the titles. Again, the pattern should be self-evident.

I am not arguing for an area-studies approach in the regional scholarship of the kind we have seen not so long ago. But is it simply impossible to decentre India as the predominant focus of contemporary and historical research and find thematics that may allow for research across both disciplinary and national borders? Is it impossible to encourage younger scholars to focus on thematics and research areas in lesser-known locations in the region that might also make sense elsewhere? Is it impossible for scholars to attempt what policymakers and politicians have so manifestly failed to do? But this is more of an ideological necessity rather than an intellectual one. After all, intellectually, we can produce knowledge in the manner we have been doing so far and they might continue to be sound scholarship. And it would be a sound scholarship in a familiar comfort zone. It is only ideologically one might have an anxiety with the kind of restrictions on comprehending the region that existing systems of knowledge production impose.

These are not rhetorical sentiments as far as I am concerned. In different ways, some of us at SAU have faced the same issues when we launched our journal with SAGE, *Society and Culture in South Asia* as well as our monograph series, *Conversations for/on South Asia* and the ongoing lectures in the twin series, 'Contributions to Contemporary

[20] http://www.press.uchicago.edu/books/saad/index.html (accessed on 29 October 2017).

Knowledge' and 'Exploring South Asia.' Despite our institutional location at SAU where we frequently hear mantra-like utterances such as 'South Asian consciousness' and 'South Asian sensibility' often devoid of any tangible meaning, it was difficult to generate through our own efforts the kind of fuller and more nuanced cartography of the region which our ideological interests demanded.

There is considerable scholarship emanating from India and on India. But the same is not true of the other countries' pasts and presents. It was also difficult to see works which self-consciously criss-crossed borders of different kinds. So in a way, the kinds of limitations in our understanding of the region that I have flagged with regard to the composition of the conference, 'Modern Matters: Negotiating the Future in Everyday Life in South Asia' and the structure of *South Asia across Disciplines* also haunt us in our day to day professional work.

This comes from multiple sources: the sheer volume of people trained within India perhaps cannot be surpassed by any other country. But such people, given the limitations of perspective they have inherited from higher education, prefer to explore India. This is what I have referred to as 'nationalised' domains of knowledge production. It is simply too bad not too many of them would like to focus their intellectual curiosity on some other location beyond the nation's borders? In different ways, the same end result applies to other countries too. On the other hand, globally speaking, it makes far more sense to focus on India in terms of career prospects, funding possibilities and so on. So the possibilities of knowing India is immense and it will continue to grow.

Let me come back to my institutional and personal locations. We recognise the existing status quo for what it is with its built-in sense of hegemonic and nationalist aspirations. But for the moment at least, we have refused to accept this state of affairs. Amidst our mounting frustrations, how far can we go along this path of discovery remains uncertain. But our assumption so far is this: if we call something South Asian, our work and efforts must reflect that reality as broadly as possible.

In making these assumptions, I think it is reasonable to assume that scholars, their forums of discourse, their analytical frameworks and collaborative projects—if carefully thought out—have certain subversive possibilities of transcending the routine limitations put in place by nation states in South Asia as well as the agendas of South Asia studies programmes in the region and beyond. But one must have the will to do so. It is in such a context that Nandy has noted, 'the more the scholars, artists and writers talk of the common heritage of the region, the more the functionaries in the region nervously eye their neighbours as enemies planning to wipe out their distinctive identities'.[21]

Perhaps, this is the limitation of an understanding of South Asia conditioned by modern cartographic strategies that my discussion in the early part has highlighted. Some effort to broaden the discursive framework by factoring in the components not-much-conducive for rigid schemata of modernity could bring about the possibility of starting a discussion on a different sense of modern South Asia. That is when modern South Asia would cease to be a finished product, a conglomeration of nation states. It would be a process in perpetuity, something messy and non-clinical, challenging and hopefully summoning our intellectual interests from across the region.

For me, what is important is this sense of embedded subversiveness in the acts of people like all of us. But I am not sure if many of us have invested as much time in these possibilities as we could and should. That is because we are satisfied merely with intellectual output as opposed to intellectual output tempered by passion, imagination and a sincere ideological commitment to South Asia.

[21] Nandy, 'The Idea of South Asia', p. 542.

III

Towards a South Asian Knowledge System

10

In Defence of 'Area Studies' in South Asia[1]

Sasanka Perera and Dev Nath Pathak

When the book, *Sociology and Social Anthropology in South Asia: Histories and Practices* edited by the authors of the present book began its circulation in October 2018, a colleague in a passing reference in what may be called 'corridor talk' dismissed the book as a work in 'area studies'.

Similarly, in 2017, when the Board of Studies of the Faculty of Social Sciences at SAU strongly suggested that M.Phil and Ph.D research at the Faculty must have a strong South Asian approach, a colleague from the International Relations Department warned us in private that 'we must be careful, so that we do not succumb to the area studies model'. What our Board of Studies—which decides on pedagogic issues with regard to our courses and research proposals of graduate students—meant, however, was that M.Phil and Ph.D research, as well as teaching programmes in the Departments of Sociology and International Relations should ideally move away from being restricted to research within a specific national location. Instead, we were advised to explore how the region might be implicated in the thematics of research and teaching, be that migration, violence, nationalism, caste, ethnicity, visual cultures, relations between states, issues of security, human rights and so on.

In these kinds of rhetorical statements, what was flippantly thrown around, as 'area studies' is seen as a demon that was somehow slain by a

[1] An edited version of this chapter titled, 'The Bogey-Man of Area Studies: Reading South Asia in Contemporary Times' was presented by Sasanka Perera at Karl Jaspers Centre for Advanced Transcultural Studies, the University of Heidelberg on 6 February 2019 as a guest lecture organised by the South Asia Institute and Professorship of Global Art History at University of Heidelberg. A version of this was published in the Dhaka-based *Daily Observer* in March 2019. The author would like to thank the *Daily Observer* for its permission to republish.

group of unnamed academic superheroes in what appears to be an epic battle sometime in the recent—but somewhat hazy and undefined—past. This assumption does not seem that different from Heracles' slaying of Geryon in Greek mythology.

And that demon, it seems must somehow remain entombed in its unmarked coffin. However, invariably many of us partake in one or the other version of 'area studies' in what we do. Seemingly, the ghost of the entombed area studies demon possesses everyone in the so-called postcolonial South Asia. One can see a variety of area studies at work in the work of a sociologist working on caste relations in India, and within India, in Punjab or Uttar Pradesh, or Haryana, or even in the famous 'village' of the doyen of Indian sociology, M.N. Srinivas, namely Rampura. Similarly, Srinivas' counterpart in Sri Lanka, Gananath Obeyesekere initially came to be known as the person who had 'studied' the village, Medagama in Sri Lanka's central hills.

Area studies also find expression in the work of many scholars in international relations and political science too. It is in this context they might talk of Nehruvian foreign policy or India's relations with Pakistan and so on. In a fundamental sense, the idea of 'area' and the deeper logic of 'area studies' are intact in most, if not all studies, which would, however claim, if the need arises, to have entombed the demon in the unmarked coffin, as it were.

But that ghost is truly more powerful than what seems as the rationally configured intellectual reality many of us comfortably adhere to. Following this self-proclaimed distancing from area studies, in our teaching roles, we often brutally advise our young scholars not to engage with it. Similarly, we may reject academic papers in the 'rigorously' quality-controlled journals based on our collective fear of area studies. But the demon plays tricks in our minds like all self-respecting demons from any mythological world ought to do and often sits in the corners of our academic practices where no broomstick of any South Asian Harry Potter can ever reach.

This is particularly so when our academic training does not allow many of us to practice reflexivity in any real sense, even though we speak highly of it in classes and in our quotidian rhetoric.

Who's Area Studies?

What appears from the rhetorical and negative judgements referred to earlier is that our recent emphasis on South Asia as an idea, a place of interest and a framework for research is very easily thrown into this unmarked coffin and equally as easily subsumed in what appears to be the monolith of area studies of the past. But at no point, one is curious enough to work out what all this means in our own context for us politically, experientially and intellectually.

Are area studies as a concept so easy to fathom and equally as easy to condemn? And in any case, why would our interests in South Asia as a framework for research that supersedes the boundaries of nation states as well as disciplinary borders of sociology be so easily equated with area studies, as it was commonly understood on the basis of conventional intellectual histories?

Are the past interests in area studies and our own focus on South Asia the same? Is a focus on South Asia, which we have never called area studies in our own conception, such a terrible thing anyway?

The intention of this chapter is not to offer conclusive or defensive answers as such. Instead, our attempt is to reflect on these polemics and academic politics linked to the older idea of area studies on the one hand, and on the other hand, to think of how to explore South Asia from the perspective of the work undertaken recently by a group of colleagues in SAU, of which we are a part.

But then, if what we have been seeking to build under the mandate of SAU as well as within our own intellectual interests is seen by some people as 'area studies', so be it.

Older Understandings of Area Studies

In any event, what exactly is the bogeyman or demon known as area studies which everyone seems to enjoy beating? At a basic level and as an approach, area studies can be understood as a multidisciplinary approach in social sciences with a focus on areas defined either by geography or culture, including language, literature, performance and various written as well as unwritten traditions. Seen in this basic sense, everything from African Studies to South Asian studies or Francophone studies could be examples of area studies.

Let us not hesitate to say that a renowned scholar such as Sheldon Pollock is also an area studies scholar in the ultimate analysis given his focus on Sanskrit and what may be broadly called Indic studies. There need not be any qualms about it, as long as it delivers to the terrain of scholarship something relatively unfamiliar. As we know well, many domains of scholarship today are saturated with the reproduction of the known, the familiar, the comfortable and finally the politically correct and the rhetorical.

Speaking in a historical sense, European colonial expansion from the eighteenth century onwards straddled with the thirst for the kind of knowledge that had a market in the imperial capitals prompted by post-enlightenment disciplinary expansions that mark the initial genesis of area studies. That is, area studies came about as part of the need for colonial rulers and their sponsors to 'know' about the places, peoples and cultures across which the uncivil thrust of their 'civilising' missions were let loose. This clearly had to do with interests in domination with regard to political power, commerce, cultural transformation as well as faith.

We can't deny the sinister objectives in the backdrop of these early endeavours of area studies that ranged from classifying and controlling the Biblical 'benighted heathen' to romancing with the 'pristine exotica'. After all, Louis Dumont's *Homo Aequalis* needed a counterpart, *Homo Hierarchicus* for official as well as intellectual purposes.

In this sense, if anthropology of the nineteenth century was the handmaiden of colonialism, area studies was the favourite child of the expanding empires. What Edward Said later critiqued as 'orientalism' at least in part emerged from this colonial politico-commercial approach to global exploitation that also led to the initial emergence of area studies. This global reality evolved in much the same way in colonial South Asia as well.

The second genesis of area studies is located in the relations of global political power in the aftermath of World War I and II. The division of the world into convenient areas of study that includes South Asia occurred soon after the end of World War II and the clear emergence of the United States as a superpower. In this context, it became imperative that the world was more clearly dissected, studied and situated which went beyond the older areas of study made necessary as a result of colonial expansion.

More specifically, this required the production of knowledge on areas of the world about which American policymakers knew very little.[2] This was not a simple intellectual curiosity. More importantly, it was a political imperative that also fed into schemes of global security, intelligence and politics of carving out spheres of influence in the emerging Cold War. It is in this context that the interest in the idea and category of 'South Asia' made political sense to the United States' Department of State.

In these larger intersections of meanings, politics and sensibilities, the study of specific world areas including South Asia expanded rapidly in the US university systems with the establishment of centres of expertise with funding allocated via the National Defence Education Act of 1958.[3] This also shows the security prerogative in understanding these kinds of global areas as specific political 'curiosities', rather than cultural areas or interconnected social systems through which ideas, memories, histories, objects and people flowed over a considerably long historical period.

Clearly, seen in this sense, knowledge was an established cognate of sustainable power, for which there was a rivalry in the then bi-polar world. Such knowledge was necessary not merely as a matter of intellectual curiosity, but also as an important basis for the projection of power. And particularly in the context of the Cold War, US military and political planners found it necessary to know more about societies and countries in world regions, including the Middle East, Africa, Latin America and also South Asia.

In fact, the word South Asia itself was initially coined by the US State Department[4] in the context of these global power dynamics. The Cold War-related interest in area studies was also seen in Europe in

---

[2] Arjun Guneratne and Anita Weiss, eds., 2014, *Pathways to Power: The Domestic Politics of South Asia*, Lanham, Rowman & Littlefield, p. 4.

[3] Guneratne and Weiss, *Pathways to Power*, p. 4.

[4] A more detailed account of this process is available in Chapter 9 '"South Asia" as an Idea and a Problem of Modernity' by Sasanka Perera in this collection.

addition to the continuities from the colonial experience. It is in these general circumstances, various centres of study focused on specific world regions were established in universities in the US, France, UK and later in countries like Japan, China and even India.

Area studies of this kind were replete with contradictions, which varied from the often-problematic designation of specific areas to the political ambitions of such studies. For instance, the term South Asia itself can be a problematic terminology when its official geographic mass is juxtaposed with its cultural territory. Taken in this sense, Myanmar would have been a far more sensible component of South Asia culturally than Afghanistan. But historically, the relationships with present-day Afghanistan were crucial as even an obvious but often forgotten fact such as Buddhism's cultural reach into that region prior to Islamisation is taken into account. The matter gets even more complicated when we ask ourselves, why the Maldives is in the official fold of South Asia and Tibet is not? This is despite the fact that there is a live and throbbing religio-cultural proximity spanning the past and the present, though in the midst of considerable political upheavals.

In any event, area studies conventionally understood in the way we have briefly outlined have been critiqued for their internal contradictions in approach and attitude over a considerable period of time. These criticisms have come both from the areas that were studied as well as from the more enlightened elements within the Euro-American academic zone itself from where areas that were studied emerged in the first place.

Perhaps the best-known critique of the area-studies approach is Edward Said's seminal book, *Orientalism* published initially in 1978 that offered a nuanced deconstruction of the ways in which the so called 'orient' was constructed in the Euro-American imagination and perception.

In a sense, postcolonial studies can be seen as a kind of a response to these issues of power and perception in the studies of the 'other' that emanated from the discourses of knowledge production in Europe and North America. Interestingly, Said discussed the perpetuity of orientalism in the latter part of his book and underlined university education, course curricula, teaching practices, research and training as the areas in which orientalising practices could be seen. In a way, he was right since most university content maintained the framework of area studies in real terms, despite the overt and often rhetorical fight against the phantom, the ghost in the coffin.

Our Approach to Politics of Knowing South Asia

The issue, however, is this: Can our present interest in South Asia in a completely different temporal moment and in radically transformed social and political circumstances be so flippantly subsumed within these complicated and hegemonic histories of pre-existing area studies? Would we wilfully entangle ourselves in such an approach given its less than desirable political and cultural baggage?

We recognise that South Asia as a term that emanated from the area studies discourse of the post-Wold War II period. We also see that a focus on South Asia necessarily means an emphasis on a world region in geographic as well as sociocultural and political terms. This makes it a kind of area studies for sure.

But does that by itself mean that we need to become prisoners of earlier understandings of area studies? In the 'Preface' to the volume, *Sociology and Social Anthropology in South Asia: Histories and Practices*, we clearly emphasise our 'passion and an ideological commitment to the idea of South Asia' is borne out of a very specific set of experiences as well as what we consider the 'academic necessity' of focusing across South Asia in teaching and research.[5]

However, our version of exploring South Asia, or if one insists—area studies—is self-consciously exorcised of the ramifications of colonialism, neo-colonialism, the expansionist and self-centred logic of nation states and power relations of hegemonic sociocultural practices usually enacted across borders. We also tend to provide a kind of contemporariness with inherent complexity to our endeavours, though this also may sit uncomfortably with the conventional understanding of area studies.

It is specifically in the realm of the contemporary that we bring in issues of civilisation and history, culture and politics, literature and poetry, visuality and performance, biography and memory and so on

---

[5] Ravi Kumar, Dev Nath Pathak and Sasanka Perera, 2018, eds., *Sociology and Social Anthropology in South Asia: Histories and Practices*, Delhi, Orient Blackswan, pp. xvii–xxi.

and so forth into what we do. And no, this does not lead to any sense of repackaged exotic or bizarre museum materials that an area studies scholar of the colonial period or soon after would have lusted for.

We consciously seek to let it be the kind of 'area studies' that differ from the older versions of that genre. Instead of being part of the archaeology of knowledge that area studies once upon a time performed for their masters, rulers, colonisers and rivalling power blocks, our version of 'area studies' unravels that archaeology and shows its pitfalls. In this process, the objective is to dismantle that archaeology of knowledge and prevent any possibility of neo-orientalism in contemporary scholarship. And in that spirit, we tend to evaluate the history and practices pertaining to our own areas of study, in sociology and social anthropology, too.

To state it more clearly, instead of being driven by the power and hegemonic considerations of area studies as outlined earlier, our emphasis on South Asia as an 'area' is motivated by our position that 'South Asia might be understood beyond the more predictable cartographic understandings of the region' by focusing on its cultural terrains, travel histories, folklore, popular politics and so on.[6] Ours is 'an intellectual position unabashedly in favour of a nuanced understanding of history as well as how culture works in the region over time and at specific moments'.[7]

We also find it extremely problematic to be imprisoned within the notions of 'nation' and nationality in terms of research, thinking and theorising as well as in understanding things like cultural flows and the circulation of ideas. These difficulties have become more pronounced and their contradictions more apparent in our classrooms where there are 'representatives' from all the 'nations' in South Asia bringing with them the political baggage they were socialised with. And much of this political socialisation is based on an idiom of mutual hostility. This is the kind of sociopolitical reality that Ashis Nandy has referred to as 'garrison states' in South Asia where most states prefer to define themselves 'not by what they are, but by what they are not'.[8] According to him, 'Pakistan,

[6] Kumar, Pathak and Perera, *Sociology and Social Anthropology in South Asia*, pp. xvii–xxi.

[7] Kumar, Pathak and Perera, *Sociology and Social Anthropology in South Asia*, pp. xvii–xxi.

[8] Ashis Nandy, 2005, 'The Idea of South Asia: A Personal Note on Post-Bandung Blues,' in *Inter-Asia Cultural Studies*, Vol. 6, No. 4, p. 541.

Sri Lanka and Nepal try desperately not to be India' while Bangladesh 'has taken up the more onerous responsibility of avoiding being both India and Pakistan'.[9] Our students often carry these burdens.

In these contexts, we have found it necessary to transcend these imposed parochial borders informed by the limited imagination of the nation. We are not calling for the dismantling of nationhood or nationality. Instead, we are suggesting that it might be intellectually useful to explore what lies beyond as much as what lies within the nation. This is particularly so at the present time in South Asia when the idea of the nation has become a divisive tool of populist and violent politics within national borders as well as in relation with other nations. Unfortunately, research and thinking also tend to be subsumed, conceived and conducted within these same confines as if it is an absolute pre-condition for intellectual activity as well as cultural life.

By its very nature, it should be self-evident that this kind of approach cannot be restricted to either a single discipline or to a single country. It has to transgress disciplinary borders within social sciences and humanities as well as the borders of nation states.

This is precisely what we have attempted in other works, opening new avenues towards understanding South Asia. For example, our attempt to initiate a discourse along the line of performative politics in South Asia sought to put together themes running across the region. In *Culture and Politics in South Asia: Performative Communication*, we have underlined that performance and politics are intricately related in South Asia, as elsewhere in the world. The collapse of power and culture is not peculiar to the United States or the former empire; it is also a crucial realisation in the political domain of our own region. To say so, we adopted a framework of themes of regional significance instead of areas, such as nation states.

Likewise, our scheme of discussion did not settle down with a haphazard and helplessly formulated conglomeration of nation states collectively called South Asia. We do not count India, Bangladesh, Sri Lanka, Nepal, Bhutan, Afghanistan, the way a SAARC meeting would

[9] Nandy, 'The Idea of South Asia', p. 541.

do, in order to fulfil the quorum. The appearance of the names of these nation states is only due to the sheer lack of alternative intellectual traditions and nomenclature. Just by naming these nationalities or nations, or by using the words, South Asia, we do not subscribe to the vulgar simplicity of post-World War II area studies or the way to understand our circumstances through the reductionist geopolitical semantics suggested by SAARC.

To be more precise, our quest for 'another' South Asia, is thoroughly determined by the themes of discussion, which brings in even those parts of the world which may not have anything to do with the contemporary cartographic entity called South Asia. In all the deliberations on South Asia, we pack the region together, with such looseness that it transcends the preoccupation with the idea of the area in particular and the narrow logic of conventional area studies in general. This approach is evident in the book, *Another South Asia!* in which we critically depart from the overly simplistic yardsticks of conventional area studies.

But as we have already noted, many colleagues 'perhaps due to their lack of enlightenment and lapses in imagination' may consider our approach 'rhetoric or propaganda'.[10] While we have not called our approach 'area studies', we have no hostility in others calling it as such, as long as its contemporary manifestations and its rupture from the area studies of the past is clearly understood.

Seen in this sense, we can steadfastly defend our kind of area studies borne out of our politics, our experiences, our intellectual needs and our pedagogic agendas. And we would also promote this way of seeing our circumstances in our work and in our institutions. This is because our efforts are clearly borne out of our experiences and needs and not anchored to others' experiences, expectations or anxieties embedded in histories and politics exterior to our own. But it is not a dogmatic and unchanging position as an all-encompassing ultimate truth.

People are welcome to experiment with it or not; they can adopt it or not; they can engage with it or not. But we will continue to engage with it until we see a more sensible alternative.

---

[10] Kumar, Pathak and Perera, *Sociology and Social Anthropology in South Asia*, pp. xvii–xxi.

11

Reclaiming Social Sciences and Humanities

Notes from South Asia[1]

Sasanka Perera

There is a general sense in most academic circles in the world today that social sciences and humanities are in crisis. Personally, I share this anxiety. But I have not seen a similar sense of urgency among my Sri Lankan colleagues. I say this on the basis of the relative lack of concerted and engaged debate and discussion on this, and related issues, compared to other academic domains in South Asia. In this context, I thought of taking this sense of global disquiet juxtaposed with relative local inertia in Sri Lanka as my point of departure in penning these thoughts. While my focus is Sri Lanka, much of what I have to say is equally applicable across South Asia despite various local contextual differences.

First, after reflecting on what humanities and social sciences have meant historically, I will very briefly explore how scholars located in different fields of social sciences and humanities in South Asia assess the situation. Does this disquiet reasonably reflect the status and futures of these disciplines? Or, is it mere doomsday conclusions by perennial systemic outsiders such as myself? Second, within this background, I would like to outline my own views on the situation in Sri Lanka. In this specific context, I will offer my thoughts on how the research and institutional agenda of the

---

[1] Edited version of the keynote address delivered at the 4th Annual Research Symposium of National Centre for Advanced Studies (NCAS) in Social Sciences and Humanities, Colombo, Sri Lanka on 20 December 2017. I acknowledge the substantial contributions of my colleague, Dev Nath Pathak at South Asian University in formulating this text. An earlier version of this chapter was published in the Colombo-based website, *Ground Views* on 20 December 2017. The author would like to thank *Ground Views* for permission to republish.

National Centre for the Advanced Studies (NCAS) in Social Sciences and Humanities could ideally look like, and by extension, think about the agenda for research in social sciences and humanities in Sri Lanka. The focus on this institution is due to the fact that it is directly under Sri Lanka's University Grants Commission and is funded by the country's central government.

About Humanities

But first, what do we actually mean when we very casually refer to social sciences and humanities? Simon During, following the ideas of Edward Said as expressed in texts such as *Humanism and Democratic Criticism* (2004) suggests, 'that there is no adequate or clear and distinct "idea of the humanities" at all'.[2] Instead, he says, what exists is a 'humanities world', which at one level consists of 'a loosely-linked conglomeration of practices, interests, comportments, personae, offices, moods, purposes and values'.[3] At another level, this humanities world is made out of 'various settings, which these practices, interests and so on inhabit'.[4] What During finds so difficult to fathom, is what we so often readily define! Terry Eagleton has suggested, what we now call humanities subjects initially manifested in their present form in the eighteenth century. And they were known as the 'humane disciplines'.[5] Their key role according to Eagleton 'was to foster and protect the kind of values for which a philistine social order had precious little time'.[6]

In other words, humanities were not just domains of knowledge but were avenues to craft a sense of political consciousness, a sense of collective public ethics. According to Eagleton, what was expected

---

[2] Simon During, 'The Idea of Humanities'. Unpublished paper. Available at: https://www.academia.edu/34926361/The_idea_of_the_humanities_2017_ (accessed on 22 October 2017).

[3] During, 'The Idea of Humanities'.

[4] During, 'The Idea of Humanities'.

[5] Terry Eagleton, 2010, 'The Death of Universities,' in *The Guardian* (17 December 2010). Available at: https://www.theguardian.com/commentisfree/2010/dec/17/death-universities-malaise-tuition-fees (accessed on 22 October 2017).

[6] Eagleton, 'The Death of Universities'.

from humanities at the time they came into contact with industrial capitalism was 'to preserve a set of values and ideas under siege'.[7]

About Social Sciences

Similarly, what we think of as social sciences came into being from diverse sources within the generality of western philosophical traditions. But as a cluster of cognate disciplines, the more obvious emergence of social sciences was in the early nineteenth century as a direct influence of positivist philosophy of science. It is from the mid-twentieth century onwards that the terminology 'social sciences' has been more broadly used to refer to a range of disciplines, which we are now familiar with. Social sciences, with their core point of departure—the systemic study of humanity—can be better understood when located in the intellectual break that occurred between the rupture of the Age of Enlightenment and the beginning of modernity.

The direct intellectual foundations of social sciences are the moral philosophies associated with iconic temporal moments in the history of knowledge and politics such as the Industrial Revolution and the French Revolution. If we are to look into the history of social sciences in general and the twin histories of sociology and social anthropology in particular, in addition to the presence of progressive Enlightenment ideas, one could also see the influence of Edmund Burke's conservatism as well as the romanticism of the German idealist tradition, among many other sources of influence. That is, from its very beginning, social science knowledge production flirted with numerous contradictory intellectual influences that both competed with and complemented each other in the long term. These interactions gave shape to the disciplines we now call social sciences. In this context, the idea of a monolithic social science, often modelled upon a sense of Newtonian reductionism that most simplistic pro-Enlightenment proponents celebrate, is too simple and too linear a proposition.

Arguably, it was only when each modern discipline of social science began to distinguish itself from others, one could see the emergence of

[7] Eagleton, 'The Death of Universities'.

sanitised and mutually exclusive social science disciplines with seemingly concrete borders. The advent of sociology, after Emile Durkheim, separating itself from a broader and less differentiated body of social sciences and humanities, is one example of this new landscape of knowledge. It was in reaction to such tendencies in social sciences, that in the first quarter of the twentieth century, Max Horkheimer and Theodore Adorno declared that Enlightenment itself was totalitarian, along with all the other tolerable bounties of modernity. Hence, they appealed for a return to philosophy and social thought, rather than abstract positivist theorising.

But today, when we think of the relevance of social sciences and humanities to South Asian societies and to universities in the region, I cannot help but think that we are approaching knowledge completely devoid of a nuanced understanding of disciplinary histories and their constituent politics. It seems to me that contemporary knowledge production in these disciplines in countries like Sri Lanka is completely ahistorical and often devoid of a sense of public ethics.

General Decline of Humanities and Social Sciences

In 2010, looking at the British University system upon which Sri Lankan as well as most other South Asian university systems were initially based, Eagleton asked the following very disturbing question: 'Are the humanities about to disappear from our universities?'[8] He went on to argue that in an ideal sense, 'there cannot be a university without the humanities', and

> if history, philosophy and so on vanish from academic life, what they leave in their wake may be a technical training facility or corporate research institute. But it will not be a university in the classical sense of the term, and it would be deceptive to call it one.[9]

Of course, he was only talking of humanities. But my suggestion is, the same question can be posed with reference to social sciences as well. That is, social sciences deprived of their imagination and rearranged as

[8] Eagleton, 'The Death of Universities'.

[9] Eagleton, 'The Death of Universities'.

mere data-generating processes as they often function nowadays, would reflect the same outcome. But the issue for me is not that social sciences and humanities disciplines are disappearing from universities. The issue is that their centrality in thinking and the collective conscience of national sociopolitical environments in general are underemphasised and neglected. In my view, much of this has happened due to two interrelated reasons:

1 First, most disciplines that fall within social sciences and humanities—with the exception of economics—have been exiled into the lower strata of academic hierarchies as irrelevant soft subjects by educational decision-makers as well as the general public. This is a global situation. Generally, economics has escaped this situation due to its alleged direct implication in what is known as 'development'. And to a certain extent, sociology in countries like Sri Lanka has reinvented itself as a mere data-gathering device in a poor simulation of economics. So instead of serious scholars of sociology, we now have a world mostly inhabited by consultants in sociology. With regard to sociology and social anthropology, in particular, this reductionist and utilitarian cloning of economics has seriously damaged these disciplines' quest for theories, concepts and methodological perspectives for which they were known for a long time. In other words, trying to become 'relevant' in a simple utilitarian fashion has led social sciences and humanities to become collectively malnourished in philosophical, humanistic and intellectual terms. This is exhibited at all levels of the academic hierarchies, from young academics' dissertations to established scholars' magnum opuses—where the tendency is to merely sprinkle theory as the icing on empirical cakes, rather than engaging theoretically with data and information and adding to the overall process of theorising.

2 Second, many people in social sciences and humanities have also not shown any clear intent or ability to disprove this popularly held belief by enhancing their research, intellectual engagement, publishing and public interventions. In this sense, the perception of crisis and decay that have befallen these disciplines, have become a self-fulfilling prophecy, dictated by official decision-making bodies and internalised by the practitioners themselves by mediocritising their own practice. As a result, these tendencies

> have adversely impacted the thematic preferences for research as well as in designing course curricula. In this context, most colleagues no longer seem to take intellectual risks or undertake adventures, without which advances in any form of science or art is nearly impossible. As a result, mediocrity in knowledge is a necessary outcome.

What I have described here though somewhat simplistically, is a contemporary global situation. This is, however, very clearly visible in South Asia in general and Sri Lanka in particular. Referring to the same phenomenon in the UK, Eagleton says—and I think quite rightly—that 'the quickest way of devaluing these subjects—short of disposing of them altogether—is to reduce them to an agreeable bonus. Real men study law and engineering, while ideas and values are for sissies.'[10]

For me, the issue of ideas and values and their resultant implication in politics is of crucial significance for social sciences and humanities—beyond the generation of disciplinary knowledge more generally. With the struggles of the French students' movement for social justice in the 1960s still fresh in mind, Pierre Bourdieu observed in the 1970s that sociology is the 'discipline that makes trouble.'[11] This is not a simplistic assumption that sociology and social anthropology[12] are inherently troublesome and unstable. Instead, it means that they are disciplines that need to be systematic in their approaches in as much as they are reflexive and conscious of societal issues. But being all this can often mean trouble for rulers and regimes at any time and anywhere. As far as I am concerned, any social science or humanities discipline, if it is incapable of being reflexive in the way it practices its craft, it has already failed its mission.

From this historical perspective and notwithstanding the complex dynamics in the evolution of these disciplines over the years, it is up to you to ponder over how far the core ideals of these disciplines have shifted and what this shift means in intellectual terms today.

---

[10] Eagleton, 'The Death of Universities.'

[11] Pierre Bourdieu, 1994, *Sociology in Question*, London, SAGE Publications.

[12] Bourdieu (1994) did not make a distinction between sociology and social anthropology and thought the border between the two is spurious.

Social Sciences and Humanities in South Asia

Let us see for a moment, how scholars in the region have seen this situation with regard to their own disciplines in the recent past. Veena Das, looking into the situation of Indian sociology in the 1980s observed, 'the crisis in sociological research in India has to be located in three institutional structures—the universities, the UGC and the professional bodies such as the Indian Sociological Society'.[13] She notes, 'at the level of the universities, the proliferation of the subject (in this particular case, sociology is taught everywhere) has simply not been matched by the will to ensure competence in teaching and research'.[14]

This situation becomes worse when the initiation of knowledge into the system is curtailed in places where higher education is provided in local languages without qn adequate intellectual infrastructure in place to bring in global knowledge in local contexts either through English or any other global language. Sri Lanka is very clearly in this situation as well. Das also refers to the politicisation of academic environments and its promotion and appointment schemes as a problem that adds to this overall negative state of affairs.[15]

How the Indian UGC is implicated in this situation is quite interesting given what it has to say for Sri Lanka. The Indian UGC is perhaps the most financially endowed in the region. As Das notes, 'the decision-making bodies in the UGC seem to have completely misguided notions about the state of social science research in the country'.[16] For her, the basic concern is the UGC's mechanistic decision-making process when it comes to funding, which assumes all institutional entities to be equal. This equality is obviously not a reality. And these variations need to be seriously considered if the idea is to systematically develop social sciences, humanities or any academic or professional discipline in a country. But to make such decisions, it is crucial that such entities are

---

[13] Veena Das, 1993, 'Sociological Research in India: The State of Crisis,' in *Economic and Political Weekly*, 5 June 1993, p. 1159.

[14] Das, 'Sociological Research in India', p. 1160.

[15] Das, 'Sociological Research in India', pp. 1160–161.

[16] Das, 'Sociological Research in India', p. 1160.

well aware of the actual status of these disciplines and what is needed. Though Das made her observations in the 1980s, what she said then, remains equally relevant today as well.

Akbar Zaidi writing about economics in particular, but with general reference to social sciences in Pakistan notes that social sciences in the country are in a 'dismal state'.[17] One reason for him to make this claim is due to the Pakistani social scientists' continued application of imported 'theoretical arguments and constructs to Pakistani conditions without questioning, debating or commenting on the theory itself'.[18] In other words, he is lamenting about the lack of local theoretical engagement. This emanates primarily when ideas are not considered seriously enough in disciplinary practices as opposed to linear empirical research, and when one is satisfied being a mere follower of theory, rather than an innovator of theoretical constructs.

Zaidi also says that state patronage in research and appointments within universities and in government also has a stunting effect on the development of social science research in Pakistan. He further argues that in the case of Pakistan, 'there seems to be no research in the social science which expands the spectrum of knowledge and ideas, and Pakistani social scientists are primarily in the 'business of giving advice'.[19] This situation is further exacerbated due to the lack of a 'culture promoting free floating discussion and debate'.[20] The overall decline of social science institutions—from universities to think tanks and research organisations—have also impacted this situation. And as a result, rather than institutions conducting research, often research is conducted by individuals who happen to be based in institutions or on their own, independently.[21] In this situation, one cannot expect significant institutional growth.

The general situation described previously is broadly applicable to Sri Lanka as well. In my own reflections on Sri Lankan sociology in

---

[17] S. Akbar Zaidi, 2002, 'Dismal State of Social Sciences in Pakistan' in *Economic and Political Weekly*, Vol. 37, No. 35 (31 August–6 September 2002), pp. 3644–3661.

[18] Zaidi, 'Dismal State of Social Sciences in Pakistan', p. 3644.

[19] Zaidi, 'Dismal State of Social Sciences in Pakistan,' p. 3645.

[20] Zaidi, 'Dismal State of Social Sciences in Pakistan,' p. 3645.

[21] Zaidi, 'Dismal State of Social Sciences in Pakistan,' pp. 3644–3661.

particular and social sciences and humanities more generally, I have also referred to a similar situation that exists in India, Pakistan and the rest of the region. In the Sri Lankan context and depending on the specific discipline, this situation of decline is related to out-migration of trained scholars; the relative lack of success in training others to take up their intellectual roles; substandard training in universities; relative lack of funding for research; the non-emergence of a serious local academic publishing industry and so on. As a result, when it comes to social sciences and humanities, Sri Lankan 'universities are no longer in the forefront of initiating or publishing cutting-edge, path-breaking or creative research; neither is this the preserve of the civil society sector'.[22]

In this situation, as in the case of both Pakistan and India, 'serious research on contemporary Sri Lanka is the activity of individuals, be they based in the country or beyond'.[23] In this context, looking specifically at Sri Lankan sociology and social anthropology and despite the existence of a large institutional structure within the university system, and an extensive network of students and teachers, research and teaching in these disciplines are 'at best unimaginative, uncreative, predictable, theoretically regressive, and mostly dated'.[24]

In these general circumstances, sociology and economics very clearly and other disciplines in social sciences and humanities which have some 'developmental utility', have been colonised by the broader development practice of both the state and the non-government sector. Commenting on this situation with reference to India, Mukherji notes that 'much of the academic time of many social scientists in universities and research institutes is being diverted to evaluation/consultancy researches very much demanded by NGOs'.[25] In Sri Lanka's case and

---

[22] Sasanka Perera, 2005, 'Dealing with Dinosaurs and Reclaiming Sociology: A Personal Narrative on the (non) Existence of Critical Sociological Knowledge Production in Sri Lanka,' in *Sociological Bulletin: Journal of the Indian Sociological Society*, Vol. 54, No. 3 (September–December 2005), p. 232.

[23] Perera, 'Dealing with Dinosaurs and Reclaiming Sociology', p. 232.

[24] Perera, 'Dealing with Dinosaurs and Reclaiming Sociology, p. 233.

[25] Partha N. Mukherji, 2004, 'Introduction: Indigeneity and Universality in Social Science,' in *Indigeneity and Universality in Social Sciences: A South Asian Response*, edited by Partha N. Mukherji and Chandan Sengupta, New Delhi, SAGE Publications, p. 29.

in continuation of a broader South Asian practice, consultants have effectively replaced scholars.

In this context, development and applied oriented work have become mainstream as opposed to dealing with ideas or theoretical issues. But unlike India and to a lesser extent even in Pakistan and Bangladesh, in Sri Lanka, there has been no major discussion on this reversal of intellectual roles that have fundamentally changed the public perception and actual practice of social sciences and humanities in the country.

Thoughts for the Future of Social Sciences and Humanities in Sri Lanka

In the backdrop I have sketched so far, let me ponder over the role the NCAS in Social Sciences and Humanities could play in Sri Lanka in reimagining the country's intellectual landscape. What we can say about NCAS can easily be expanded to the social science and humanities knowledge scenario in general across the country. Also, as it is directly governed under the UGC and is funded by the state, I assume what it stands for in terms of research is a reflection of the thinking of the state. Hence, my decision to enter this broader discussion via a reflection on the research agenda of the NCAS. I am intrigued by the word 'advanced' in the nomenclature of the institute (National Centre for Advanced Studies in Social Sciences and Humanities). I have also further noticed that it publishes a journal called the *Sri Lanka Journal of Advanced Social Studies*. Again, the word 'advanced' caught my attention. In this context, what does 'advanced' mean in a conceptual sense?

To me, the immediate question is this: how, and on what basis can the research and training agenda of NCAS be rendered advanced? And how would the essays published in its journal (which does not seem to be published regularly) contribute towards advancing social studies or the advancement of knowledge in general? How are such advances in intellectual terms to be achieved and gauged when the general background of research in social sciences and humanities in the country and that of the region is on a decline? Let me address this apparent dilemma with reference to a number of recent personal experiences.

In Sri Lanka and elsewhere in the region, words and concepts are often not used with the seriousness they deserve in academic contexts. It was Bourdieu who once suggested that concepts and terminologies used in social sciences should be revisited regularly to see whether they continue to make sense over time, and if not, they should be suitably modified.[26] So the Department of Sociology at Colombo University has a compulsory course called Advanced Sociological Theory, as do most other sociology departments of sociology in Sri Lanka and elsewhere in South Asia. But most such courses are merely summaries of social theory where no tangible efforts are undertaken to engage with these theories in the broader contexts in which they are discussed and taught. My present academic location, Department of Sociology at South Asian University that I have personally helped establish, also has a course for the Ph.D programme called Advanced Social Theory, as do many other similar Departments in India and in other parts of the world. I could never see what was so advanced in any of these courses. In our Ph.D course, however, a number of more themes were covered, accompanied by a larger dose of reading compared to the two compulsory MA courses on theory.

In both cases, it was not possible to see a serious advancement of knowledge in any real sense. And neither was such an outcome anticipated. 'Advanced' was just a word! When my colleague, Ravi Kumar[27] and I took over the teaching of the Advanced Social Theory course in 2017, we wanted to try and make it come closer to its claim of being 'advanced'. The first thing that was done was to drop the word 'advanced' from it nomenclature, and call it 'Social Theory, Society and Modes of Thinking'. But our intention was to complicate how theory was to be taught in a sociology Ph.D programme in South Asia.

Towards this, we consciously reduced the structural elements of course from ten integrated sections to four. The first in the new

[26] Bourdieu, *Sociology in Question.*

[27] Much of the rethinking and restructuring of this course was done by my colleague, Dr Ravi Kumar.

conceptualisation dealt with the idea of what theory is, and what it is expected to do in social sciences. The second dealt with what we called 'the work and puzzles of culture'. The third dealt with 'understanding the self and being'. In each section, we asked the students to read a handful of core readings and discuss them in class, as they understood them. In the fourth section, which we had called, 'Advanced Social Theory: South Asian Possibilities', we asked students to explore selected 'thinking from South Asia' on the basis of what they have read and discussed in class.

We wondered why the academic training we receive in universities seemed to suggest the non-existence of social theorisation in South Asia despite the existence of philosophical works, which looked at categories such as consciousness and self as in Buddhism and Charvaka philosophy or the ancient Indian thought on materialism; politics and diplomacy as in Kautilya's *Arthashastra*, and taste and aesthetics as in Bharata Muni's *Natya Shastra*, among many others. All of these had their own complex analytical apparatus. We asked the students to engage with these South Asian ideas and see if and how they might provide a basis for contemporary theorisation devoid of notions of faith and belief. This was our attempt at making this course 'advanced' by actively asking our Ph.D students to think out of the box and attempt to fine-tune ideas and reflect on possibilities of new theorisation. For us, this came closer to a certain advancement of knowledge. And it offered possibilities of creating new knowledge. In other words, this was close to the philosophical expectations initially associated with humanities and social sciences.

But this kind of self-conscious effort is generally not the norm. In this context, let me try and explain my own understanding of NCAS' sense of 'advanced' on the basis of a concrete example, and offer some suggestions on how this might be reimagined. Let me refer to the 4th Annual Research Symposium in Social Sciences and Humanities organised by NCAS in Colombo on 20 December 2017 as an example. By the time the call for papers for this symposium was closed, I learned that NCAS received 96 papers across disciplines and about 60 of them were slated to be presented in the symposium. I am impressed by this degree of interest in the production of knowledge. But a closer reading of the titles of these papers indicated that they subscribed to a very specific idea of knowledge. Almost without exception, they were applied and developmental in orientation. They were empiricist in approach and were looking for solutions to specific problems. But this is only one very specific kind of social science and humanities knowledge. In reality, the entire spectrum of these two broad disciplinary domains cannot be reduced to an applied-developmental paradigm alone.

What about the rest? Why not deal with ideas? Why not an actively engage with theory and theorisation? Why not undertake research for the sake of knowledge and not for the sake of finding a solution to a problem? It is from this latter cluster of research, the kind that is by and large absent in NCAS symposium, that knowledge in social sciences and humanities can be truly advanced, rendered nuanced and made theoretically sophisticated.

But this is not a uniquely Sri Lankan problem. One can see this everywhere in South Asia and to different degrees in the rest of the world as well. In our region and in Sri Lanka for sure, this has come about as the result of the political interpretation of a very regressive and dangerous word. And that word is, 'relevance'. Often nowadays, and particularly if research is funded by state agencies, we are asked 'how is your work relevant'? This means that all research understood in this sense—be they in the social sciences, humanities, natural sciences or engineering—must be subsumed by the utilitarian logic of national or regional development. It is in such a context that the former Sri Lankan Minister of Higher Education, Vishwa Varnapala (2007–2010) asked in a UGC-sponsored conference in Colombo years ago, what the 'relevance' of Gananath Obeyesekere's seminal work, *The Cult of the Goddess Pattini* was.

Of course, Obeyesekere's elegantly written book does not inform us about the number of tube wells in the North Central Province, how many kilometres of roads have been asphalted in the Eastern province, the extent of electrification in the South, how many litres of Palmyra toddy is annually produced in the north or any such matters of applied utility. In that sense, his book is absolutely irrelevant.

But it informs us through a detailed study of Pattini worship, important aspects of the country's cultural history, dynamics of migration by looking at how specific ideas of faith and worship have travelled from South India to Sri Lanka and places in context important parameters of identity formation of Sinhala and Tamil people through matters of belief. Seen in this sense, Obeyesekere's book and others like it are crucially relevant to our sense of being.

However, that kind of knowledge that dwells in the realm of ideas, history, philosophy and politics cannot be generated if the focus of Sri Lanka's social sciences and humanities is overwhelmingly dictated by developmental and applied criteria.

Seen in this sense, I think there are two possibilities for NCAS' future as well as Sri Lanka's future in knowledge production in social sciences and humanities:

1 The first possibility, and the easiest is to do absolutely nothing. Let the kind of research that predominates today continue. They will certainly add to the quantum of our information, developmental planning, promotions within universities and so on. But this approach will certainly not add to any kind of serious advancement of knowledge or engagement with ideas.

2 The second possibility is to seriously recognise a multiplicity of knowledge as essential and necessary for social sciences and humanities in the country and actively promote this diversification. In this scheme of things, applied research will be one kind of research. And, it is an important kind of research. The other is the kind of knowledge that will deal with ideas, would promote theorisation and abstract thinking. Besides, the self-conscious coming together of applied and so-called non-applied research at different plains would have significant benefits. For instance, if we want applied research to be more nuanced and sensitive to the complexities on the ground, then, the so-called non-applied research can offer the orientation and the necessary intellectual curiosity to ask the right kind of questions. But at the same time, the non-applied research should not mean the constant replication of ancient, outdated or obscure practices in the name of research. Social sciences and humanities also need to actively reinvent themselves in the present by visiting the intersections of science, technology, contemporary ethics and politics. For me, this is the way to make the word, 'relevant' more sensible.

It is up to university academics in social sciences and humanities and academic administrators to make these decisions. It is also up to them not to make the kind of decision I am advocating. But the 'future' will tell us if colleagues have opted to be simple technicians in the world of applied research, or opted to do that as well as contribute to serious and theoretically nuanced production of knowledge in social sciences and humanities. But 'futures', like most things in our society, tend to be unclear, distant and seemingly unreachable. Precisely due to this, 'futures' worth becoming a part of our lives, have to be passionately imagined and fought for.

12

Anthropological South Asia

Thinking through Utopias Amidst Intellectual Hegemonies[1]

Dev Nath Pathak

The idea of 'Anthropological South Asia' presupposes an ability to transcend national-territorial confines. Within each national-territorial confine, there is a history of doing anthropology. Each such confine is presumably a little republic of anthropologists operating with preferences, pride and prejudices in accordance with the sociopolitical and cultural priorities of the confines. Anthropologists of India would not read anthropologists from Bangladesh, Sri Lanka or Nepal. The scene may be slightly different if some of the local scholars from these confines dislocate and relocate themselves in the premier institutes in the western hemisphere. Curiously though, many of the non-Indian scholars from across South Asia tend to feed themselves on the literatures produced by chosen few Indian scholars. But on the whole, there has been an evident dearth of mutual respect, cross border intellectual engagement and sharing of theoretical, empirical and analytical interest. For example, more than half of sociology and social anthropology in India may be considered to be focussed on the study of caste. But there is seldom an attempt to read caste as a regional phenomenon or at least be informed about the existence of caste features in societies across borders in the cartographic neighbourhood. In this wake, one is bound to notice an Indian hegemony in intellectual and academic terms.

---

[1] Some of the ideas presented in this chapter were initially mooted in an interview with Asif Bin Ali in the Dhaka-based newspaper, *Daily Observer* on 18 October 2018.

In this sense, our probing question shall be, as to how an anthropological South Asia is possible, in such a grave scenario of little republics further vexed by issues of hegemony?

However, to make the challenge a little more nuanced, we shall be concerned with many levels of hegemony in the production and circulation of academic knowledge. Euro-centrism, which was about the predominance of the knowledge generated in the European context, is not yet dead. Indeed it has become more complex with other additions, making it more a Euro-American hegemony. The stakeholders in the politics of production and circulation of knowledge have multiplied. The global South Asian scholarship rivals with Euro-American hegemony in knowledge politics. In many ways, this is a new avatar of the erstwhile intellectual predominance of Euro-American scholarship. Often, it seems that global South Asian scholars are content with the kind of view of South Asian societies and polity that has been formulated in the waiting lounges of airports or fly-by-night operations run by paid research assistants. Global South Asian scholars tend to celebrate their identity defined by the number of visas they accumulate on their passport. Many local scholars of the region lustfully and self-consciously join in the competition of collecting visas on their passports too and hence they speak highly of the places they visit. Mass-produced souvenirs from global capitals adorn their walls. These days, there is also quite an evident tendency of reducing academic visits to a few selfies or Facebook status updates on where one is flying to rather than a deeper engagement with what one has actually done. It is visible that we are living in the time of the 'selfy-academic' in general and sociologists and social anthropologists helplessly abide by the terms and conditions of this regime. Ridiculous as they may appear, they are blind copies of the reference group that is global South Asian scholars.

Furthermore, we often hear a meaningful joke that global South Asian scholarship is by and large global Indian scholarship, which can be furthermore narrowed to Indian-Bengali scholarship with the participation of some Marathi and Gujarati scholars too. Indian hegemony itself is a knee-jerk reaction to Euro-American and global South Asian hegemony. And then, Indian hegemony attempts to look like a master of its own destiny in the so-called postcolonial, local, South

Asia. It is often a butt of ridicule in the larger analysis of epistemological decolonisation. As such, Indian scholarship does not provide with much headway when it comes to scholarship in or on South Asia. Instead, what it shows consists of various levels of slavishness, precisely what the Malaysian sociologist Syed Husain Alatas has called the 'captive mind', at work. Within this, Indian hegemony pretends to be a master, though it is only 'his master's voice', as it were. In the twentieth century, the masters were those who delivered to us the European canons. There was a dethroning of the former masters, but not the master–slave relation. The new masters were of colour, belonging to the benighted heathen of the Catholic imagination. These new masters struggled with and characterised the dominant power relations as a matter of relations between the core and the periphery. And yet, they maintained the same interest by diversifying the core and peripheries. Now there are many cores from where some of the old masters, along with their new partners from different racial-ethnic-national profiles look at the peripheries. Mostly, these peripheries are restricted to the local qua regional. They have announced that you can match up, more or less, if and only if you subscribe to the scheme of hybridity, dislocated locality, transnational flow of goods and knowledge. No wonder, so many local scholars aspire to get there by singing in the tune of a familiar orchestra, rooted in the logic of neo-colonialism.

How does one deal with such a complex structure of hegemony? There could be varied answers, amid which I would like to present the utopian imagination of my preference for discussion. The approach of my academic politics in this regard starts with an idea that the hegemon is too weak to interfere. Indian hegemony, precisely, is a monster without fangs, at best; it is a docile quantum of flesh without bones; it is a body in decay ever since its inception. An approach to rendering sociology and anthropology, as South Asian, one needs to be keen to perform what might be called an act of intellectual cannibalism; eat the meat of the monster and spit it out. Make it loud and clear that Oedipus has no interest in the tyrant; academic politics of South Asian scholarship needs to declare that it can grow without beating the known hegemons. For, the hegemon has no impact whatsoever. Indeed this utopian answer seeks to render the masculinity of neo-colonialism impotent enough to allow wildness of epistemological decolonisation, an intellectually anarchic spot in the blitzkrieg of academic limelight.

Cultural Politics: A Way Forward in Anthropological South Asia

For a long time, in post-colonial South Asia, social science, in general, operated within various comfort zones. The comfort was ensured by restricting scholarly attention to everything predefined, such as territories, nationalities and thematic issues of enquiry and theoretical and methodological preferences. We can safely say that sociology and social anthropology have been made, like many other cognates, too nationalist and therefore also parochial. Anthropologists of India made anthropology a handmaiden in the service of the nation-building programme. Similarly, in Bangladesh, anthropological practices swung from archiving the indigenous and serving the nationalist need to create a trope for national-cultural superiority by contributing to the development programmes and to please donors, governmental or non-governmental. Likewise, there are complaints by anthropologists in Nepal and Sri Lanka about the development sector almost taking over the whole of social sciences. The national and international NGOs determine the idea, nature and scope of research across South Asia. Anthropologists have not shown necessary courage and conviction to be exceptionally defiant of any regime of power, of state or of NGOs. We seldom find sociologists and anthropologists indulging in deeply disturbing intellectual disputes in the region of South Asia. Instead they, by and large, choose to be a cog in the machinery of power. There was no idealism, it was merely a calculated utilitarianism of a self-serving class of academics. If there was any utopianism at all, it was only to enable the parochially interested academics to masquerade as change-makers. This is not to lament about the problem that is contemporary. This all goes back to the history of sociology and social anthropology in South Asia. After all, anthropology had deep philosophical roots which ought to be harnessed in order to make sense of the embedded cross-disciplinary tendencies. Seldom, an anthropological work makes an explicit foray in the area of philosophical enquiry in South Asia. Existential anthropology could hardly be a central theme in the region. Indeed, across the region there has been a systematic attempt to de-philosophise anthropology.[2]

In general, it is obvious that most scholars, who had greater intellectual responsibility and the institutional ability, indeed did nothing to develop the grounds on which intellectual risks could be undertaken ever since the advent of sociology and social anthropology in any of the South Asia contexts. Everyone played it safe and stayed within defined areas, be it national or disciplinary, or overall intellectual. Perhaps, this was also beneficial for them, in terms of maintaining validity, getting financial support from state and other agencies with vested interests. This can be seen in Bangladesh, Sri Lanka, Nepal, Pakistan and of course India where the 'games of academic politics' unfold without too much of word-mincing. The notoriety of Indian sociologists and social anthropologists congratulating themselves for self-reflexive criticism is quite known. It led to various occasions of crisis mongering, without any answer to the crises, not at least in any practical sense. This has not been the case since the beginning. Initially, sociologists and anthropologists in India developed creatively passionate polemics criticising intellectual colonialism and pleaded for decolonisation. But over time all this only added to the rhetoric without execution, dream without realisation, diagnosis without remedies and rejection without alternatives. Though everyone aspired for alternative epistemological development, there was none of the kind that one could bank on. As a result, it became easier for sociologists and anthropologists to throw the bathwater away with the baby, or to be precise, abandon the project of decolonising the epistemological bedrocks of disciplinary practices. This applies to the tribes of sociologists and anthropologists from India, as well as from elsewhere including Bangladesh, Pakistan, Nepal, Sri Lanka, Afghanistan and so on. So much so that today if you say disciplinary decolonisation, or if you utter words such as indigenous, roots, traditions, etc., you may invite many peers' ire. The dream

[2] This complaint is resonant in, Dev Nath Pathak, 2018, *Living and Dying: Meanings in Maithili Folklore*, Delhi, Primus.

was lost since there has been no chance to retrieve faint ideas from the dream into the language of reality. No Dr Freud can help as far as these forgotten dreams are concerned. No wonder, some contemporary scholars in India even cringe at the thought of the word decolonising.

If there is no idea of decolonisation, then there can be no inclination to cultural politics. For the cultural texts across South Asia still, resonate with the idea of thinking through local categories. But, how would a colonially crippled anthropology deal with culture and its politics? Most anthropologists have hitherto operated with a monolithic idea of culture, something ornamental like folklore, heritage, museums, exotic etc. Culture, just like a curio in the drawing room of an upper middle-class household, is a second fiddle in the theatre of scholarship. Just like in patriarchal social division, girls are supposed to be trained by the mothers to be cultural, while boys are to be trained by menfolk to be practical, political and outwardly social. Anthropologists perpetuated a notion of culture against which someone like Herbert Read said, 'to hell with culture'.[3] However, some others among anthropologists and sociologists tried to see culture only in terms of fixed formations, such as caste, ethnicity and engendered relations. Many of them invariably based their understanding on indological oversimplification such as purity versus pollution, equality versus inequality, natural versus social. It all seemed pretty justified with a progressive ideology and political correctness injected into dominant versions of anthropology. So an oversimplified understanding of caste structure became unimpeachable since it led to questioning of the caste hierarchy, or an equally mistaken idea of gendered relations became prominent since it attacked the gender power relations, so to say.

One could not see any denial of the importance of the emancipatory ambitions of sociology and social anthropology in such endeavours. But then, what is the point if it created blinders on the pretext of emancipation and transformation. The complexity of culture remained a fugitive at large in such politically biased anthropology. This led to the perpetual obscurity of the integral relations of culture with politics and the various

[3] Herbert Read, *To Hell with Culture: And Other Essays on Art and Society*, London, Routledge, 2002.

performances of this interrelated entity which can be captured in, say, conventional ways of dealing with the caste-sociability. Sociologists and anthropologists are ill-equipped to ask as to how caste, ethnicity, gender or any such indicators are disarmingly, performatively, enforced in a social set up. Or for that matter, what are the enchanting values of everything regressive against which the politically correct brigade of social scientists have waged battles and yet did not inch any closer to convincing anyone other than the already converted peers? Social scientists have done exactly what most journalists in newspapers or television do. That is, to put culture as a soft (and subsidiary-secondary) area, and politics as the real domain of actions, or let the political determine the cultural in the ultimate scheme of analysis. They have pitched the two as separable entities. Neither journalists nor social scientists were able to see the twinness of the characters, culture and politics. It is like many scholars, alike journalists, will go to watch a theatre performance, thinking of a 'purely' cultural event, without knowing that it is a bourgeoisie tendency to separate roots and routes, tradition and modernity, cultural and political, performance and power. Such performances are reviewed in newspapers or documented by ethnographers or performance studies scholars. Seldom does one get a sense from such reporting that each bit of performance is an act of politics, and likewise these days, every act of politics is a performative execution. It is not only due to the content of political nature but also due to the relations of a performance with the history and politics of a society.

Take, for example, almost everyone laments in Bangladesh about the decline in the audience of modern theatre. To make sense of such a decline, or conversely inclined interest for the violently vivacious Bengali television soaps produced in India and religiously consumed in Bangladesh, one has to see the conjoined twins at work, culture and politics entangled. We know about the love for soft porn in some Bangladeshi films (famously known as cut-piece cinema), or an uncanny popularity of Hero Alom, the YouTube sensation amongst the lower middle-class consumers in Bangladesh. And many such instances from Bangladesh help us see similar trends in other parts of South Asia. Recently, a video clip of an ordinary uncle dancing in a wedding party on a film song became a rage. This song was from an old film starring

Govinda, the actor known for a peculiar dance style. The thick narrative of politics is imbued in such sporadically unearthed cultural texts if one is willing to caste the gaze to 'see' them and not just consume them as blind consumers in the neoliberal entertainment market. A travelling theatre group in Nepal, or a series of young contemporary artists in Sri Lanka, and so on so forth, deliver to us a panorama of cultural politics in South Asia. In the Sri Lankan case, it has been variously approached to read a reaffirmation of Sinhala nationalism and its cultural critique. We have tried to put together a book along this line titled *Culture and Politics in South Asia: Performative Communication.*[4] We emphasised that South Asia is a region of perpetual dramatics, loaded with emotive contents. We deemed the region a theatre of performative politics whereby culture and power are inseparable. This book brought together cases from Bangladesh, Sri Lanka, Nepal and India, in support of the thesis.

If this fundamental realisation makes sense, one has to think of anthropology and sociology of South Asia that could do justice to the inseparable culture and politics. Such an endeavour has to be against the divisive academic politics, which has plagued intellectual growth in Bangladesh as well as in India, and elsewhere in South Asia. We are aware of the selfish and unjustifiable divide between sociology and anthropology in Bangladesh. Strangely enough, this is common across the region, and even more paradoxical that within sociology there is a lobby that argues for an 'applied' business orientation. So does anthropology. Of course, this is under the influence of the development sector. National and international NGOs determine the way scholars would conduct themselves. The market determines the idea of research and intellectual development. Much of South Asian societies, polity and academia suffer from this disease. This is reflective of 'a slave morality' (following Nietzsche), or a captive mind (following Syed Husain Alatas). Hence, another book titled, *Sociology and Social Anthropology in South Asia: Histories and Practices*[5] sought to develop

[4] Dev Nath Pathak and Sasanka Perera, eds., *Culture and Politics in South Asia: Performative Communication*, London and Delhi, Routledge, 2017.

[5] Ravi Kumar, Dev Nath Pathak and Sasanka Perera, eds., *Sociology and Social Anthropology in South Asia: Histories and Practices*, Delhi, Orient Blackswan, 2018.

a nuanced disciplinary framework that can allow us to engage with not only a national-territorial context, but with the region at large; not only the conventional and familiar issues of enquiry, but also opening new frontiers by pushing disciplinary boundaries; not only reading the western canons, but also seeking to fathom theoretical values of the local canons (diverse bodies of thoughts across the region of South Asia). This book has advanced our endeavour in creating a framework of research for South Asia in which one might effortlessly engage with contexts beyond one's home turf, without being 'anti-national', so to say. This is also what we envisaged in the book *Another South Asia!*,[6] that was almost like a manifesto of our efforts to build up a specific understanding of sociology and social anthropology of South Asia. In a way, we perform a kind of academic politics through these publications. As part of our politics, we emphasise everything hitherto underemphasised; we bring to the core the issue of cultural politics that we witness in South Asia today; we posit questions that have been deemed non-issues by and large till now; we stress on the imperative of developing sociology and social anthropology in the regional framework of South Asia. This is indeed a political move of a bunch of academics who believe that the logic of nation state has impeded the growth of social sciences.

Meaning of South Asia for Anthropologists

Let us imagine South Asia through a metaphor since we are aware of the pitfalls of definitive definitions and politico-ideological distortions. It is akin to a cracked mirror with various shards of glass, yet together since an invisible frame over it is still intact. If you can imagine such a mirror, which is not hard to find in our everyday life, much more becomes possible. We don't like to see our face in such broken mirrors. It shows us in terms of ugly and real images unlike the official camera obscura fairly dear to diplomats and emissaries of power to be. And if one is courageous in staring at the image reflected in such a cracked

---

[6] Dev Nath Pathak, 2018, ed., *Another South Asia*, Delhi, Primus.

mirror, one gets to see the aesthetics of it, mixed with ideologies and utopias, reality and fantasy, history and mythology, poetics and politics. Over the decades, the official-bureaucratic effort has been to whitewash the cracked mirror and hide it away from us. SAARC gives us such a whitewashed illusion, as do the individual member nation states of SAARC that would look at the whitewashed mirror and ensure that there simply cannot be any sense of the region for the citizens in various nation states. This is because, despite the rhetoric, functionaries within the governance structures of SAARC and individual nation states are emotionally imprisoned by the restricted prism of the nation state. A larger number of academics, be they in sociology and social anthropology or elsewhere, tend to avoid seeing themselves in this cracked mirror too. It is better to see our beautiful faces in a nationalist mirror, though such a mirror could well be an illusion when situated in the context of history and memory. All the bilateral and multilateral treaties and agreements, visa regimes (with an orchestration of occasional friendly flexibility as well as aggressive military guarding) are dramatic acts to disable us from seeing into the cracked mirror. Citizens in nation states in South Asia are made prisoners of whitewashed frames of the underlying cracked mirror. It would be a herculean task for sociologists–anthropologists of the region if they opt to wash the whitewashed cracked mirror clean and show it to everyone in its more natural state. If this is done, they might see that we are still connected and in multiple flows despite many ruptures. This is South Asia, beyond definitions and yet within comprehension. A linear definition of South Asia will only serve states, not their people. It is perhaps due to this difficulty in defining South Asia that many of us in academic domains have avoided it. But the longer we avoid, the worse would be our understanding of civilisation, history, mythology, folklore, cultural texts, performances, cinemas, songs, music, food, tastes and smells, loves and hatreds that collectively make all of us more complete.

The courage and conviction, passion and patience, to see in the cracked mirror can benefit us a great deal. If we would begin to see that every Bengali Indian and Bangladeshi, Hindu or Muslim, proudly shows a kinship chart that defies the heavily guarded national borders, more nuanced cartography of the region might emerge. If so, we would not consider it residual that every Punjabi Indian tends to relish a kinship network involving kith and kin across the borders even though it may smack of 'anti-national' tendencies. If so, we would note that it is not only in popular cinema that love and hatred bring folks from across the region in various relationships. It would become self-evident that the literary, performative and other traditions of thoughts and philosophy bring about a sense of region essentially connected despite nation states going on literal or figurative wars with each other. We will see that there is a South Asia even though SAARC and some nation states within it moot a maddening idea of South Asia minus Pakistan. We would see that the region is still there despite the antagonism of nation states, or cricket teams that impede SAARC summits to take place. All this might mean faith in fictional possibilities and at another level, merely rhetorical. But all this could be, at yet another level, a gold mine for ideas for anthropologists and sociologists to rethink family, marriage and kinship, caste and ethnicity, religion and spirituality, development and underdevelopment, globalisation and locality, modernity and tradition, nationalism and beyond and so on and so forth.

In such an anthropologically rediscovered South Asia, everything that was systematically ignored and ridiculed till now would assume instant importance. Similarly, everything that has been done to death without being aware of the regional implications of the themes of enquiries might resurface as areas of enquiries. Say, for example, almost all of sociology and social anthropology in India has been about understanding caste and a little later, its intersectionality with various other indices. Weirdly, and funnily enough, not a single sociologist and social anthropologist in India seems to attend to the idea of caste among Muslims in and beyond India, or caste amongst the Buddhists in Sri Lanka, or the treatises on caste in Nepal and Sri Lanka, enabling us to see the interrelation of the caste hierarchies across borders. Indian scholars have been too comfortable with a borrowed scheme of purity and pollution and could not see caste as a performed and communicated entity. This ignorance was due to a particular kind of politics of knowledge production and circulation, which largely canonised the canons or lustfully as well as helplessly sucked up in the wake of Eurocentric, India-centric, or global South Asia centric ways of seeing. In our endeavour to go regional with sociology and social anthropology, we tend to revisit all of them with due irreverence to the canons and gatekeepers of conventional scholarship, be they in India or elsewhere. And simultaneously, we attempt to break free from 'intellectual incest' due to which a sociologist reads only what is labelled as 'sociological' or an anthropologist would read only what was classified as 'anthropological'. Ridiculously, most of them still rivalled with economists. We declare this intellectual incest a taboo, and thus we do not hesitate to read from diverse sources to comprehend the sociological–anthropological meanings emerging from them. We consciously perform a sort of intellectual promiscuity and sincerely flirt with issues pertaining to art, visuality, photography, cinema, mediated cultural texts and contexts, tastes, smells, touch, eating habits and shitting and a whole gamut of emotions underlining the politics of these practices. Everything that was a non-issue in the intellectual orthodoxy becomes an issue worthy of sociological–anthropological enquiry for us. It leads us to a more liberated framework of doing sociology and social anthropology. One can heave a sigh of relief that one is not going to die a prisoner of intellectual nationalism and yet one is not anti-national to be tried on charges of sedition.

13

Universities, Classrooms and Intellectuals

The Struggle to Create a South Asian Knowledge System

Ravi Kumar

South Asia presents itself in different ways. Looked at from the perspective of nation states, it not only produces a conflictual image of the nation but also shows this conflict in the everyday lives of people as nation states determine the way individuals approach crucial issues.

Every morning, newspapers provide us with a window into the world we live in. We know the news that comes to us is also an interpretation, as reflected in the fact the same news item is reported in different ways across the vast spectrum of media. It is this window into the world that has been painting a canvas called South Asia for us. In the recent past, the Maldives asked India to take back its helicopter and some of its personnel stationed there.[1] Nepal seems to have given a 'setback' to India when it refused to participate in a BIMSTEC (The Bay of Bengal Initiative for Multi-Sectoral Technical and Economic Cooperation) military exercise in 2018.[2] India appears to have made an impractical investment in Sri Lanka when it took over Mattala Rajapaksa International Airport in Hambantota[3] after Sri Lanka formally handed over its southern port of Hambantota to China on a 99-year lease.[4] The airport had no

[1] https://www.ndtv.com/india-news/big-new-snub-for-india-from-maldives-as-it-favours-china-1898558 (accessed on 12 September 2018).

[2] https://www.indiatoday.in/india/story/nepal-snubs-india-refuses-to-join-first-military-drill-of-bimstec-nations-in-pune-1335773-2018-09-09 (accessed on 9 September 2018).

[3] https://www.thehindu.com/news/international/india-to-operate-worlds-emptiest-airport-in-sri-lanka/article24348234.ece (accessed on 10 August 2018).

[4] https://www.ft.com/content/e150ef0c-de37-11e7-a8a4-0a1e63a52f9c (accessed on 9 October 2018).

takers globally though the Sri Lankan government tried. The One Belt One Road initiative of the Chinese also appears to be an area of great concern.[5] Mahinda Rajapaksa and some South Asian politicians have been trying to tell us that they can have a better relationship with India if they are in power in their respective countries.[6]

South Asia that one talks of, one that is bound by the framework of nation states is generally encountered in the way newspapers present it to us as explained previously. This is also the reality to a great extent. The politics of each nation state, guided by the internal structural politics of class and other identities and the political economy of how it is constituted, have created a lot of fissures among these nation states. These fissures presented themselves differently even earlier as well. However, previously they were dominated by the hegemony of India as the dominant paradigm. Today, the South Asian region is changing politically with the arrival of China as a significant player. India ceases to have the position it enjoyed when SAARC (South Asian Association for Regional Cooperation) came into existence earlier as an institution.

All this while, the nation state has been the dominant paradigm to locate any international issue. It has pervaded the innermost corners of the individual self as the nation through its project of consensualisation by way of cultural means, political rhetoric and other ideological apparatuses ensured that the thinking horizon of individuals is narrowed as much as possible. This allowed the project of the internally dominant and hegemonic classes to be pursued effectively. Hence, when any internal crisis of a nation is to be ignored and made to look insignificant, the othering of a neigbouring nation serves as the opium of the masses. Inebriated with this opium of the nation, people act and behave and think in bizarre ways making a reasonable and historically grounded conceptualisation of South Asia difficult.

Even in these circumstances, commonsense suggests that an intellectual is attributed critical and reflective capabilities. These

---

[5] https://timesofindia.indiatimes.com/india/china-road-initiative-is-like-a-colonial-enterprise-india/articleshow/58664098.cms (accessed on 6 August 2017).

[6] https://www.thehindu.com/opinion/interview/for-the-security-of-india-stability-in-sri-lanka-is-very-important/article24929236.ece (accessed on 20 September 2018).

capabilities are expected to make them independent in thinking and not bound by the conditionalities within which they are located, as neoliberalism tends to force them to. Moreover, critical and self-reflective intellectuals are expected to be sensitive to the contexts of people around them. They are also expected to be independent of governmental or bureaucratic allegiances as seems to be the tendency. The ability to hope and dream and to think of alternatives to the given order of things makes the intellectual endeavour lively and engaging. However, the way many individuals have been co-opted into the frame of the nation state has made them exactly the opposite of a critical thinker. Let me offer a concrete example from an institution in its incipient stage of development. The setting is a meeting that was called to discuss how the institution's intellectuals envisioned the future of each of its departments/faculties. When a particular department began its presentation and turned on the cover page of its PowerPoint, which said, 'To Imagine South Asia Differently', the meeting was virtually held up due to the opposition from a senior academic. His opposition was mostly due to the use of the well-known inverted map of South Asia developed by the *Himal South Asian* magazine. He had later expressed his thoughts in an email that noted, 'The slide no. 2 depicts an imaginary "map", which is unnecessary, inappropriate and derogatory. You can easily make your academic point without using this provocative "map". I shall appreciate if you could kindly exclude the "map" from your presentation'. An inverted map[7] can stir up this hysteria only because the nation state as it is conventionally perceived becomes sacrosanct. This happens because of the failure to locate the nation state in the broader history of the region. Caught in this iron cage of the nation, identities do not merely remain that of the nation but they also become matters of race, physical features and attributions of individual characteristics to nationalities. In a fit of frustration I overheard yet another intellectual in the recent past saying, 'in a multinational workplace there seems to be prioritisation over people other than Indians, and I am also thinking

[7] This map can be found at http://himalmag.com/wp-content/uploads/2016/03/map-reduced.jpg (accessed on 7 June 2018). It was created by the magazine, *Himal South Asian* in 1998.

that I will get somebody to box my nose in so that I can look like a Nepali'. This ethno-physical caricaturing of nationality speaks volumes about the inability to create a work environment of mutual respect and equal footing and is also an indication of how deep-seated the malaise of nationhood is.

This hysterical nationalism is ingrained in an individual as part of socialisation because various instruments of the state pervade the cultural politics and generate a mindless love for the nation, even at the cost of promoting sectarianism in a workspace or a learning space that is multinational. So, while doing fieldwork on how students view the nation and nationalism in such a situation, one student says, 'the citizens are able to reveal their national identity as Afghan, Nepali, Bhutani, etc., only because there is a soldier protecting that identity back in his native land. Your identity is only because of your nationalist identity. Only soldiers are martyrs'.[8] We can see how ideologically the sense of nationalism is deeply ingrained in the students.

Back in my small workplace, I am constantly reminded of how many things cannot be done because of the politics among these nations. Even the idea of a regional consciousness or diversity, we are told, is an unattainable utopia. If the discourse is what newspapers feed us, what people in power profess and what universities and intellectual circuits that are considered more sensitive express, then, the borders appear rigid, non-transcendental and difficult to even make a hole in. For ages now, we have not seen those ritualistic cross border cultural exchanges, peace missions, conferences or *mushairas*. Most things have become subservient to the interests of the nation state constantly grappling with the conditions created by the local as well as global capitalist class. In this situation, despite the rhetoric of globalisation and 'world as a village', borders remain as strongly fenced as before. These are difficult times when the 'local' and 'global' are in flux as nation states are being preserved while the fight by the hegemonic economies to get a share of the pie from the smaller economies, intensifies. Who will give more loans, have more of its corporate capital pumped in and, therefore,

---

[8] This response came when I was trying to have a focused group discussion among students in Delhi about whether national identity is important or not.

also control the governments of smaller nations is characterising the battlefield of regional geopolitics. It is this politics, which does not allow humans to be treated as humans. It is this context of politics that creates boundaries and borders of cultural difference, when there may be none. It is this kind of politics which does not allow two people from two different societies to sit and converse. Visa regimes, cultural bracketing, religious overtones, creating hierarchies of knowledge and so on are all part of this exercise. They first create borders and then come up with an idea of a region seeking connections of roads, economies and trade etc. But they still do not want the free movement of people, conversations across these borders, dissolving the distance and letting masses experience how *pindi chana* that originated in Rawalpindi becomes popular in India or how the food from East Bengal has a constant conversation with that of West Bengal—a little bit of sugar in the savoury items would make a lot of difference and might initiate a dialogue on culture and history.

This segregation of people and farcical integration of economies acquires such proportions that when a Sri Lankan sits in a bar in a North Indian state while visiting the place during Dussehra, the others sitting beside him express sympathy for he might be hurt looking at Ravana effigies being burnt. But for Sri Lankans neither Ravana nor the *Mahabharata* has any serious emotional significance. In another situation, an officer sitting beside another from a different nation in a multinational work environment would call him all sorts of names knowing that he cannot understand the language in which these names are being called. Students from across nations enter into a bitter fight over something that happens at the border over which they have no control. Some want to celebrate their military's prowess while some others ask for an analysis and some others express their own reservations about this cross-border violence. A sociological analysis would reveal different dimensions of these episodes ranging from the frustration, insecurity and threat of demolishing the hegemony of one nation by another. But what reflects immediately is the impossibility for conversation created by borders. We have become barbaric deep inside as the virus of nationalism destroys the humanity in us and urges us to hate others in name of security, religion and colour. It has become a deep-seated malaise that does not allow the initiation of any serious conversation.

In order to have a conversation, there has to be a sense of 'equality' prevailing among the conversants. What it also demands is that they must be 'agreeable' to have a conversation, and hence, the subject matter must be of 'mutual interest'. One would see from examples provided earlier the way institutions of learning have become narrow and, therefore, extremely hierarchical. Do they have the kind of attributes outlined earlier to have a conversation? It is a difficult question because they are also the sites where the possibility to have such a conversation exists most despite the hurdles. We have historically witnessed how inequalities of different kinds have been debated at such sites. Will it be possible to do the same when the idea of nationalism is on the rise in university campuses throughout South Asia? This is a difficult question because it would involve a contestation, a political battle between those who, imbued with nationalism, would be confronted by those who believe that nationalism creates divisions, distances and inability to dialogue. In a situation where people from multiple nationalities are present, when we talk about the idea of South Asia, it would require an understanding of the cultural contexts and the political history of how these nation states came into existence. For instance, how does one ensure that everyone coming to South Asian University in a situation when the nation-states seem to be at loggerheads feel at home in the university located in India? As an exaggerated example, think of Pakistani students studying in this university. One way to ensure they feel at 'home' is to remind all constituents programmatically and consistently that this place belongs to all of them. It is not a project of one nation. However, it is difficult to establish this when the numerical presence of constituents is imbalanced, when the everyday cultural symbols are lopsided, and when the state itself does not assume it to be a multilateral institution. The University Grants Commission of India has put it in the category of a Central University.[9] Ministry of Human Resource Development, while mentioning it in that category

[9] https://ugc.ac.in/centralniversitylist.aspx?id=5&Unitype=1 (accessed on 18 September 2018); also see http://mhrd.gov.in/central-universities-0 (accessed on 11 September 2018).

does, however, note that it is an 'international university'. But what is interesting is that by not devising new categories for universities like SAU or Nalanda University, the nation state shows that it cannot go beyond its limited imagination to locate such universities.

In this grim situation what holds promise is the classroom and the students who would come out of it as long as creative teachers consider the classroom as a possibility of experimentation. The colonisation of the self by national boundaries impacts our intellectual endeavours as well. That is why an Indian sociologist would prefer to author a book with the words 'South Asia' in its title but would not have any material in it except India. I was trained in universities like JNU unaware of sociologies and anthropologies existing across Indian borders in other South Asian countries. This has been nothing but an intellectual colonisation by national frameworks. In a classroom where students from across South Asia have their presence, the discussion must be intentionally well informed by what happens in all these countries. Unfortunately, that too does not happen as it should. In a classroom on Social History of South Asia at the South Asian University, a discussion was initiated on how contemporary Afghanistan is struggling to build a national identity due to the compulsions of global capitalism. One finds that none of the Indian students participate in it. They start to look elsewhere, fiddle with their gadgets or become completely oblivious to what is going on. This is despite the insistence that such a discussion would possibly reveal how a nation and national identities get formed and therefore would make us understand how historically there might be other ways and means through which such identities get constituted. This learning would allow a mutual exchange of ideas, a sharing of histories and would initiate a dialogue that would breach the borderlines.

The same class has the potential to mutually learn the processes of identity formation at different historical moments by looking at the Sinhala–Tamil dynamics in Sri Lanka and that of Pashtuns and Hazaras in Afghanistan or the caste identities in India. What impedes the students from undertaking this exercise is a question worth pondering over, especially when they are prodded to do so. They possibly want to stick to their own national boundaries and deal with the identity formations within those limited areas. In other worlds, they prefer to inhabit in their own cultural comfort zones. They are also not interested in unravelling the underlying processes that might expose the real politics behind these identity formations that would gradually also impact the idea of the nation. Destruction of the dominant modes of thinking that limits our way of exploring and impedes our intrusions into the otherwise well-guarded areas of intellectual pursuits is a prerequisite to ensure that South Asia becomes an area of academic and political interest beyond performances of narrow national tokenism.

14

Buddhist Categories, Contemporary World and Sociology

Incomplete Thoughts towards Possibilities of Social Theory and Modes of Thinking in South Asia[1]

Sasanka Perera

Coming from Sri Lanka and that too from a Buddhist background, the celebration of Buddha Purnima, which is called Vesak in Sri Lanka, comes naturally to me. Even so, it would be dishonest on my part if I do not make it clear that I am not a scholar of Buddhism or a historian of Buddhist institution-building. That is, I am well aware of my relative ignorance of both Buddhism and Buddhist history in South Asia. But this does not mean that I do not have opinions on some aspects of Buddhist thinking based on what I have read and thought about it over the years.

My intention in this chapter is to very briefly answer the following general question. That is: Would the Buddha's thoughts make intellectual sense to a person interested in society and politics in contemporary times? I would attempt to answer this question briefly in a way it makes sense to a sociologist such as myself interested in the worldly affairs of contemporary existence and politics in South Asia.

The Buddha, as we know, did not speak to our world. He spoke to the world in which he lived and was inspired in his thinking by what he saw in his own world. So he was responding to his world in terms

[1] This chapter is the edited version of a talk delivered on 21 May 2016 on Buddha Purnima at Buddha Vihar, Maha Bodhi Society of India, New Delhi.

of what he has said about issues like inequality, violence, good and evil and so on. But these are not necessarily the terms he used. Instead, these are categories I might use today to make sense of what he has said in terms of contemporary knowledge. But crucially, today we know of his world only in fragments through the incomplete picture painted by archaeology and history. And that past is further clouded by myth and belief. The question of course is, can his thinking transgress his world across time and make sense today not only in our world but more specifically in the practice of a thoroughly contemporary discipline such as mine? My question also comes from the lingering thoughts I have entertained for some time on the possibility of introducing aspects of thinking from South Asia, including ancient modes of thinking and philosophy such as what we have inherited from Buddhist and Jain texts, the Vedas and discourses like the Charvaka philosophy in the practice of theory-building and abstraction in South Asian intellectual contexts of today.[2]

Let me try and address the question of Buddhism's possible relevance to contemporary times. I am a sociologist, and I explore human conditions, anxieties, contradictions and the incredible chaos, which define our existence in contemporary times. As a rule, my process of analysis is thoroughly rational, theoretically based, highly analytical and completely devoid of emotion. Can such a seemingly clinical process of reading the world be informed by what the Buddha taught? In trying to answer this question, I am only looking at Buddhist systems of knowledge informed by a clearly laid out analytical process as opposed to issues of faith, belief and ritual which are also integral parts of the Buddhist faith.[3] What I mean by this self-imposed restriction can be explained with reference to the example of what is known in Buddhism as the 'Four Noble Truths' that perhaps summarise the essentials in

---

[2] My colleague Ravi Kumar and I have tried to experiment with this possibility in the Ph.D course, 'Social Theory, Society and Modes of Thinking' that we co-teach in the Department of Sociology, South Asian University. For more details on the course and some of what has been attempted in it, please refer to Chapter 11, 'Reclaiming Social Sciences and Humanities: Notes from South Asia' in this volume.

[3] For more information on this general area, please refer to K.N. Jayatilleke, 2010, *Early Buddhist Theory of Knowledge*, New Delhi, Motilal Banarsidass.

Buddhist thinking. In effect, these 'truths' are a means to comprehend and address the suffering among human beings. The truths are, 'the truth of suffering; the truth of the cause of suffering; the truth of the end of suffering and the truth of the path that leads to the end of suffering.'[4] In simpler terms this means, 'suffering exists; it has a cause; it has an end; and it has a cause to bring about its end'.[5] Without going into details of what all this means, it is clear that this formula does not deal with emotion or faith. Instead, it offers an explanation and what seems to be a logical trajectory to achieve a specific end that in this case is the end of human suffering. So when I refer to 'Buddhist systems of knowledge informed by a clearly laid out analytical process' that might be able to inform contemporary modes of social analysis or theorising in a discipline like sociology, my attention would be on formulations such as the 'Four Noble Truths'.

Taking this possibility further, it seems to me that much of *abhidhamma* that constitutes Buddha's thoughts and works in much the same way as any formal system of knowledge not linked to faith, which includes sociology. But when attempting to make this association, we have to be mindful that we are talking of two different systems of knowledge. As we know, sociology emerged in the latter part of the nineteenth century in Europe in the context of industrialisation and post-Enlightenment knowledge. Comparatively, Buddhism came into existence over 2,500 years ago under very different sociopolitical circumstances in the extended neighbourhood that we call South Asia today.

But if one is careful and within limits, I can't see any reason why Buddhist thought cannot inform the sociological analysis. But I emphasise my caution that comes with the words 'careful and within limits'.

Let me clarify my position by referring to two important Buddhist concepts, which emerge in discourses on consciousness and reality.[6] According to *abhidhamma*, there are two kinds of reality. The first is

---

[4] https://www.pbs.org/edens/thailand/buddhism.htm (accessed on 1 March 2019).

[5] https://www.pbs.org/edens/thailand/buddhism.htm (accessed on 1 March 2019).

[6] For an extensive discussion on *sammuti* and *paramattha* as well as the *abhidhmamma* more generally, please read 'A Comprehensive Manual of Abhidhamma' (General Editor: Bikkhu Bodhi. Kandy: Buddhist Publication Society). For the present discussion, I have mostly relied on this text.

conventional reality known as *sammuti*. The second is the ultimate reality known as *paramattha*. In this scheme of things, conventional realities describe ordinary and mundane conceptual thought and conventional or taken-for-granted modes of expression. This is what all of us deal with, on a day to day basis. They include everything which meets our eyes, from men to women, animals, trees, things and many other seemingly stable objects which demarcate the extent of our unanalysed world. I emphasise the word unanalysed here.

According to *abhidhamma*, all these things are devoid of any sense of ultimate reality because the objects they signify cannot exist on their own as irreducible facts. In my reading of what this means, men, women, animals and other things do not make sense or exist independently by themselves. Instead, they exist in relation to each other as well as in the context of a larger field of meaning, which requires explanation, analysis and knowing.

That larger field of meaning is what *abhidhamma* refers to as ultimate realities. They exist on the basis of their own intrinsic nature. *Abhidhamma* calls these the dhammas, or final components of existence that cannot be reduced further. In other words, they become possible only on the basis of a properly and consciously undertaken process of analysing experience; an analysis of what is seen, heard and felt. This becomes possible by crossing from the unanalysed to the analysed; from taken-for-granted knowledge to realms of actual knowing. In terms of *abhidhamma*, these realities cannot be reduced any further.

What I have just described comes from the core of *abhidhamma*, and therefore from the realm of Buddhism. So technically, these explanations are from a specific religion and therefore cannot be part of science such as sociology if we go by the logic of post-enlightenment rationality, which drives most contemporary academic disciplines.

But at the same time, it is also possible to perceive what I have outlined within a paradigm that has nothing to do with religion. As in the case of the analytical trajectory of the 'Four Noble Truths', this is simply a highly rational and unemotional method of analysis which can well be employed to read society and its multiple complexities. In fact, one of Buddhism's main intellectual contributions is its ability to deal with highly emotional issues such as desire and suffering within a highly rational and non-emotional system of analysis. It seems to me that many theoretical approaches or ideas I have used in my own thinking over the last two decades that have also influenced many others in humanities and social sciences such as Ferdinand de Saussure's *semiotics* and Jean Baudrillard's ideas on *simulation* and *simulacrum* in certain ways work as ideas in making sense of our social world in much the same way as do *sammuti* or conventional reality and *paramattha* or ultimate reality. All these, from the words of the Buddha to more recent theorisation attempt make sense of the world and explain human action.

But by saying this, I am not making a simplistic argument for the replacement of social sciences or sociology with *abhidhamma*. For me, as a person for whom Buddhism offers intellectual inspiration, without emotional entanglements, this makes no sense. Clearly, Buddhism is a vast system of knowledge for living as well as for knowing the social world. But it is also a system of knowledge that deals with faith, belief in an afterlife, *karma* and so on that does not make sense in terms of a discipline like sociology which only deals with the visible world. Comparatively, contemporary academic disciplines are merely limited tools for making sense of the social world only. They certainly cannot offer an ideal for living or notions of the world after death. So one cannot and should not attempt to replace one with the other. My suggestion is, careful and self-reflective thinking might well allow us to formulate very contemporary approaches to reading society and theorise social action which might be sensibly informed by a corpus of knowledge such as *abhidhamma*. That is, to see if this kind of thinking with adequate abstraction accompanied by a clear process of fine-tuning within the realities of contemporary conditions might allow us the use of categories of analysis that a discipline like social sciences or sociology have so far not offered. Or, to see if categories of analysis that might allow us to read South Asian society, in particular, more accurately. This does not mean that Buddhist ideas, even the kind of exemplary formulae I have briefly referred to previously, would necessarily make sense in an analytical process like sociology as they are. One has to work with them and see how these ideas might be contemporised. Hence, my suggestion on abstraction. Also, in making this attempt, one has to also self-consciously delink these ideas from their original contexts of faith and see if they can allow us to read situations across the world. I do not have an answer beyond all doubts if this is possible at all. As far as I can see, possibilities of such an attempt have not been seriously explored yet as an intellectual exercise without recourse to religion or ethnocultural politics of hegemony.

Of course, this is also a journey which might entail considerable dangers at a time when unmitigated violence in the name of Buddhism has become possible in many predominantly Buddhist societies. As we know, violence in any form cannot be formulated in terms of Buddhism. It can, however, be explained via Buddhism. Unfortunately, Sri Lanka and Burma are both examples of this sad and anti-intellectual and decidedly un-Buddhist turn of events. This has become possible as a result of people who claim allegiance to the ideas once propagated by the Buddha having opted to drift further and further away from the core of his ideas and seek solace in ignorance or *moha*.

I flagged this danger of our times to conclude with a warning. Today, we see many systems of faith around the world, despite their robust intellectual moorings and ideals of compassion being reduced to discourses of division. This becomes possible when the core ideals of a system of knowledge and faith are misunderstood or deliberately misinterpreted in order to suit the contemporary exigencies and ill-defined political circumstances.

In this context, when we are thinking of Buddhism's relevance to contemporary world and to contemporary practices, it would make sense to also keep in mind that disruptions to such thought will mostly come from within, from amongst moral communities who have lost touch with their own ideals and are lost in a world of ignorance.

Abhidhamma might have described this unfortunate contemporary dilemma as our inability to transgress from the emotional shackles that bind us to the day-to-day realities of *sammuti* and cross over successfully to *paramattha* which might have explained the nature of our predicaments, and hopefully point the way out.

15

Bringing the Thinking of Jiddu Krishnamurti into Politics[1]

Sasanka Perera

The book *J. Krishnamurti and Educational Practice: Social and Moral Vision for Inclusive Education* edited by Meenakshi Thapan[2] was published in September 2018. I read this as an outsider to many of the locations from where the book would have been more proximate and what it says would have been much more familiar. I think it is important to make note of these distances and outsider locations because they would have an impact on what I have to say. Though I have worked on education fairly closely at some point in my academic life, I am not as closely associated with it as a researcher or writer now. But I remain a teacher and a reluctant administrator in a university. I am an outsider to India as well where Krishnamurti's ideas are widely known in academic circles and have been discussed over time, whether one agrees with them or not. And his thinking has inspired a number of institutions. Some of the chapters in the volume refer to these institutions and in particular to the Rishi Valley School in Bengaluru. I am also an outsider to Krishnamurti's thinking in the sense I am not a scholar of Krishnamurti, but merely an informed reader who has come across his ideas often and have come to admire some of them in my own circumstances.

---

[1] Edited version of the lecture delivered at the discussion on the book, *J. Krishnamurti and Educational Practice: Social and Moral Vision for Inclusive Education* edited by Meenakshi Thapan at the Department of Sociology, Delhi School of Economics, 28 September 2018. I would like to thank my colleague, Dev Nath Pathak for his comments in editing this chapter.

[2] Meenakshi Thapan, ed., 2018, *J. Krishnamurti and Educational Practice: Social and Moral Vision for Inclusive Education*, Delhi, Oxford University Press.

But I do not consider these distances as a disqualification when it comes to speaking on Krishnamurti. Rather than passing judgement on Meenakshi Thapan's book, my interest is to flag a number of issues that came to my mind as I read through some sections of the book because of their relevance to circumstances in my own life at different times, which Krishnamurti's thinking might help unpack. In other words, I want to outline very briefly how Krishnamurti would make sense to me in the worlds and paths I have tread.

Other than in the context of Thapan's book itself, I have begun to reread Krishnamurti along with other South Asian thinkers in at least two other contexts. One of these has to do with my present interests in South Asia as a place and an idea and to see if the region has generated thinkers whose ideas can transgress its borders. In this context, I do not consider Krishnamurti as Indian, just as much as I would not find it useful to consider the poet, Faiz Ahmed Faiz Pakistani, or the Buddha as Nepali. What they had to say in their own times made perfect sense across our region and the world beyond as well, spanning time and transcending cultural, religious and national borders. Citizenship, nationality or primordial identities such as caste and ethnicity as we know them today had nothing to do with what these kinds of people had to say. It is in this sense of global citizenship that the ideas of Krishnamurti might also make sense in South Asia, beyond India.

The second context in which I began to revisit Krishnamurti and a host of other thinkers in the region across times was when I was exploring the possibilities of reorganising the Ph.D theory course in sociology at South Asian University with my colleague, Ravi Kumar. We have now called our course, 'Theory, Society and Modes of Thinking'. Though Krishnamurti did not make it to our reading list in the first attempt while the writings of Ambedkar, Phule and a number of Buddhist texts did but the exploration allowed me to begin reading him in a broader context.

My main fascination with Krishnamurti is because I think he has been a creatively dangerous thinker. And this generalisation is valid not just for India, but also for any location in South Asia or beyond. He has attempted to engage with constructive ideas, though they may not always be popular. That makes him for me, a kind of kindred spirit, but not a *guru*. His thinking is dangerous to conventional thinking and parochial dogmas that often overshadow our ways of looking at the world. And his thinking is discomforting to regimes of the kind that rule over our destinies throughout South Asia, which would prefer docile beings who are mere followers, rather than people who might exercise their minds. Krishnamurti's thoughts, as articulated in his numerous lectures presented at different times in his peripatetic career, subvert the popular notion of manufactured freedom, formal education and institutions such as family, marriage and kinship with which we associate most human emotions. Right when one begins to celebrate freedom, saying knowledge is power, Krishnamurti reminds us in a sanguine devil's voice that we are only trying to escape from freedom. A more systematic theory along these lines constitutes the main intellectual contributions of the Marxist psychoanalyst, Eric Fromm.

Krishnamurti himself noted this in his essay 'Education and the Significance of Life', when he suggested, 'governments want efficient technicians, not human beings because human beings become dangerous to governments—and to organized religions as well. That is why governments and religious organizations seek to control education'.[3] Coming from Sri Lanka where ethnicity and a parochial and divisive sense of nationalism led to a debilitating civil war and living at a time and in a region where primordial identities often surpass one's sense of humanity along with common sense, I have found it very difficult in emotional terms to be imprisoned within the discourses of nationalism, ethnic pride, religious fervour, caste identity and so on. These are nevertheless quotidian markers of our collective reality today, as well as sources of violent emotional and political rupture that we have seen often unfolding in many locations throughout South Asia.

This does not mean that I do not recognise nationhood, nationality, borders, ethnicity, caste and other such categories as social formations with their own sense of agency and power. But when approached from an informed perspective of knowledge, I find it more useful and sensible, if we would attempt to surpass these divisions even as

---

[3] 'From Education and the Significance of Life': https://www.goodreads.com/quotes/141542-governments-want-efficient-technicians-not-human-beings-because-human-beings (accessed on 1 March 2019).

we recognise their existence. This is why I am fully in agreement with Krishnamurti when he notes,

> when you call yourself an Indian or a Muslim or a Christian or a European or anything else, you are being violent. Do you see why it is violent? Because you are separating yourself from the rest of mankind. When you separate yourself by belief, by nationality, by tradition, it breeds violence. So a man who is seeking to understand violence does not belong to any country, to any religion, to any political party or partial system; he is concerned with the total understanding of mankind.[4]

This kind of emphasis on humanity rather than on primordial identities would make little sense to states and political formations that would take ethnicity and religion as their foundational logic and to many ordinary people for whom identity politics based on ethnicity, caste, religion and so on are far more proximate experientially and emotionally than an encompassing idea of humanity. It is also in this sense that I called Krishnamurti 'dangerous' to conventional and populist thinking as well as regimes engrossed in parochial and non-inclusive ideas of nationalism and regressive identity politics.

In a sense, if we can summarise Krishnamurti's thinking overall, my sense is that he was interested in fermenting change in the fundamentals of our thinking and action. This justifies his strong preoccupation with education. I think it is these general circumstances that Meenakshi Thapan refers to in her introduction when she says, 'it is in the everyday that Krishnamurti seeks out change, beginning with the individual and the world, both personal and social'.[5] Towards the goal of achieving such fundamental changes in thinking, though Krishnamurti focused on educational practice, he did not see education in a reductionist, utilitarian and objectivist sense as it is often understood today from market perspectives. For him, education 'was a deeply nuanced method for the transformation of consciousness and social change' as Meenakshi Thapan reminds us.[6]

---

[4] https://www.goodreads.com/quotes/520382-when-you-call-yourself-an-indian-or-a-muslim-or (accessed on 1 March 2019).

[5] Thapan, *J. Krishnamurti and Educational Practice*, p. 3.

[6] Thapan, *J. Krishnamurti and Educational Practice*, p. 4.

As Krishnamurti observes in *Education and the Significance of Life*,

> while one is young is the time to investigate, to experiment with everything. The school should help its young people to discover their vocations and responsibilities, and not merely cram their minds with facts and technical knowledge; it should be the soil in which they can grow without fear, happily and integrally.[7]

Personally, I have always been guided by this fundamental principle as a teacher even though I am no longer sure if the idea came to me from Krishnamurti or my own sense of politics in teaching.

But education for emotional and intellectual empowerment in this sense is a source of radical political and social power that allows the mind and intelligence relative freedom to roam, discover, creatively conspire and enact change. That is why Krishnamurti saw intelligence as 'the capacity to perceive the essential, the what is'.[8] And he saw education as the means 'to awaken this capacity, in oneself and in others'.[9] But this is a dangerous and provocative thinking in circumstances and times when education is seen more as a mere tool of social control, disciplining and a means to generate skilled labour.

In this sense, today's educational systems in South Asia as well as everywhere else are closer to what Ivan Illich has rightly described them to be, rather than what Krishnamurti promoted: That is,

> schools are designed on the assumption that there is a secret to everything in life; that the quality of life depends upon knowing that secret; that secrets can only be known in orderly successions; and that only teachers can properly reveal these secrets. An individual with a schooled mind conceives of the world as a pyramid of classified packages accessible only to those who carry the proper tags.[10]

---

[7] https://www.goodreads.com/work/quotes/343644-education-and-the-significance-of-life (accessed on 1 March 2019).

[8] https://www.goodreads.com/work/quotes/343644-education-and-the-significance-of-life (accessed on 1 March 2019).

[9] https://www.goodreads.com/work/quotes/343644-education-and-the-significance-of-life (accessed on 1 March 2019).

[10] https://thoughtcatalog.com/ayodeji-awosika/2015/04/25-quotes-that-accurately-represent-the-problems-with-our-education-system/ (accessed on 1 March 2019).

This is about imparting skills and the logic of discipline to young people for the explicit purpose of enabling them to enter the job market and become a convenient cog in the overall machinery of the market. In this scheme of things, in which all of us are a part, and are perhaps complicit in perpetuating in different degrees, there is very little room to think of humanity or the world with any sense of empathy. In this sense, we are all architects of our unenviable circumstances and not merely the politicians we opt not to agree with.

It seems to me, despite all the debates and discussions on the thinking of Krishnamurti in India and beyond, his ideas have hardly become a cornerstone in any national policy of education in India or more broadly in South Asia. Meenakshi Thapan rightly recognises this situation when she observes with a detectable sense of anguish that his work 'remains at the margins of educational perspectives that inform the academy and education practice in general'.[11] One needs to seriously consider, why this might be so. In a way, much of *J. Krishnamurti and Educational Practice: Social and Moral Vision for Inclusive Education* is a plea via an empirical and reflective detour to make a strong case for the continuing relevance of Krishnamurti's ideas in contemporary times.

But then, can we realistically expect any outcome other than this kind of marginalisation given the consistently subversive nature of Krishnamurti's thinking? For instance, in countries like Afghanistan, India, Bangladesh, Pakistan, Maldives and Sri Lanka, where religion has become a basis for division and an important mobilisational force in national politics, how would Krishnamurti's appeal for the erasure of these labels and the embracing of humanity as one make sense? Such a departure from convention in South Asia would unravel the way our dismantled democracies have used these primordial identities as vehicles for electoral politics. Surely, no government or political party in contemporary South Asia will consider making this kind of thinking an integral part of its educational policy, which would necessitate a critical reflection on its own legitimacy to power.

But this is not only about regimes. It is also about people. For instance, let me briefly refer to Krishnamurti's critique of organised

[11] Thapan, *J. Krishnamurti and Educational Practice*, p. 4.

religion, with which I broadly agree. He has described organised or institutionalised religion as 'the frozen thought of man, out of which he builds temples and churches' in the context of which, 'it has become a solace for the fearful, an opiate for those who are in sorrow. But God or truth is far beyond thought and emotional demands.'[12] Here, Krishnamurti is not rejecting faith, belief or spirituality, but the way in which organised religion holds sway over people's lives and minds that we see everywhere. But for many people, this might seem like a political position against their faith.

I have long held, that Krishnamurti's ideas such as what I have referred to so far, are perhaps too cosmopolitan in the social worlds which we inhabit in South Asia. My sense is also when compared to how people have engaged with ideas of thinkers such as Jyotirao Phule or B.R. Ambedkar or even Mohandas Gandhi as a form of politics in India, Krishnamurti's thinking still by large remains in the realm of ideas and not in the domain of broader politics.

In these circumstances, Krishnamurti's thinking has become a discourse with considerable meaning and sense, but without the power of social transformation or popular appeal in the broader sense. It has become a kind of minority thinking that has not reached the masses or captured the imagination of the thinking in the street—metaphorically and quite literally. Or, one can say his thinking in the present form is a kind of political and social discourse without the intent of politics. It is this discursive limitation in terms of political dynamics and reach as well as the limited number of schools that are self-consciously inspired by and established on the basis of his thinking that have led to the criticism of these schools as elitist, and to the argument that Krishnamurti's perspective and the resultant forms of educational practice cannot realistically be factored into the mainstream.[13]

On the other hand, Krishnamurti's notion of 'revolution' is something that needed to be undertaken in people's minds, in the visits of consciousness, in the realms of ideas, in the domains of behaviour

[12] https://www.goodreads.com/quotes/7578135-organized-religion-is-the-frozen-thought-of-man-out-of (accessed on 1 March 2019).

[13] Thapan, *J. Krishnamurti and Educational Practice*, p. 4.

and not in the street as such. When Krishnamurti was once asked if equality among people could be guaranteed through revolution, his answer was this:

> Revolution based on an idea, however logical and in accordance with historical evidence, cannot bring about equality. The very function of idea is to separate people. Belief, religious or political, sets man against man. So-called religions have divided people, and still do. Organized belief, which is called religion, is, like any other ideology, a thing of the mind and therefore separative. You with your ideology are doing the same, are you not? You also are forming a nucleus or group around an idea; you want to include everyone in your group, just as the believer does. You want to save the world in your way, as he in his. You murder and liquidate each other, all for a better world. Neither of you is interested in a better world, but in shaping the world according to your idea. How can idea make for equality.[14]

Here, when he refers to 'thing of the mind' and 'idea', he is talking about dogmas and taken-for-granted notions that people tend to follow without reflection. No wonder then, many of my friends and colleagues in the region, impressed with the more widespread notion of revolution, have insisted that Krishnamurti's ideas are for the elite and for the maintenance of the status quo.

I have no confusion in my mind that my own discipline, sociology or social anthropology as the case may be, or for that matter mainstream education and art, as they are generally taught in universities in South Asia, tend to routinely accept existing received wisdom as well as the blindly constructed, circulated and consumed academic and political dogmas. The net result is that this situation does not allow scholars to generate new utopias for a better world at large. People who seek such utopias will be seen as naïve, idealist and may be elitist. In this scheme of things, it is not unrealistic to suggest that many of us in mainstream university contexts, by not being self-reflective would well end up employing sociology, anthropology and social sciences more generally

---

[14] http://jiddu-krishnamurti.net/en/commentaries-on-living-series-2/1957-00-00-jiddu-krishnamurti-commentaries-on-living-series-2-5-progress-and-revolution (accessed on 1 March 2019).

to perpetuate a kind of un-freedom that Krishnamurti as I understand him would never espouse.

Let me end with two final thoughts:

1. If the long term ideological interest of people closely affiliated with the thinking of Krishnamurti is to make his thinking more squarely relevant to contemporary times, then, these ideas need to percolate from his writings, the main Krishnamurti schools and the discourses of followers to a broader and more engaged domain of politics. In other words, these ideas will have to get closer to the messier and sometimes nastier domains of everyday politics, which is a more difficult journey. My sense is that for any corpus of ideas to become mainstream or at least to have broader traction, it will have to engage with politics more robustly.

   Or, one can simply ask if Krishnamurti's thoughts can be allowed to engage with contemporary politics if they do not transcend beyond the comfort zones of institutions where they mostly reside at present. True, such institutionalisation allows a source for ideas to become esoteric, accessible to *pundits*, scholars and cultural elites like ourselves, and not to the masses. People at large can be awed by them, or even fear them if they ever accidentally come across them, but never think of working with them, while scholars can go on producing dissertations, essays and books on them.

2. The second thought has to do with my own vested interests in South Asia as an idea and a place when juxtaposed with the Oxford University Press' series, *Society and Education in South Asia* in which *J. Krishnamurti and Educational Practice: Social and Moral Vision for Inclusive Education* is the first. Given the South Asia-focus referred to in the series title, it would have made much more sense if the book actually dealt with the ways in which Krishnamurti's thinking and work have been negotiated with or discarded beyond India in the rest of South Asia. For instance, in his last visit to Sri Lanka in 1980, he was met by the Prime Minister and the President of the time as well as other dignitaries and was interviewed on national television by the then Minister of State. He was asked by good-natured Buddhist monks, 'do you think at all', to which he responded, 'I only think

> when it is necessary'.[15] In other words, he was widely accepted by the political and cultural mainstream of the time in Sri Lanka as an equal.

He addressed large audiences including in the University of Sri Jayawardenapura. And there were many discursively active Krishanmurti centres in major towns and Sinhala and Tamil translations of his lectures were available to some extent. But today, beyond limited discussions in what appears to be closed circles, there is hardly a tangible trace of his ideas in the highly animated and politically crucial discussions on educational reform or in existing educational policy. So how would one explain this eclipse despite the fact that those ideas of Krishnamurti's I have briefly dealt with earlier have as much relevance to Sri Lanka as they do to India? Even though he addressed humanity, have his ideas become somehow limited to closed circles of circulation in India, South Asia more generally and the West? I think it is intellectually important to understand these dynamics in the border contexts of South Asia.

I would like to end my thoughts with a hope. I hope *J. Krishnamurti and Educational Practice: Social and Moral Vision for Inclusive Education* might mark the beginning of a new life for the thinking and the educational practices inspired by Krishnamurti. That is, to usher his thinking into the mainstream in South Asia through a more nuanced engagement with day-to-day politics. Perhaps this is another utopia in my own mind. But utopias are never bad things. But they are even better if sensible people would take some effort to realise them.

---

15 Susunaga Weeraperuma, 1983, *That Pathless Land: Essays on the Beauty and Uniqueness of J. Krishnamurti's Teachings*, Delhi, Motilal Banarsidass Publishers Pvt. Ltd., p. 105.

16

Thinking of Myth and Folklore in the Twenty-first Century[1]

Sasanka Perera

What I want to do in this chapter is quite simply to pose a basic question and answer this question from my own perspective. And that perspective is informed by my academic training as well as what I have seen in my travels in South Asia. My question is, what does folklore mean and how does its study make sense to us at this time in the twenty-first century in South Asia or in the world? Or, is the study of folklore a burden on our time? To answer this question, I will travel to two planes of discourse:

1. The first is the plane in which folklore travels from the past to the present over time and is consumed within circumstances of the present. How does this work?

2. The second is the plane of the present itself in which folklore is given genesis and space for consumption. This has nothing to do with the past. This is about contemporary folklore.

But let me begin with a basic conceptual clarification. This has to do with the confusions some people seem to have about myth and mythology when dealing with folklore. For me, myth and folklore are often terms that are used interchangeably. At other times, they can differ in their primary meanings but are nevertheless located in close proximity to each other in discursive terms. To put it simply, in a broader structure of folklore, a number of mythic narratives might be

[1] Edited version of the Valedictory Address delivered at the seminar, 'Folk Philosophy in South Asia: Exploring Cosmic and Mundane in the Folklore', organised by Banasthali Vidyapit and South Asian University at Banasthali, Rajasthan, 26 March 2017.

embedded. This is a given; this is common sense. But I have flagged it in this chapter for a reason. And that is, I will be using these terms more openly and sometimes interchangeably in the way they are used in contemporary human sciences and not as closed, airtight, archaic and linear categories. In other words, I cannot talk of folklore without myth or myth without folklore.

Let me now go back to my initial question and attempt to unravel it. And that is, what does folklore mean and how does its study make sense to us at this time in the twenty-first century and particularly in South Asia? And more importantly, what happens to narratives of folklore when they travel from the mythic or the historic past into the present?

There is a widespread assumption that folklore is a matter of the past, a matter of history and of mythic times, a matter of kings and queens, a matter of divine beings and their encounters with other mythic beings as well as humans. It is partly in this context where folklore intersects with possible reality as well as the fantasy that folklore has never been taken too seriously in formal historiography though anthropology has been far more engaged in trying to make sense out of folklore, particularly in fathoming the past. There is also a popular dogmatic notion, very clearly apparent in much of South Asia, which suggests that folklore is beyond interpretation and analysis and that it should be taken as a historical fact, however, fantastic it might seem. This is particularly the case if such folklore is centrally implicated in the realm of religion or in a nation's imagination of its past and self-identity.

This assumption suggests that folklore and its constituent linkages including folk philosophy and ideas of cosmology and so on, are to be recorded, compiled and incessantly narrated as unchanging references to heritage and tradition, but cannot come to the present via forms of reading or analysis. For me, this understanding is intellectually too limiting. But this is certainly one way in which folklore is often seen, as a corpus of knowledge from a different time that should merely be compiled and be awed.

But the question for me is, what can one do with this material, with this knowledge that is not of our time when we attempt to read it within a discipline such as sociology in the context of contemporary politics? Folklore and the mythic narratives they may contain, cannot be understood merely in the context of the undifferentiated past from where they might have sprung up. Neither can they be accepted as facts without interpretation or discarded as mere fantasy. The basic questions that would come up when attempting to situate folklore and myth today would necessitate us to ask how these narratives have been seen at different times over the years, how are they seen today and how will they make sense in the future? How are they remembered, how are they performed and what aspects of them are forgotten or underemphasised and why? These are the kinds of basic questions that interest me when looking at folklore from the perspectives of today and from my own disciplinary vantage points.

When thinking of these issues, I was taken back to Roland Barthes' essay 'Myth Today' that I first read in 1997. In it, when talking of 'myth as a form of speech', Barthes says, 'mythical speech is made of a material which has *already* been worked on so as to make it suitable for communication'.[2] He says further, this is because 'all the materials of myth (whether pictorial or written) presupposes a signifying consciousness, that one can reason about them while discounting their substance'.[3] In my mind, what Barthes is talking about deals with the obvious possibilities of myth as a transforming discourse in the process of making it intelligible in a given context. And this context would change in terms of politics, temporality, culture and so on, making mythic speech also to change. This is not a matter of the basic structure of a specific myth changing even though this also happens at times. It is more a matter of the contexts of its reception and interpretation changing, which also impacts its points and modes of reference in the present. And Barthes further observes that 'myth hides nothing: its function is to distort, not to make disappear'.[4]

This is what happens when myths travel from the past to the present. They get embedded in the present, not as an unchangeable package from the past, but when we distort their references they attempt to make more sense in the new circumstances. I would say, even in a simplistic

[2] Roland Barthes, 1993, *Mythologies*, New York, Noonday Press, p. 110.

[3] Barthes, *Mythologies*, p. 110.

[4] Barthes, *Mythologies*, p. 121.

understanding of folklore, what Barthes says about myth would also hold true for folklore more generally.

Let me clarify this aspect of transformative and temporal travel associated with myth and folklore by taking it beyond theory and locating it in the midst of folklore as it is consumed in contemporary society. I refer to the *Ramayana*, which many people in South Asia would have at least heard of. As I grew up in the 1960s in Sri Lanka, I was familiar with the stories of *Ramayana* too. Some of its stories were in our textbooks and elders narrated renditions of it as bedtime stories. But in Sinhala folk traditions, it was never performed, as was the case in many Indic and Balinese traditions. But it was narrated as folktales and mythic renditions of an undefined mythic past in which the cosmic and the mundane worlds interchanged at different planes.

The physical landscape of Sri Lanka is littered with references to places where Ram is supposed to have landed with his army, where he rested in the midst of battle, where Hanuman had dropped a piece of mountain he had plucked from the Himalayas in search of herbal medicines, places where Sita was imprisoned by Rawan who is locally known as Rawan and where his famed flying machine is supposed to have landed. And all these local places had specific local renditions of the *Ramayana* with their own emphasis and deviations. So stories emanating from Sita Eliya in Sri Lanka's central hills mostly refer to the location as a place where Sita was imprisoned. Wariyapola in the country's Wayamba Province refers to itself as a place where Rawan's flying machine locally known as the 'dandumoanaraya' had landed. Other aspects of the broader *Ramayana* stories play no significant part in these mini local mythic narratives.

But in Sri Lankan myths and folk narratives that have circulated within the island for thousands of years, Ram was not the hero. Instead, it was Rawan. An influential group of local cultural theorists known as the 'Hela Hawula' from the 1920s right up to the 1960s proclaimed him to be the progenitor of the Sinhala people who supposedly spoke a language called Hela delinked from Sanskrit and Pali influences that supposedly became the present-day Sinhala language. This active local myth-making in the margins of a more dominant *Ramayana* mythic structure gave the Sinhalas a more local genesis than the time-tested story of an Indian lineage through yet another cluster of folklore where the hero is an exiled prince called Vijaya.

What does all this mean in the context of the question I had posed earlier? In so far as folklore goes, it is hardly surprising that the story of *Ramayana* was known in Sri Lanka beyond the shores of present-day India. This is simply because folklore, myths and other ideas circulated extensively within the region we call South Asia today and much beyond that also, as a result of the regular movement of people, sharing of cultural knowledge, collective practices of faith and so on. But none of this necessarily constitutes references to evidence-based histories as fact. It is not a matter of ancient international relations between Lanka and Bharat. This is too simplistic. But it is a clear reference to planes of relationships and knowledge, which were, culturally linked that shows the existence of a shared, living landscape embedded with a significant degree of cultural complexity that was known to and acknowledged by different people throughout our region. That is why for me, the study of *Ramayana*, if undertaken cautiously without the hurdles of emotion might show how cultural knowledge travelled in South Asia at specific times creating a very particular experientially based and mythically informed cartography of the region.

But the ways in which *Ramayana* was and is understood in parts of India will not work in attempting to understand how it was sensed and understood in Sri Lanka at different times. This is because the mythic speech in the sense suggested by Barthes changes and distorts over time and in different places. In other words, folklore is not made sense of in the same way they may have been once constructed. Instead, this is done on the basis of how they are remembered, narrated and understood in different temporal and spatial settings. Today, *Ramayana* stories are not in Sri Lankan textbooks and most young people would have forgotten that Rawan emerged from the narratives of *Ramayana*.

But Rawan has re-emerged over the last few years as a purely local and historic character with warrior sensibilities clearly delinked from the Indic epic. His name has been borrowed by a group of militant Buddhists to name their disruptive political outfit known as *Rawana Balakaya* or the Rawan Force. It works as a kind of contemporary fascist paramilitary outfit targeting ethnic and religious minorities as well as political opponents in general. At least one person claimed to have millenarian dreams indicating that he was Rawan in a previous life in the scheme of the Buddhist notion of rebirth and claimed to have seen in these dreams places where Rawan is supposed to have resided. Popular excavations and investigations of these places had taken place at times with TV cameras bearing 'witness'.

The point I want to stress is this. None of these contemporary manifestations can be addressed by considering myth or folklore merely as a product of the past or by assuming it is an unchanging discourse. It also cannot be made sense of by insisting these stories to be historical 'facts'. The only way in which the Sri Lankan manifestations I have referred to can be made sense of is, by situating the original story of *Ramayana* and its varying and different local emphases in the realm of very contemporary local politics as well as Sri Lanka's own past in which these stories have been narrated with different degrees of emphasis.

In another contemporary incarnation of the *Ramayana* story in a very contemporary idiom, the cluster of local stories and places associated with *Ramayana* have been rearranged across the country's landscape as part of Sri Lanka's discourse on international tourism mandated by the state. This can only be understood as part of the process of decision-making within the realms of economics and tourism. Over the last ten years or so, the government has invented something called the 'Ramayana Trail' targeting affluent middle-class Indian tourists.[5] They are taken to see the kind of local places associated with *Ramayana* that I have already referred to. They were never taken seriously by local people before except as pointers to strictly locally circulating mythic narratives.

But now, these mythic references from folklore and embedded in an Indic epic are defended by local people as historic and archaeological facts because they have been collectively turned into a bread and butter issue. A forgotten folklore has been reinvented as a local fact squarely in the midst of economics. And there are no real local consumers for this reinvented interest in the *Ramayana* via the Ramayana Trail.

---

[5] As an example, see the travel packages offered by the company, Ramayana Tours: http://www.ramayanatours.com/. There are many such local companies offering such tours mostly to Indian or non-resident Indian tourists.

Its consumers are Indian tourists and pilgrims who themselves are motivated to visit Lanka as a result of the recent re-awakening of ancient *Ramayana* stories as socio-historical facts in contemporary times. Again, it should be obvious that the only way in which these mythic narratives can be made comprehensible is not only by locating them in the past but more importantly by locating them in the present and that too, in very specific discourses of the present. In this case, these discourses have to do more with international tourism, local entrepreneurship and state policies on commerce.

Let me now refer to the second issue I flagged at the beginning very briefly.

That is the plane of the present in which folklore is given both genesis as well as the space for consumption. This has nothing to do with the past. This is about contemporary folklore. So far, I talked about what happens to folklore when they travel from the past and get enmeshed in contemporary conditions. What I have in mind now is folklore that is invented in the present. Talking of contemporary folklore with particular reference to the digital age, Emma Louise Backe writes that

> contemporary folklore can be found within geek enclaves and hubs, such as video games and Internet urban legends. By drawing on folkloric traditions from around the world, and crafting their own universe-specific lore, video game writers and developers are building new interactive spaces for folklore and reifying the significance of folklore within our cultural imagination. Internet related and generated urban legends such as Slender Man also demonstrate the importance of cyberlore and the transformation of folklore in the digital age.[6]

But contemporary folklore is not merely generated by the technology of the digital age though this is clearly one source. Politicians of our time, university students with what they write on the walls of toilets and on library tables are all in the process of creating contemporary folklore. And most of these are rooted in the experiential realities and fantasies of the present and have nothing much to do with the past.

[6] https://thegeekanthropologist.com/2014/10/03/contemporary-folklore-in-the-digital-age/ (accessed on 15 March 2017).

As people interested in the formal study of folklore would know quite well, one of the best-known scholars who professionalised the study of folklore was Alan Dundes at University of California, Berkeley. His book, *The Study of Folklore* (1965), established the widely accepted definitions of folklore, including what is meant by the term 'the folk'. Dundes was quite aware that the study of folklore could become obsolete if its practitioners were perennially enamoured by a need to link folklore to the past and be guided by outdated ideas of what constituted 'folk'. In his essay, 'Who Are the Folk', Dundes observed with reference to the United States, 'it would be absurd to argue that there is no folklore in the United States and that industrialization stamps out folk groups and folklore—Industrialization has in fact created new folklore, for example, the folklore of computers'.[7]

As we know, while the effects of industrialisation, urbanisation and globalisation swept across the world, many folklorists throughout the twentieth century perceived the introduction of modern technology as the apocalypse for folklore and its study. But Dundes' ideas were in many ways ahead of his times. He said

> technology isn't stamping out folklore; rather it is becoming a vital factor in the transmission of folklore and it is providing an exciting source of inspiration for the generation of new folklore. The rise of the computer symbolizes the impact of technology upon the modern world. My point is that there is folklore of and about the computer.[8]

While we lament on the demise of folklore studies in our times and in our region and lament on our younger generations' forgetfulness of the folklore from our ancient past, how many of us have thought of compiling and interpreting contemporary folklore? As far as I can think of, there is no serious attempt in South Asia to study newer versions of folklore seriously or to study folklore from the past in the newer conditions they find themselves in. And as a result, our attempts at understanding contemporary times are straddled with significant lapses, leading to a situation of intellectual malnourishment. We are

---

[7] Alan Dundes, 1965, *The Study of Folklore*, Englewood Cliffs, Prentice-Hall, p. 7.

[8] Dundes, *The Study of Folklore*, pp. 16–17.

shackled by the past and blinded to the present. And in the end, our understanding of both the past and the present would be incomplete.

Let me end by referring to a comment made by Nancy Willard. She says that according to Armenian folklore, 'three apples fell from Heaven: one for the teller of a story, one for the listener, and the third for the one who "took it to heart"'.[9] And Willard laments, 'What a pity Heaven awarded no apple to the one who wrote the story down.'[10] In our region, I would lament that there are no apples from heaven for those who try to situate folklore in the midst of contemporary times, in the midst of psychoanalysis and in the midst of history and within realms of reasonable interpretation.

[9] https://www.brainyquote.com/quotes/nancy_willard_741378 (accessed on 1 March 2017).

[10] https://www.brainyquote.com/quotes/nancy_willard_741378 (accessed on 1 March 2017).

IV

South Asia in Popular Politics

17

Online South Asia and Its Mediated Politics

Dev Nath Pathak

The idea of a mediated South Asia, overdetermined by electronic media, and in particular by television and cinema, solicits a little more than technical data mining. Some media scholars may throw up their arms to say, it's not mediated, its mediatised, with a variety of news clips in support. It is needless to waste time with such terminological neologisms that plague scholarship in general and works on mass media in particular. The attention towards social or new media is recent and it has begun to challenge some of the conventional assumptions of understanding mediated South Asia. This too has been subject to terminological warfare that we can avoid while trying to fathom the idea of an online region, precisely South Asia as it looks through the relatively newfound public sphere, commonly known as blogosphere in conjunction with social networking sites such as Facebook, Twitter and Instagram. For the time being, we are not indulging in the academic pursuit of theoretically and conceptually evaluating the nature and scope of this new cognate of the public sphere. So we don't spend time in answering whether this new found public sphere aligns with Habermas' idea of the public sphere or responds to Hannah Arendt's notion and so on. Instead, we straight away take an eagle's eye view of selected national contexts—Sri Lanka, Maldives, Bangladesh and India—into consideration to see how invariably the national connects with regional, implicitly as well as explicitly.[1]

[1] An elaborate study on this appeared in an essay: Dev Nath Pathak and Ratan Kumar Roy, 2017, 'Clicking and Politicking: Notions of Mediated Politics in South Asia', in *Media as Politics*, edited by Steve McDowell and Sahana Udupa, London, Routledge.

Online Politics for Offline People?

Blogs began to evolve into a platform to share opinions and disseminate ideas in the national contexts under discussion since the late 1990s, nearly corresponding to the economic liberalisation underway worldwide. However, it is in the decade of 2000 that blogging in South Asia acquired uncanny momentum. This was not merely to become an appendage of the mainstream media. Many bloggers in the region began to perform online activism coupled with overt political objectives. They were different in content, resembling in temperament, thematic concerns and quest. Take, for example, the foundation of *muktomona.com* in Bangladesh and *tamilnet.com* in Sri Lanka, which shared a commonality of being collective initiatives even though the course of action and agenda for each was different. Both blogs became crucial in reflecting political ideologies and germinating a new political discourse responding to their respective politico-national contexts. Likewise, *Dhivehiobserver.com* began in 2004 in the Maldives with the explicit political agenda to criticise and build public consensus against President Gayoom's regime. Maumoon Abdul Gayoom had served as the President of Maldives for 30 years and in 2008 he was defeated and a democratic government was formed in the country. *Dhivehiobserver.com* facilitated the political campaign for democracy led by Mohamed Nasheed and carried political propaganda in support of the Maldivian Democratic Party (MDP). Blog posts, however, covered various themes including travel, literature, science, religion and liberal thoughts on democracy, equality, justice and so on. Post-2005, individual blog activism became influential and robust among Maldivian youth, freelancers, journalists and scholars. In the same period, Bangladesh too saw the emergence of a thriving Bangla blog community. The blog spawning in Sri Lanka led to the emergence of various individuated, yet considerably collective, blogging too.

In December 2005, a full-fledged Bengali blog *somewhereinblog.net* emerged with the title tag *badh vangar awaaj* (roaring to win). Since it maintained a strict policy about posts and comments, some bloggers opened alternative blog pages too. Other websites such as *sachalayatan.com* and *amarblog.com* appeared to facilitate the virtual community of Bengali writers. By 2010 different groups of like-minded youth, writers and activists had already initiated platforms to share their views and to spread their ideologies. The interconnectedness of like-minded Bengali-speaking people in the cyberspace and their continuous activism through writing, commenting and affiliation with these blogs yielded an idea of Bangla Blog Community.[2] More than fiction writing and literary creativity, sociopolitical and cultural debates made these blogs such as *Amrabondhu.com*, *Istishon.com*, *Nirmanblog.com*, *Choturmatrik.com*, *Sonarbangla.com* considerably influential. The most confrontational topics discussed on the blog sites were Bangladesh's liberation war and the issue of war crimes, the spirit of liberty, identity question, cultural legacy and political developments. It ought to be mentioned that a lot of bad blood, in the form of trolling and abusing, was also shed in the blogosphere. This is yet another common feature running across South Asia.

Politics, culture and identity-related questions have been common topics for Sri Lankan bloggers too. In addition, the Lankan bloggers also took to writing on peace-building, social justice, human rights and governance. Unlike in Bangladesh, the individual's effort and identity played a crucial role in establishing and carrying forward blog pages. However, each instance of individuated initiative aspired to build up a virtual community of contributors, followers, commentators. Significant blogging activities were carried out amidst the peace process in the wake of the civil war. In the post-2005 milieu, blogging in Sri Lanka reached a remarkable stage where a conscious effort to generate public consensus, cultivate national and international support were foregrounded. In this scenario, it is important to mention *groundviews.org* launched in 2006 in English, Sinhala and Tamil languages under the supervision of a non-governmental policy organisation. Aimed at fostering citizen journalism in Sri Lanka, the site emphasised 'alternative perspectives

---

[2] Fahmidul Haq, 2013, 'Bangla Blog Community: Expression, Virtual Resistance or the Urge of Building a Community of Different Individuals' (In Bengali: Bangla Blog Community: Motprokash, Virtual Protirodh Othoba Bicchinno Manusher Community Gorar Khudha), in *Media, Society, Culture* (In Bengali: Media, Shomaj, Shongoskriti), edited by Fahmidul Haq and A-Al Mamun, Dhaka, Agami Prokashoni, pp. 342–372.

on governance, human rights, the arts and literature, peace-building'.[3] The institutional support, variations in writings, critical articles and analytical discussions made the site popular. The website initially published solely in English and later in Sinhala through *vikalpa.org*. Readers of this website post numerous comments on political analyses, opinion pieces, satirical posts and cartoons and share these on their personal social media sites as well.

Individual journalists played a crucial role in popularising blogs in Sri Lanka. For instance, *groundviews.org* was initiated by Sanjana Hattotuwa, a journalist. Another journalist, David Buell Sabapathy Jeyaraj (D.B.S. Jeyaraj), who had been a freelance Sri Lankan writer in exile, was associated with various blog pages such as *tamilweek.com*, *transcurrents.com* and *federalidea.com*. In 2009, he opened a blog page with his own name *dbsjeyaraj.com* where writings about current political and social issues appeared. He stated,

> after decades of writing for the print media I feel it's time to plunge into web journalism, using perhaps all the advantages of the internet.... This blog would be one where I post my thoughts and views on different subjects. It would not focus on politics and current affairs much. Sometimes I feel that I've short-changed myself by focusing on politics greatly. Nowadays politics disgusts and depresses me.[4]

However, in practice, blog posts, followed by comments and counter-comments on the blogs, are never free from political agendas. At the same time, he mentioned his commitment as a Tamil blog writer of Sri Lanka to contribute to the resolution of the country's inter-ethnic anxieties, which indicates a clear expression of political motivation.

The tendency of coming up with personal blogs was well established by 2010. Some of them came up with an idea to share knowledge about political and social history as in Michael Roberts' *thuppahi's blog*. Others had very clear political agendas, for instance, the writings of Ahmed Anver Manatunga. Manatunga is a Muslim now, but he was born to Buddhist parents, and later converted to Christianity. Manatunga's

---

[3] Extract from the site: http://groundviews.org/about/ (accessed on 18 December 2018).

[4] Extract from the site: http://dbsjeyaraj.com/dbsj/about (accessed on 19 October 2018).

blog *anvermanatunga.net* was initially in Sinhala and later in English to counter what he called, extremist Sinhala Buddhist elements. The blog spreads information about the condition of Muslims in Sri Lanka to the larger world. To justify his online actions Manatunga accuses some extremist Buddhist of 'spreading hate-filled articles widely over the Internet in Sinhala language'.[5] He argues that Buddhist extremists in Sri Lanka circulate hate-filled posts on social networking website Facebook because they want to create ethnic tensions between Muslims and Sinhala Buddhists.

Let us now take a quick turn to the Maldives. The *Dhivehiobserver.com*, popularly known as *DO*, started as a platform to support the Maldivian Democratic Party (MDP) with the stated political commitment to fight for democracy. It published news and opinions on modern democratic thought that critiqued autocratic regimes. As a response to this website, there emerged some new blog pages that criticised *DO*'s efforts as 'western' and 'secularist' propaganda. For instance, in 2004, a new blog page was opened on *BlogSpot* (*antimdp.blogspot.in*) to counter the propaganda of the *DO* and MDP. They called themselves the anti-Maldivian Democratic Party and stated, 'This site is not in opposition to the democratic reform in the Maldives. Our stand is not against MDP per se, but their secularist philosophy. We respect the rule of law and Islam is what we believe superior.'[6] In general, during the democratic movement in the Maldives, different individuals including journalists, freelancers, scientists, scholars and youth from diverse backgrounds had founded a considerable number of blogs. Opinions about religious issues were widely published in the virtual world. The two political parties, the Jamiyyathu Salaf and the Addhaalath Party, adopted the online medium to disseminate their Islamic ideology and political propositions while running for elections in the Maldives under Islamic Shariah. One Dhivehi language site, *sidahitun.com* and the English language site *gospelgo.com* respectively

---

5 Extract from the site: http://www.anvermanatunga.net/english/about-me-anver-manatunga/ (accessed on 14 October 2018).

6 http://antimdp.blogspot.in/2004/10/sappe-caught-between-devil-and-fire-to.html (accessed on 23 October 2018).

disseminated contents on Christianity and Jesus too. However, the first democratic government in the country that came to power with the promise to support freedom of dissent and speech did not take much time to block various blogs and tried to control the online sphere. The control continued even after political turmoil dethroned the democratically elected party.

Likewise, India is not devoid of its share of blog phenomenon. The number of blogs, similar to the ones in Bangladesh and Sri Lanka are large and hence one can only recount brief biographies of a few. Blogs that have made it to news and views, include the academic blog, *Kafila*, the students' blog, *YouthkiAwaaz*, and a Dalit[7] blog, *RoundtableIndia*, among others. *Kafila* was set up in 2006 as a voluntary, ad-free, zero marketing budget, radical model of critical writing by a group of academics and journalists. *YouthkiAwaaz*, on the other hand, was founded in 2008 by Anshul Trivedi. It functions as a crowd-sourced, community-led model providing a digital media platform for the opinions and reportage on issues of pressing concern for youth. Over 30,000 writers have contributed to a mammoth body of stories on *YouthkiAwaaz*. In doing so, it hopes to enable social change by breaking stereotypes and creating social impact. Likewise, another blog that came in existence in 2008 was *RoundtableIndia*. Kuffir Nalgundwar, Anuram Das among other bloggers, underline this blog as a platform for broadest expression of Dalit-Bahujan voices, resource centre for alternate Dalit histories and a tool for young Dalits to interact and connect with each other. In brief, it seeks to function as 'uniquely Dalit-Bahujan media actor'.[8]

As obvious from the slices of reflection mentioned previously, these blogs bring about an instance of online politics for offline people. Democratic or otherwise, progressive or not, they all seem to be contributing to the creation of a space, which can be frequented without visas, passports and personal identification. Whether we like them or not, they are creating a regime that is beyond the logic of the

[7] Dalits are a historically discriminated caste community in India.

[8] http://roundtableindia.co.in/index.php?option=com_content&view=article&id=2621&Itemid=28 (accessed on 23 October 2018).

nation state. And hence, the state seeks to control it, usually with utter failure though.

Control, Censor and Condemnation

Mass media in South Asia has invariably been controlled by the state through formal and informal means. Various regimes of censorship made the conventional media a fragile fourth estate of democracy. This is mostly on the pretext of national security. This kind of surveillance and control has also spread to online sites usually under the pretext of securing the Internet and establishing cyber security of national contexts. True, cybercrime too has increased manifold, hence ensuring security is an inevitable challenge. However, it is imperative to fathom the implication of the regimes of censorship or control over citizens' politics online.

In the context of Bangladesh, the alleged legitimacy of state control premised upon the perceived vulnerability of youth to adult websites; in Sri Lanka it was largely about the impact on children, the manifestation of sectarian identities and to maintain peace; and similarly, in the island country of the Maldives, this has been mostly to curb the dissemination of differences, (mis)projection and propaganda.

Under the guise of mass-control and censorship, numerous blog sites—whether religious or secular, personal or collective, amateur or political—were victimised and their IP addresses were blocked. The erstwhile Supreme Council for Islamic Affairs in the Maldives, which was subsequently renamed as the Ministry of Islamic Affairs by the democratic government, continued with online censorship in 2008. In a satirical response, an old blog *darkmoon* (chopey.blogspot.in) posted an image of Mecca with the caption 'Dr Majeed, please bless my blog' on 16 March 2009. Dr Majeed was the minister in charge of the Ministry of Islamic Affairs and bloggers were fiercely condemning and criticising his aggressive control of cyberspace. The post, however, received threats and hate speeches by anonymous visitors in its comments section. Another blog titled *Bits 'N' Bytes* (almode.blogspot.in) condemned the Internet censorship by the ministry and posted, 'I condemn the blocking of certain websites by Islamic Ministry, This[sic] is insane. They are out of their fucking minds. Don't they have better things to do then[sic] blocking internet. lol....'[9] In the comment section, people have termed this blogger and his supporters as 'modern-gay-atheists' and one of them commented, '... Go to momma and cry now gay atheists'.[10] Though these actions and reactions in the cyberspace are with reference to the Maldivian context, we are aware of their universality. One can safely speak of the phenomenon called trolling in India that has been a bone of contention among even journalists in mainstream media. Many of them are discussing 'troll trauma' and how to deal with them, legally as well as psychologically.

Since 2005, Bangladesh too has witnessed instances of state authorities intervening and attempting to control blogging and cyber activities, though without much success. Critical reports about the military-backed caretaker governments, between 2006 and 2008, have appeared in the blogs. In 2008, a democratically elected government came to power with the prime slogan to turn the nation into 'Digital Bangladesh'. Ironically though, the same democratically elected government blocked the Internet, blog pages and carried out the arrests of bloggers. Bloggers have also faced considerable violence in Bangladesh, perhaps more so than in any other South Asian country. If the bloggers in Bangladesh were accused of anti-Islamic blasphemy and atheism, an interesting case in the Maldives presents another aspect. One may recall the famous Hilath Rasheed case, in which the blogger was attacked by extremists and detained by the police in the Maldives. Unlike many bloggers from Bangladesh, Hilath Rasheed's blog writings were not positioned to bash Islam or Prophet Muhammad. Instead, he was accused of promoting Sufism and propagating gay culture in society through his blog. He was made to pay for his 'wrongdoing' in the blog. Various ministries of the government made an effort to bring him to what they considered the 'right path'. Some regular bloggers, post-2005, have now become quite irregular in the blogosphere

---

[9] http://almode.blogspot.in/2009/03/i-condemn-internet-censorship-by.html (accessed on 21 October 2018).

[10] Extract from the site: http://www.anvermanatunga.net/english/about-me-anver-manatunga/ (accessed on 14 October 2018).

because of the threats and state-imposed controls. But bloggers from the Maldives and Bangladesh have also raised their voice for the right to dissent.

In addition to blogs, other online news sites (portals) and social networking sites such as Facebook have played crucial roles in shaping the online public sphere in South Asia. Unlike in Bangladesh, massive commentary on the online news portals is widespread in Sri Lanka and the Maldives. In Sri Lanka, *dailymirror.lk*, *lankanewspaper.com*, *asianmirror.lk*, *colombopage.com*, *lankaenews.com*, *lankaweb.com*, *adaderana.lk*, *ada.lk* and *onlanka.com* have opened up new avenues for readers to engage in debates. The trend of sharing, liking and commenting on online news has become popular since 2000. This has enabled citizen-journalism as well as the emergence of a new public sphere(s), an issue that solicits conceptual deliberation on some other occasion. The online version of major newspapers in the Dhivehi language attracts readers to comment and generate debates on various websites such as *haveeru.com.mv*, *sun.mv*, *cnm.com* and *minivandaily.com*. However, departing from the *Minivan Daily* (in print), the *minivannews* launched a separate website which also gathers a huge number of political comments in their English version news portal *maldivesindependent.com*. The online news portals in both countries, by endorsing Twitter posts and making them visible on the front page, underline the fostering of intimate participation of readers or citizens. Compared to Bangladesh and the Maldives, in Sri Lanka, managers (admins) of different Facebook pages do not face legal trials. However, there is fierce hatred and condemnation among readers who are against public abuse of politicians through humorous/slanderous writings, hilarious/vulgar expressions and objectionable/ordinary language. Instances of forced disappearances and abduction of journalists in Sri Lanka during the last years of the civil war continue to instil a sense of fear among young social media activists. The disappearance of journalist, Prageeth Eknaligoda, who used to draw cartoons mocking politicians, has made many bloggers anxious. The former President Rajapaksa has been implicated in the killing and abduction of dissidents during his regime. However, Sri Lankan politicians have not created any concerted outrage about politics online as their Bangladeshi counterparts have.

Sheikh Hasina, the Prime Minister of Bangladesh, got emotional in Parliament and expressed her intense feelings for the blogger-driven Shahbag protest. But in the wake of bloggers being killed in the country and threats from the Islamic groups, she asked the bloggers to control their writings. Politics online assumes significance with this kind of contradictory reactions by politicians in response to blogging and online activism. The detainment of the administrator of a Bangladesh-based Facebook page *mojalosss* (are you joking) by the police (Rapid Action Battalion, popularly known as elite police), alleging a campaign against the government and the dissemination of anti-state content, has added to the vibrancy of and anxiety over online politics. Filled with fun posts and humorous content, often interpreted as a source of hurt-sentiment, these pages gained popularity as a discursive space for political communications, interactive politics online and more accessible political culture.

It is necessary to clarify that the group of bloggers I have referred to is not homogenous. It is a highly segregated and fluid community who have diverse interests and agendas but its appearance and actions bear political implications. The heterogeneity of bloggers in this region correlates with the political practices of these postcolonial societies, fraught with differences.

Sometimes Facebook pages and users, with evident political motives (often affiliated to particular political parties) do not confine themselves to humour and instead attack and scandalise their opponents. As an example in the Maldives, the anti-Nasheed account *Laadheenee Anni* (Nasheed is irreligious) created a few fragmented images, put a bikini on him and enclosed some quotations as his statement. Bangladesh based anti-government community page *Baksal*[11] often posts funny images and captions, expressing absurdity, to defame the current Prime Minister in

---

[11] *Baksal* used as the shortened form of the *Bangladesh Krishak Sramik Awami League* which was formed as a national political party with the presidential order and outlawed all other political parties in 1975. After Sheikh Mujibur Rahman's assassination, this collective was dissolved and all the parties became independent including the Awami League. However, the term *Baksal* has often been referred to criticise the one-party policy of Awami League in 1975 and to term the Awami League as undemocratic. Hence, the use of the *Baksal* for running a Facebook page by anti-Awami groups and parties is to criticise the Awami League-run government.

Bangladesh and her family members. It recently posted an image with the caption 'prime minister's son (Joy) did not have a circumcision, how cum he claimed as a Muslim'.[12] Christina, Joy's wife is shown as revealing the secret. Similarly, the assumption of the owner of *Baksal* page about the political bankruptcy of the Bangladeshi government and its absolute dependence on India is presented via images of Indian Prime Minister Modi accompanied by slanderous commentaries and scandalous cartoons. However, this does not mean to suggest that they trivialise their politics.

Making funny Facebook memes of local and global political leaders, the posts render political critique light and accessible rather than trivial. For example, Obama saying 'are you joking', Modi daring 'Will slap you so hard', former Bangladeshi President and dictator shying away 'you are so naughty,' are not presented as grave political posts. Furthermore, commenting on a girl's newly uploaded photo, the meme of a notorious politician says 'Please don't kill me with your shining beauty', or her reply with another meme with the images of an ex-Prime Minister says, 'shut up idiot'. These are examples of bringing political figures into the domains of the personal, every day and mundane environs. Laced with humour and slander, these posts serve explicit political motives.

In this regard, it is important to note that many social mobilisations in various parts of South Asia are being fuelled by blogs and social media activism. The Maldivian social media activists played a crucial role in organising the protest in support of President Nasheed on 1st May 2015. It was a massive turnout, which eventually turned violent. The Facebook page *EkehFaheh15* (One Five Fifteen) became the rallying platform of that event and many Facebook and online campaigns appeared in solidarity with the page. Ironically, some of the organisers of this protest were also involved in the 2011 protest against Nasheed and his government. On that occasion too, the youth mobilised against Nasheed on May Day 2011 in Male and social media played a crucial role. Subsequently, online activists called for a grand assembly on 23 December 2011; this information was widely circulated through social media. A huge crowd assembled against Nasheed, beyond the control of state machinery, in the name of protecting Islam.

---

[12] https://www.facebook.com/Baksal1975/ (accessed on 13 December 2018).

Facebook accounts and community pages are crucial in blogger-driven protest movements in Bangladesh too. In 2013, bloggers and online activists initiated the Shahbag protest; these were primarily youths of Bangladesh. It began with the demand for the death penalty for war criminals of the 1971 Liberation war. It also targeted Islamic political groups. Hundreds of Facebook accounts were registered to cultivate support for Shahbag. A unique opposition, however, also fuelled such galvanised cyber activism. Islamic political groups disseminated rumours online about unethical practices of the Shahbag protestors. They brought about a reactionary protest to protect Islam and used cyberspace to share the blog writings on Islam and Prophet Muhammad. In the ensuing confrontation between the progressive youth and Islamist groups, a so-called atheist blogger was killed in 2013. Thereafter, the bloggers began to get continuous threats over their writings in blogs. Many of them came under surveillance by various interest groups. The hacking to death of a number of bloggers blurred the hard line between virtual and real in Bangladesh.

Conclusion: A Precariously Online Region

This brief overview, with evident similarities in detail from various national contexts and contextual peculiarities, aids in understanding the complex characteristics of the phenomenon. This alludes to the shrinking gap between online activism and offline actions, virtual and real. The South Asian cyberspace is fraught with the intricate blending of scandalous, salacious, hilarious, personal, public and the political. It may engender a gamut of emotions, excitement, disgust, hatred, love and solidarity. Whether we like it or not, this activism and the way in which the cyberspace has been implicated in that activism also leads to a sense of South Asia, thoroughly mediated, manipulated and manufactured by the interface of the social and the political in the cyberspace. Everything that appears in this domain becomes markers of contemporary South Asia. It is certainly more precarious than the bards of the bygone times, the traditional messengers of the oral tradition might have imagined.

18

A Melodramatic South Asia

Perusing a Performative-scape

Dev Nath Pathak

South Asia is a region marked by diversities stemming from numerous local contexts located within nation states comprising the subcontinent. However, while sociocultural conditions differ across specific national contexts, the region is defined by a unity arising from shared historical circumstances, contemporary experiences and emotions that transpire in these experiences. A glance at performances of the region would bring to light these shared emotions that encompass the subcontinent, widening one's imagination beyond the bounded space of the nation. Arguing that 'melodrama' is a trope at the centre of the performative repertoire of South Asia, this chapter maps out ways in which performative forms (folk forms as well as modern theatre) and cultures in the subcontinent narrate experiences and emotions that are shared across the region.[1] South Asia, when understood as a performative scape, appears to be a site over which emotions, ideas, histories and performative forms traverse across borders, undercutting rigid political boundaries. History[2], or perhaps histories, of the region underline shared past, pre-colonial and colonial, giving rise to both, regional chauvinism as well as scepticism about neighbours. A synoptic glance through the vast performative landscape of South Asia would bring forth multiple regional histories embedded in local contexts of nation states and their trans-local, qua interterritorial or regional, dynamics.

---

[1] This chapter resonates an elaborate study in Dev Nath Pathak, ed., 2018, *Another South Asia!*, Delhi, Primus, pp. 163–186.

[2] A. Jalal and Sugata Bose, 1998, *Modern South Asia: History, Culture, Political Economy*, Delhi, Oxford University Press.

A Synopsis of Tradition and Modernity of Performative-scape

In order to build an overview of performance traditions in South Asia, *Jatra*, a popular folk dramatic form performed across much of South Asia, is an ideal starting point. In particular, *Jatra* is performed in Bangladesh and West Bengal, eastern Bihar, Assam, Tripura as well as Odisha in India. *Jatra*, literally meaning 'procession', possibly deriving from an ancient form of folk drama, reflects a persistent engagement with changing political and sociocultural forces and the form has also been impacted by the same. Marked by highly melodramatic overtones, *Jatra* typically involves songs and theatrical scenes. Among the characters is the 'conscience' (*Bibek*), an allegorical figure who makes appearances in the drama, commenting on actions of other characters and consequences of their evil deeds. Yet another archetypical character is that of 'fate' (*Niyati*), which, much like the 'conscience', comments on characters' actions and warns them of impending dangers. *Jatra* plays draw heavily upon stories from the epics such as *Ramayana*, *Mahabharata*, etc. A case in point is *Matri Puja*, a play by Kunja Behari Ganguli transformed into a *Jatra* by Mukunda Das, prominent playwright-performer whose dramatic plays also deployed historical themes to spread the message of anticolonial nationalism. A battle between *daityas* (demons) and *devas* (gods), wherein the former have forcibly taken control of the latter's kingdom, was intended to be an allegorical reference to colonial exploitation in India.[3] Arrested on charges of sedition, Mukunda Das eventually received a long prison sentence.

The nineteenth century is considered the period when *Jatra* underwent significant transformations in terms of form as well as content. The groups of the young bourgeoisie in Calcutta (the cultural elites known as *Bhadralok*), in colonial India, developed

[3] Darnton Robert, 2001, 'Literary Surveillance in the British Raj: The Contradictions of Liberal Imperialism,' in *Book History*, Volume 4, edited by Ezra Greenspan and Jonathan Rose, Pennsylvania, Penn State Press, pp. 163–164.

their own *Jatra* groups and secularised the content of the folk drama. The new format of the *Bhadralok Jatra* came to be more oriented towards entertainment than earlier entirely didactic content. With the establishment of the public stage in Calcutta in 1827, experiments that aimed at synthesising the classical European theatre with *Jatra* were abounding. However, as European theatrical interventions transformed audiences' sensibilities and aesthetic tastes, the *Jatra* form found little support among the educated or elite audience in Bengal. *Jatra* catered primarily to an audience based in rural settings until the Communist mobilisation of support through appropriation of this folk performative form in the 1930s and 1940s revived an elite audience's interest in *Jatra* to a certain extent. Perhaps, a powerful melodramatic tone as well as malleability of form, enabled *Jatra* to be utilised as a tool for propaganda politics. Placing emphasis on the suitability of Jatra as a weapon for ideological warfare due to its intimacy with the audience, the renowned thespian Utpal Dutt[4] called for utilisation of the form for revolutionary propaganda. The contemporary themes of certain *Jatra* plays deploy themes such as American action against Iraq featuring Saddam Hussain at the forefront of a great anti-imperialist War. *Loke Nattya O Sanskritik Unnayan Kendro*, an association for sociocultural development in Bangladesh, uses *Jatra* among other performative forms to raise awareness and advocate social change.[5] The character of *Bibek* is shown to sing a song about human trafficking, a peril that plagues parts of rural Bangladesh in order to provoke community.

The trajectory of performance includes *Lavani* in Maharashtra that reflects a similar engagement with changing sociocultural conditions and resultant transformations. Another melodramatic form, overtly erotic *Lavanis* can be traced to the Peshwa period. A popular saying in Marathi attributes downfall of the Brahmanical Peshwa Empire to

---

[4] Utpal Dutt, interview by Malini Bhattacharya and Mihir Bhattacharya, 1984, 'An Armoured Car on the Road to Proletarian Revolution,' *Journal of Arts and Ideas*, Vol. 8, pp. 25–43; U. Dutt, 1991, 'Not Out of Thin Air,' *Indian Literature*, Vol. 34, No. 5, pp. 147–155.

[5] Namzul Ahsan, 2004, 'Social Theatre in Bangladesh,' *The Drama Review*, Vol. 48, No. 3, pp. 50–58.

the performance of erotic *Lavanis* by women at courts in the *Peshwai.*[6] Elaborating on intersections between popular performance, gender and caste in the context of *Lavani*, the late sociologist Sharmila Rege posits the folk performative form as a site over which sexuality of lower caste female performers was constructed. Bodies of lower caste *Lavani* performers were projected as arousing or satiating male desire, a construction that was central to the pre-colonial Peshwa state's appropriation of labour of lower caste women. Interestingly, erotic *Lavanis* expressing sexual desires of women were composed in the voice of lower caste women, as opposed to those about the *Virah* or 'pain of separation' that were composed and performed in the voice of the wife, supposedly in awe of the virility of her husband. As a public performance, *Lavani* constituted an important part of *Tamasha*, another significant folk form performed in Maharashtra. The term *Tamasha*, essentially a Persian word indicating 'fun' or 'entertainment', was perhaps introduced to the area by Urdu-speaking Mughal soldiers. Furthermore, the *Tamasha* is said to have developed in the sixteenth century, being performed as a bawdy entertainment for Mughal armies occupying the Deccan as well as for insurgent Maratha forces. The *Tamasha* combined several regional folk performative traditions including the *Powada*, in addition to the *Lavani*. The anti-caste thinker and activist Jyotiba Phule employed the *Powada* to put forth a non-Brahminical history of Maharashtra, aiming at educational and economic mobilisation of peasants, artisans and *ati-Sudra* castes.

With the British victory over the Marathas in 1818, *Tamasha* performers were relegated to rural Maharashtra in search of new sources of patronage. Similar to the historical trajectory of *Jatra* outlined earlier,

---

[6] S. Rege, 2000, 'Understanding Popular Culture: The Satyashodhak and Ganesh Mela in Maharashtra,' *Sociological Bulletin*, Vol. 49, No. 2, pp. 193–210; S. Rege, 2002, 'Conceptualizing Popular Culture: "Lavani" and "Powada" in Maharashtra,' *Economic and Political Weekly*, Vol. 37, No. 11, pp. 1038–1047; S. Rege, 2012, 'Songsters from the Mudhouse,' *Outlook*. http://www.outlookindia.com/article/songsters-from-the-mudhouse/281948 (accessed on 17 October 2018). Also see, K. Hansen, 2004, 'Theatrical Transvestism in the Parsi, Gujarati and Marathi Theatres (1850–1940),' in *Sexual Sites, Seminal Attitudes: Sexualities, Masculinities, and Culture in South Asia*, edited by Sanjay Srivastava, New Delhi, SAGE Publications.

the emergence of a new theatre of the middle class and upper castes in the mid-nineteenth century, emulating forms of Victorian theatre, had implications for *Tamasha*. The latter came to be projected as 'immoral' when juxtaposed with the new theatre of the educated middle class.

In the same vein, we can add another genre of *Tamasha*, known as *Jalsa*, which appropriated idioms of the former for instructional and propagandist purposes. The *Satyashodhak Samaj*, an organisation founded by Phule in 1873, employed *Jalsa* as instructional theatre, taking up issues of untouchability, exploitation of women and the peasantry, etc., informed Sharmila Rege. This performative form aided to critique Brahminical practices. For instance, the *Gavlan*, traditionally a dialogue between Krishna and the milkmaids, was altered as an encounter between the non-Brahmin hero and the daughter of the Brahmin village priest. Likewise, the *Ambedkari Jalsa* reorganised the performative structure of *Tamasha*, employing more verses to convey the message of Ambedkar, often through parody. The *Ambedkari Jalsas* gained predominance in the period between 1920 and 1956. Foregrounding concerns of dowry, indebtedness and prostitution etc. behind the veil of religion and emphasising the importance of education, organised the collective effort and struggle, these *Jalsas* critiqued exclusion of female performers. This is akin to the utilisation of *Jatra*, in Bangladesh and India, to raise awareness against concerns such as exploitation and trafficking.

Like the *Jalsa*, other performative forms in South Asia have also utilised comic dialogues for making subversive political comments and enacting subtle forms of resistance. *Bhand*, a form performed widely in Punjab, in both India and Pakistan. With an element of *Bahurupiya* or mimicry, it is performed in Rajasthan too. The *Bhand* artists usually wander about and perform at various sites of practical convenience. These wandering comedians are said to have a fragmented history. With the 'Partition' in 1947, several *bhands* hitherto particularly concentrated in the Indian region of Punjab migrated to Pakistan.[7] Roots of the form go back to the *Natya Shastra*, an ancient text of performance arts,

---

[7] C. Pamment, 2008, 'Mock Courts and the Pakistani Bhand,' *Asian Theatre Journal*, Vol. 25, No. 2, pp. 344–362.

known to be written by a sage named Bharat. However, historically, the *bhands* trace their art to the courts of Hindu and Mughal rulers, roughly during the period of 1556–1857 where they performed as entertainers of the power-elites.

In Pakistan, weddings, birth celebrations, intervals between folk plays, as well as *melas* (festive congregations) constitute the performance spaces of the peripatetic *bhands*. The dialogic structure is typical of a *Bhand* performance. But invariably, the *bhands* subvert hierarchies of language, commenting on sociocultural and political subjects, using comic acts. For instance, a famous *bhand* Munir Hussain popular among prominent Pakistani politicians, infuses his performative methods with satire and a subtle critique of his invitees, making a comment on broader sociopolitical concerns such as corruption plaguing the country. Likewise, in Indian-administered Kashmir, the *Bhand* is performed by troupes called *Bhand Pather* who enact farcical dramas, combining music, dance, clowning, drum beating, chants and barbed satire incorporating mythological legends and contemporary sociopolitical issues. Parody, as Shafi Shauq[8] notes, is often used to articulate dissent against social evils and exploitation.

The tradition of using exaggerated emotions or melodrama and satire in performative modes is a factor underlying several forms of folk drama in South Asia. In addition to the *Bhand*, or *Vag* (satirical theatre) aspect of the *Tamasha*, the *Kolam* dance, a masked dance performance in Sri Lanka involves satirised portrayals of characters. The *Kolam* dance is essentially a folk drama in which every character wears brightly coloured masks made of wood.[9] With no central theme or story, *Kolam* entails loosely structured plays with short humorous anecdotes and dances. *Kolam* plays, crude satiric performative forms, drawing characters from the sociocultural world of everyday reality in rural settings. Satirised and lampooned, these characters included officials, village headmen, clerks, policemen, the farmer and his wife,

---

[8] http://www.heritageofkashmir.org/frontpage/177-kashmiri-folk-theatre.html (accessed on 16 October 2018).

[9] See for more detail http://www.accu.or.jp/ich/en/arts/A_LKA2.html (accessed on 16 October 2018).

in addition to a range of gods, demons and animals. Following the colonial encounter, certain performances came to portray a white male character called *Sinno* (Senor) and a white female character called *Nona* (lady) who danced together, the woman eventually climbing on the man's back. Another satirised figure was the white soldier, depicted with a broken nose, his face covered by wounds and blood, as recorded by John Calloway in the first description of a *Kolam* dance in 1829.[10]

A particularly popular object of satire was the *Andi gura* or guru from Andhra (perhaps Andhra Pradesh in contemporary India), an Indian astrologer as well as snake charmer who roams from village to village in the guise of a holy man, fraudulently collecting money. The plays never developed beyond a comic dialogue between the narrator and a character. Moreover, under the impact of colonialism in the late nineteenth to early twentieth centuries, a new 'protestant' or revivalist Buddhism spread across Sri Lanka, placing emphasis on doctrinal Buddhism as a modern 'rational religion'. As a result, ritualistic or folk forms such as *Kolam* came to be considered frivolous, nonsense and eventually faded from the villages where they traditionally held a wide appeal.

Regional Implications of Modern Theatre

If the case of traditional performances in South Asia shows that performative-scape is not monolithic and static, the modern theatre also joins in this to enrich understanding. In spite of the nationalistic concerns in the modern theatre performances, there has been a curious urge to overcome the divisive ideological and territorial boundaries. Hence, we encounter not only 'roots' but also 'routes', for example, in the history of modern theatre in colonial and post-independence India.[11] If the roots indicated theatrical inclinations to what was deemed

---

[10] R. Obeyesekere, 1992, 'The Sinhala Theatre of Sri Lanka,' *The Drama Review*, Vol. 36, No. 2, pp. 126–137; also see, Neloufer De Mel, 2001, *Women and the Nation's Narrative: Gender and Nationalism in Twentieth Century Sri Lanka*, New York, Rowman Publishers.

[11] Vasudha Dalmia, 2008, *Poetics, Plays and Performances: The Politics of Modern Indian Theatre*, Delhi, Oxford University Press; Nandi Bhatia, 2011, *Modern Indian Theater: A Reader*, Delhi, Oxford University Press.

traditional, or perhaps invented traditions of a bound-context, routes alludes to the traffic of styles, idioms, narratives, motifs, props and production of theatrical performances not-bound-to-local contexts. The theatre scene in South Asia is characterised by a history of traffic of the aspects of drama across the subcontinent. In Nepal, particularly since the 1970s, through modern dramaturgies such as surrealism or adaptation of *Puranic* tales to contemporary ground realities, theatre has presented a critique of autocratic rulers and feudal nobility. Davis'[12] research shows that the subsequent decade saw a more politically conscious theatre emerging as a vanguard of the 'pro-democracy movement' in Nepal. Street theatre was particularly important in this context. Ashesh Malla, the pioneer of modern theatre in Nepal, was at the forefront of this vibrant street theatre during the 'pro-democracy movement'. Founding the *Sarwanam* theatre group, Malla was engaged in a theatre that voiced discontent against the *Panchayat* System as well as the government's indifference to demands of the people. Moreover, *Sadak Natak* (Nepali version of street theatre) was utilised as an important tool of protest, with plays performed not just in university campuses but wherever a crowd could be attracted. Malla gained exposure to and was influenced by works of Indian theatre persons such as Badal Sircar, Subodh Patnaik, Probir Guha and Safdar Hashmi.

A similar cross-pollination of dramatic forms and practices is discernible in certain performative forms in Sri Lanka as well. Modern Sinhala theatre, like theatre in much of South Asia, bears the colonial imprint. Ranjini Obeyesekere informs that it has also been influenced by Bengali nationalist theatre as well as touring Parsi musicals from Bombay and South Indian operatic plays. The modern Sinhala theatre under the influence of British colonial theatre entailed new ideals of womanhood. This ideal valorised the image of the chaste woman, inspired by *Sita* in *Ramayana*, or dutiful wives, good mothers and chaste partners drawn from historical legends and Buddhist *Jataka*

---

[12] C. Davis, 2014, 'Towards an Engaged Stage: Nepali Theatre in Uncertain Times,' in *Mapping South Asia through Contemporary Theatre: Essays on the Theatres of India, Pakistan, Bangladesh, Nepal and Sri Lanka*, edited by Ashis Sengupta, New York, Palgrave Macmillan.

stories. However, in response to colonial domination, Sinhala theatre, influenced by nationalist Bengali theatre, was utilised as a tool to forge a Sinhala consciousness amongst the audience, playing an important role in the anti-colonial drive that assumed a greater pace by the late nineteenth century.

In addition to cross-cultural influences, theatre in South Asia also indicates how performance can be a tool for bringing disparate groups together and engendering a sense of community. In Sri Lanka, more recently, attempts are being made to redefine the nation and make it more inclusive through multi-ethnic mobile theatre groups such as *Makkal Kalari* or *Jana Karaliya*. Similarly, in Bangladesh, in indigenous performances such as *Madar Pirer Gan* (The Lay of Madar Pir), performers constituting Hindus, Muslims or both together, invoke support for the Sufi cult of South Asia to challenge Islamic orthodoxy.[13]

Sengupta's map of modern theatre in South Asia shows that theatre has served to be a medium through which histories of the marginalised are brought to the fore, hence enabling a rethinking of mainstream 'national' histories. Writing on Tamil theatre in Sri Lanka, Sengupta writes that a socially and politically conscious Tamil theatre emerged against the background of the Civil War. Since such performances sought to reach out to wider audiences in refugee camps, this new wave of Tamil theatre developed away from the confines of the proscenium stage. In the context of Pakistan, harassment of women due to dominant oppressive ideologies or by the state was critiqued through theatre. For instance, *Dard Kay Faasley* (Distances of Pain, 1981) was a critique against the condition of women in a period of heightened nationalistic chauvinism and fundamentalism. *Barri* (The Acquittal, 1987) was themed around Zia-ul-Haque's oppressive laws against women. The play was set in a prison cell where a group of women are held captive for various crimes.

Through South Asia, theatre has attempted to contest societal values, cultural norms and oppressive practices. For example, recent

---

[13] A. Sengupta, 2014, *Mapping South Asia through Contemporary Theatre: Essays on the Theatres of India, Pakistan, Bangladesh, Nepal and Sri Lanka*, New York, Palgrave Macmillan.

plays in Pakistan such as *Burqavaganza* (2010) by Shahid Nadim, portrayed the veil as a metaphor for hypocrisy in a 'hidden nation' and presented a satire on the country's contemporary chaotic condition, hence challenging hegemonic narratives of nationalism. Significantly, the play faced censorship by the government on charges of corrupting young minds. Also, Sengupta writes how a host of English musicals, gaining prominence on the contemporary theatre scene, could be considered a challenge to 'Talibanisation' of culture. Theatre in Nepal has engaged with issues such as witchcraft, alcoholism, etc. To cite an example, Ashesh Malla's *Boksi!* (Witch!, 1991) brought forth the ills of superstitions and witchcraft, bringing to light ways in which old superstitions continue to plague people, particularly women, in rural Nepal. One can hence discern a challenge to oppressive practices by the state, or status-quoist dominant ideologies and cultural norms, as a common strand across the performative landscape of South Asia.

Conclusion

The synoptic overview of the performative traditions in South Asia, touring through various parts of India, Pakistan, Bangladesh, Nepal and Sri Lanka, is indeed an incomplete perusal. The performative landscape, replete with traditional (invented or otherwise) and modern forms, is too vast to be surmised in one chapter. However, this chapter makes a modest attempt to peruse eclectically chosen instances along the lines of key interest: How does performative landscape in the region exhibit an inclination to melodrama as well as a tendency to be trans-local? In other words, the chapter tries to highlight a creative dilemma underpinning the regional performative landscape. On one hand, the examples show contextually (in a broad sense, nationally) rooted permutations and combinations of emotions and on the other hand, they reveal that the emotions are shared and so are styles, metaphors, idioms and socio-historical experiences. The earlier discussion brings to light common strands that run through diverse dramatic forms, primarily a predisposition towards melodramatic content arising from the traditional sources of tales, idioms, metaphors and styles.

It only receives further augmentation in an encounter with historical upheavals, such as colonialism and realisation of various sociopolitical anomalies. While colonial interventions, responses to colonial rule and engagement with post-colonial realities of oppression and exploitation are aspects at the centre of the theatrical domain of the subcontinent, these factors bring about shifts in the category of melodrama that unites the region. Drama is a melodramatic medium through which experiences and emotions felt during those experiences are communicated. Historical changes result in associated changes in the emotions and experiences being expressed. There emerges a possibility of a qualitatively different kind of a map of South Asia if we look at it through the prism of performance. The performing arts enable an understanding of the subcontinent as a terrain marked by diversities that are encompassed within a similarity of experiences that underlies myriad local specificities.

19

In the Frame of the Popular Cinema Despite the Hegemony of Hindi

Dev Nath Pathak

Popular Hindi cinema is a hegemonic soft power in South Asia. Zakir Hossain Raju makes this assertive proposition looking at the undergrowth of cinema in Bangladesh.[1] One instantly enters in an agreement, as well as critical dialogue with Raju. And the dialogue enables to believe that despite hegemonic impacts, popular Hindi cinema chisels out a cultural cartography of South Asia. Curiously, this cartography includes not only local South Asia but also a large chunk of South Asia in faraway lands across seas.

This chapter reflects on the phenomenal circulation of the content of Hindi cinema in the region and fathoms the validity of a 'dynamic local' as an alternative to the overarching category of globalisation. Within cinema, the case of Bollywood and popular Hindi cinema songs is taken as an anchorage to traverse the region and sneak into diverse locations and thereof popular cinema and music. An evident fondness for popular Hindi cinema, notwithstanding, one is aware of the soft hegemony and various allegations about Hindi cinema jeopardising the growth of cinemas in other parts of the region as well as provinces in India. Be that as it may, this chapter is an attempt to understand the local-to-local dynamics that is somewhat of an ignored category in the wake of a linear vacillation between local and global. The ulterior motive in this chapter, if any, is to upset the fad of linear

[1] Zakir Hossain Raju, 2012, '"Bollywoodization" as (H)Indianization? Bangladesh Film Industry under National Protection', in *The Magic of Bollywood: At Home and Abroad*, edited by Anjali Gera Roy, New Delhi: SAGE Publications, pp. 193–212; Zakir Hossain Raju, 2014, *Bangladesh Cinema and National Identity: In Search of the Modern*, London, Routledge.

taxonomical reasoning, which dubs art as either local or global, either folk or classical or popular, either for class or for mass, cosmopolitan or regional/nationalistic, etc. In the same way, cinema too has been judged through either Indian cinema/regional cinema or global Bollywood. Transcending this limitation implies an alternative way of imagining South Asia beyond the dominant mediated imagination of the region.

'Bollywood' is another name of the Hindi cinema industry lately in spite of the discomfort of cinema workers as well as cinema scholars.[2] Most of the arguments on the nature and scope of 'global Bollywood', as it is the case with the debate on global regional art, fail to recognise the regional-spontaneous-mobility of the forms and contents. The internal dynamics involved in the process of exchanges of forms, in another word the mobility of forms and contents, is easily glossed over in the aura of the spectacular global Bollywood. There is also a lack of interest in another very significant question as to how the local, irrespective of the global, also retains a locality in spite of the crumbling/crumbled territorial boundaries. If a piece of art, a piece of cinematic motif, of popular music, expresses global ambition, it does not do away with the locality and predisposition towards the local. In the case of Hindi cinema especially, there is a neo-orientalist urge to refashion local for whetting the appetite of the consumers. Same is the case with the artisans and craftsmen of the global market, belonging to the local and producing for the global. The women weavers of Southeast Asia narrate the saga of lamentable loss because they cannot switch from methods of local to indulge in copious production for global.[3] The artists from the local in India, however, have gotten into the mode of improvising upon the local to produce saleable forms and content for the global. Roma Chatterji's[4] research elucidates this with a systematic work on the folk artists of Medinipur and Purulia. On a larger canvas, a similar tendency

---

[2] Ashish Rajadhyaksha, 2011, 'The "Bollywoodization" of the Indian Cinema: Cultural Nationalism in a Global Arena', in, *Global Bollywood*, edited by Anandam P. Kavoori and Aswin Punathambekar, Delhi, Oxford University Press, pp. 17–40.

[3] Roy W. Hamilton, ed., 2011, *Weavers' Stories: From Island Southeast Asia*, Los Angeles, Fowler Museum At Ucla, 2011.

[4] Roma Chatterji, 2012, *Speaking with Pictures: Folk Art and the Narrative Tradition in India*, Delhi, Routledge.

is well captured in a bid to 'theorise the local'.[5] This is fairly addressed in the context of South Asian Cinemas too showing the dynamic character of the local, with due focus on change and yet continuity.

To meet with the questions of concern point blank let's look at the dynamics of local popular Hindi cinema. A perusal of the contemporary discourse on popular Hindi cinema suggests a few steps backward and forward.

O(f)f the 'Global Bollywood'

In the time of transnational flow, Hindi cinema is spawning nothing more than the nation for an imagined community. Bollywood thus becomes the state's self-representation with film production companies becoming corporate, benefiting from state provisions and coming under the regulation of the state. This 'return of the nation' in popular Hindi cinema has attracted criticism at length. In the same breath, there is an invariable reference to the diaspora audience, changing economy of cinema and representation of the diasporic influences in cinematic narratives. Underlining the ideological import of Bollywood, Thakur argues, 'Bollywood participates in the ideological construction of a globalized cultural subjectivity through the construction and privileging of a new ethics of globalized living; an ethics which is in opposition to established pre-global notions of cultural subjectivity'.[6]

Participating in the critique, a cinema study scholar such as Ravi Vasudevan[7] reminds that India's Tamil, Telugu and Malayalam cinemas produce more films and have farther reach than the Bombay cinema. Hence the name of Bombay cinema to underline globalism of it is not

---

[5] Richard K. Wolf, ed., *Theorizing the Local: music, Practice and Experience in South Asia and Beyond*, New York, Oxford University Press, 2010.

[6] Gautam Basu Thakur, 2011, 'Globalization and the Cultural Imaginary: Constructions of Subjectivity, Freedom and Enjoyment in Popular Indian Cinema', in *Bollywood and Globalization: Indian Popular Cinema, Nation and Diaspora*, edited by Rini Bhattacharya Mehta and Rajeshwari V. Pandharipande, Delhi, Anthem Press, pp. 75–92.

[7] Ravi Vasudevan, 2011, 'The Meanings of "Bollywood"', in *Beyond the Boundaries of Bollywood: The Many Forms of Hindi Cinema*, edited by Rachel Dwyer and Jerry Pinto, Delhi, Oxford University Press, pp. 3–29.

only an exercise in ignorance but also a hasty parallel of Hollywood. It is the complex multi-levelled production, circulation and consumption of forms, with speed in access that invites a fresh thinking on the globalism of Hindi cinema. In fact, Morocom's exciting study showed that,

> Songs, and more importantly dance, are also the key agents that have seen Bollywood spread not just throughout India but also across the world, spawning an array of syncretic sub-cultural forms globally. The appeal of song and dance extends far more easily across cultures than narrative, and while the sleek picturization and images of the glamorous stars are alluring, the sounds are particularly pervasive, playable on audio as well as audio-visual media and easy to absorb passively and/or at a distance.[8]

Interestingly enough the travelling songs, even through pirated copies in a context like Tibet, take Bollywood far and wide. The circulation of sonic components of Hindi cinema is although not new. For example, as noted on several occasions, a song from a 1955 film *Sri 420* (Mr Fraud) titled *Mera juta hai japani...* (translated as, my shoes are Japanese), assumed popularity in the then USSR. The circulation of songs from Hindi cinema hence may have been accelerated with the newfound diasporic destination. But it is not entirely a new phenomenon as there is evidence of sonic spread even in pre-liberalisation of economy.

Thus, steering clear of the jarring discomfort with the terminological import of 'global' and 'Bollywood', it is imperative to note some of the counter-arguments stemming from the same discourse. For example, in relation to the cinema in Asia, an important cinema critic from Sri Lanka, Wimal Dissanayake had aptly pointed out that the tool of melodrama in Asian cinema is not only to perpetuate the local-contextual ideology/ideologies, it is also aimed at indigenising cinema in the region.[9] The metonymic reproduction of nation and thereof

---

[8] Anna Morcom, 2011, 'Film Songs and Cultural Synergies of Bollywood in and beyond South Asia', in *Beyond the Boundaries of Bollywood*, pp. 156–187.

[9] Wimal Dissanayake, *Cinema and Cultural Identity: Reflection on Films from Japan, India and China*, New York, University Press of America, 1988; Wimal Dissanayake, 1993, 'The Concept of Evil and Social Order in Indian Melodrama: An Evolving Dialectic', in *Melodrama and Asian cinema*, edited by Wimal Dissanayake, Cambridge, Cambridge University Press, pp. 189–204.

ideology, the perpetuation of socio-structural stereotypes and values and enforcement of refashioned local resources from the folk and the classical texts/genres, are all towards substantiation of the melodrama. It is hence hard to debunk the local cinema as regressive melodramatic trash. Hence, Dissanayake also manages to read a relation between Hindu mythological injunctions on the idea of evil and the Hindi cinematic narratives on the same. Rather than trashing it, he underlines a national subjectivity stemming from Hindi cinema on the idea of evil. Also, the exhaustive body of Dissanayake's readings of cinema offer a significant cue to rethink the dynamics of popular Hindi cinema and thereof various components, in a larger perspective of not 'global' but of inter-local mobility in the region. The local-to-local dynamics assume profundity of significance when Hindi cinema and thereof music, as well as narratives, are located in 'transnational local' contexts such as Nepal, Pakistan, Bangladesh among other countries of South Asia. The phenomenon also underscores the sociocultural aspects of the 'transnational local' independent of the trans-locality espoused by the global South Asian scholars.

Local-to-Local

In a simple linear scheme of analysis, artform will be either local or global or both as a hybrid. However, the dynamics of the local-to-local would suggest the need to transcend the binaries and its solution in the hybridity thesis. With reference to the instances emerging from the recent reflections on cinema and music, this is vociferously articulated. For example, one can take the example of the monumental radio programme *Binaca Geetmala*, the first ever chartbuster radio programme of Hindi cinema songs blended with interesting infotainment on Hindi cinema. The show was anchored in a sonorous voice by Amin Sayani in a linguistic style called Hindustani. The programme was aired on Radio Ceylon, however, only after a dramatic episode of events. Radio Ceylon, a household name in the length and breadth of India, was a veritable godsend saviour for Hindi cinema music lovers at the time, in 1952, when the government of India had banned Hindi cinema songs on All India Radio (AIR).

The popularity of Radio Ceylon and its broadcast of popular Hindi cinema songs forced the then information and broadcasting minister, B.K. Keskar, in the cabinet of the Prime Minister Jawaharlal Nehru, to reinstate film songs on AIR in 1957. Not only reinstate but All India Radio also had a special wing called *Vividh Bharti*, which was dedicated to the songs of Hindi cinema. However, before this, the Hindi cinema songs and the *Binaca Geetmala* had become a regional cultural wildfire. The songs of Hindi cinema via Radio Ceylon reached out to the listeners in Sri Lanka, India, Pakistan, Nepal and Bangladesh for sure. As a growing up boy in the small town of remote northern Bihar I have a strong memory of the whole family tuned on to the Radio Ceylon, which aired Hindi film songs muffled in the swing of shortwave. The channel never appeared to be non-Indian and Ceylon seemed more like another town located somewhere very nearby while territorially afar.

This revealed three-fold functions. One alludes to the typical commonsense anxiety that popular music is a threat to traditional forms of music such as the folk and the classical. And more importantly, the self-proclaimed guardians, operating with puritanical taste, such as the state, had anxiety. Second, alludes to the industry catching up faster with the pulse of people than the nation state. And third, last but more than the least, it alludes to the fact that popular music travelled across borders, carved a sizeable fan following, and also synergised diverse locals. These three put together, underlines the trans-local implications of popular cinema of India despite the wishy-washy state policy, much before the idea of the transnational flow of international goods appeared formally. Even though there is a hesitation in acknowledging, there was an influence of Hindi cinema songs and music on the songs composed by Sinhala music composers in the decades of 1960s and 1970s. And likewise, Greene's[10] research showed that popular music in Nepal had to go through a similar experience. When the Rana policy of banning mass media in Nepal was reversed in the early 1950s, Indian films and music made successful inroads into the market as well as into the hearts

[10] Paul D. Greene, 2010, 'Musical Media and Cosmopolitanism in Nepal's Popular Music, 1950–2006', in *South Asian Media Cultures: Audience, Representations, Contexts*, London, Anthem Press, pp. 91–106.

of Nepali audience. However, the state-sponsored Radio Nepal was founded to provide a platform and encouragement to the local artists to create Nepali popular music. It succeeded to an extent with the Ratna Recording Trust facilitating the production of music in 1961 and the Royal Nepal film Corporation coming into existence in 1973. But then, the inspiration for the Nepali filmmakers and music composers was Hindi cinema from India as well as other Western sources. The influences and inspiration from outside Nepal render the popular cultural scene of Nepal too complex to be dubbed in one or the other category. In this regard, another dimension to be verified is the weekly show of Hindi cinema on Nepal Television that attracted most of the viewers in India too. Especially in the townships and villages of Bihar, with a TV booster, it was possible to catch up with the Nepal TV. Similarly, tuning into Radio Nepal for Hindi cinema songs was a common found practice. It seemed that Nepal and India were one as far as the preference of music and cinema was concerned in spite of the cartographic delineation of territories. The idea of a neighbouring country, thanks to the cultural proximity created by cinema and music, was more like the neighbour next door.

But then, the local-to-local dynamics vis-à-vis popular Hindi cinema was not devoid of its share of tension, anti-people regulation and complaints of Hindi cinema being a hegemonic force. And the experience from Bangladesh and Pakistan brings forth evidence of the complex romance with Hindi cinema and songs across the territories of a nation state. While the case of Nepal is suggestive of an early reconciliation with Hindi cinema and songs on the part of the ruling power and people, the locations of Pakistan and Bangladesh complicates the case. The evident love and hate relation with Hindi cinema has, on one hand, sustained the official ban and, on the other hand, enthralled the viewership including the filmmakers. The ban on Hindi cinema has opened floodgates for alternative ways. A film scholar such as Gera Roy[11] noted that state protection of markets in Afghanistan, Pakistan

[11] Anjali Gera Roy, 2011, 'Is Everybody Saying "Shava Shava" to Bollywood Bhangra?', in *Bollywood and Globalization: Indian Popular Cinema, Nation and Diaspora*, edited by Rini Bhattacharya Mehta and Rajeshwari V. Pandharipande, Delhi, Anthem Press, pp. 35–49.

and Bangladesh from Bollywood's hegemonic or 'corruptive' influence inspired the citizens to devise indigenous strategies to evade state regulation by smuggling them.

In the case of Pakistan, despite the ban, Pakistani filmmakers persisted with the search for influence from Hindi cinema. The Pakistani filmmakers were aware of the diversity of tales, motifs, plots and exploration in Hindi cinema, which outnumbered Pakistani cinema in production. In the middle of predominant presence of sexually charged cinema, nearly soft porn, Pakistani filmmakers also cloned the nationalistic cinema of India. Thereby, following the anti-Pakistan jingoism of Indian cinema, Pakistani cinema took to anti-India jingoism that did good business. However, watching the Hindi cinema across the decades of the 1990s and 2000s, there is also a realisation that it is not plainly anti-Pakistan in focus in the cinematic narratives of Indian cinema. Hence, despite the apparent negative portrayal of Pakistani characters in Hindi cinema they tend to be acceptable to the Pakistani audience. They also enjoy watching Hindi cinema for the essential influence of Urdu language and Islamic *tehzeeb* (culture), which recur in cinematic narratives. The viewers in Pakistan find it necessary to take to Indian cinema in order to fill the vacuum of narratives created by low-quality Pakistani cinema. To quote one of the respondents named Maliha in the research conducted by Din and Langah,

> We are not telling our stories. Indians are telling our stories, and CNN and CBC (the television channels) are telling our stories. These stories tell us that it is not great to be Pakistani and our cinema and television traditions in this country are very weak and do not contradict these accounts. Take the example of our dramas, they have very high standards but many in Pakistan prefer to watch Indian dramas because we are 'wannabe' Indians.[12]

Not much different is the case of Bangladesh where the ban on Hindi cinema continued after the creation of Bangladesh out of Pakistan. It was much beyond the expectation of the civil society as the prevailing

[12] Kamal ud Din and Nukuhbah Taj, 2012, '"Dada negativity" and Pakistani Characters in Bollywood Films', in *The Magic of Bollywood*, New Delhi, SAGE Publications, pp. 107– 124.

general sense was that the ruler of Bangladesh was friendly with India. However, the government led by Sheikh Mujib sounded the necessity of protecting the traditional Bengali culture. This though did not dent interest in and memory of Hindi in Bangladesh. The grip of influence was so much that the local filmmakers had to watch Hindi cinema and copy the stories, plots and cinematographic techniques from them. The relationship between officially banished Hindi cinema and the local cinema as well as Bengali Muslim audience was intimate. A major breakthrough was in 1977 with the record success of *Dost-Dushman* (Friend-Enemy), which was a scene-to-scene copy of the Hindi *Sholay* (Flames, 1975, directed by Ramesh Sippy). It kick-started a debate on the quality of cinema in Bangladesh given the capitalisation on violence, sexual innuendos and crass copying of the Hindi cinema. But then, despite the growing concern in the circle of intelligentsia and ruling class, the relation with Hindi cinema only fanned furthermore with the arrival of the technology of Video Cassette recorder and player (VCRs and VCPs), which aided in circulation of Hindi cinema through small video theatres and screening of films on rent in the household. Critically reflecting on the impact of Hindi cinema, Raju (2012) called this 'Bollywoodization as (H)Indinization of Bangladeshi cinema' despite the policy of national protection.

But then, the case of Bangladesh, like that elsewhere in the region, also underlines a latent thesis on local-to-local dynamics. Cultural forms, especially in a popular format, flow ceaselessly irrespective of the state support or ban, regime of transnational flow under the pale of state treaties. This is indeed made possible by a conducive technological atmosphere and people's aspirations for entertainment. The history of cinema and music, to a great extent, has been mediated by changing technology. The degree of democratic access to, for example, popular Hindi cinema and songs, have increased with the advances in technology. It also surfaces that the apple of discord, piracy of cultural products such as cinema and music, aids in democratisation of the access to these forms. The phenomenon indeed excites us to think of a popular South Asia which can apparently defy the bans, regulations and logic of economic as well as cultural nationalism.

20

The Sound of Silence

Of the Shrinking Public Sphere in South Asia[1]

Sasanka Perera

Avijit Roy, a writer and an acclaimed champion of 'secularism' and freedom of expression was killed in a Dhaka street on 26 February 2015. Very clearly, to deserve this terrible public execution, he had committed two 'crimes': One was that he had an opinion that was not shared by some others in Bangladesh. The second was that much of what he believed in was expressed openly in the public domain and often through *Mukta-Mona* (free mind), a Bengali blogging platform, which he had established after migrating to the United States in 2007. Roy was not the first to be hounded or killed in Bangladesh for his opinions. He will also not be the last.

But this is not merely a Bangladeshi phenomenon, it is a form of global intolerance that nevertheless has a profoundly obvious presence across South Asia. In 2011, Salman Taseer, the Governor of Punjab Province in Pakistan was killed in Islamabad by one of his own bodyguards. His 'crime' was his defence of a Christian woman who was sentenced to death in terms of Pakistan's blasphemy laws. Lasantha Wickrematunge, the editor of *The Sunday Leader* was killed in Colombo in January 2009, and his 'crime' was his criticism of the government of the former president of Sri Lanka, Mahinda Rajapaksa. Taunted by people who had issues with his novel, *Madhorubhagan*, Indian writer Perumal Murugan decided on his own to cease his passionate engagement with creative writing. He had posted on his Facebook account not too long ago, 'Perumal Murugan, the

[1] This chapter is based on a lecture delivered at South Asian University on 5 March 2015 at an event organised by the students to protest against muzzling of dissent in South Asia. An earlier version of this chapter under the title 'The Sound of Silence' was published in *Fair Observer* on 6 May 2015. The author would like to thank *Fair Observer* for its consent for re-publishing.

writer is dead. As he is no God, he is not going to resurrect himself. He also has no faith in rebirth. An ordinary teacher, he will live as P. Murugan. Leave him alone.'[2] Though his corporeal body was not harmed, his emotions and his will to write and express were shattered and the end result was not too different from the fate of the others referred to earlier.

In almost all countries in South Asia, books and films have been banned for very similar reasons and under similar circumstances. In these different places, these people were all silenced and their ideas erased by their own fellow citizens who believed that only one kind of truth and reality should exist. That is, one kind of powerful truth is expected to prevail, be it political, religious or both, within a larger domain of silence and acceptance. Many more have been killed in South Asia under similar circumstances since these killings and muzzling of voices. And by all indicators, going by the nature of relative state (in) action in these contexts in South Asia and the relative lacklustre public opinion, these kinds of actions will continue.

Whenever I am confronted with this discomforting expansion of silence and the accompanying entrenchment of a single claim for 'truth' that must necessarily hold sway in the different countries in the region, I am always reminded of an encounter attributed to a group of people known as the Kalamas who lived in Kesaputta and the Buddha nearly three thousand years ago. These were our ancestors living, thinking and debating very much within the borders we call South Asia today. But they also had encountered the spectre of a singular truth and its rhetoric for superiority in their time. The Kalamas' question to the Buddha was to figure out how to 'know' what is 'right'. According to the narrative, they asked the Buddha:

> Lord, some teachers come to Kesaputta, expounding and glorifying their own doctrines. But as for the doctrine of others, they abuse them, disparage them, deprecate them, and pull them to pieces. Other teachers, on coming to Kesaputta, do the same thing. When we listen to them, we feel doubt and uncertainty as to which of these teachers are speaking truth and which are lying.[3]

---

[2] http://www.thehindu.com/news/national/tamil-nadu/perumal-murugan-gives-up-writing/article6784745.ece (accessed on 27 February 2015).

[3] http://www.accesstoinsight.org/lib/authors/rosenberg/righttoask.html (accessed on 27 February 2015).

What is expressed here all those years ago have an uncanny similarity with what we see in our region at present.

The Buddha gave the following response to the Kalamas:

> Come, Kalamas. Don't go by reports, by legend, by traditions, by scripture, by logical conjecture, by inference, by analogies, by consistency with your own laws, by probability, or by the thought, 'This contemplative is our teacher.' When you know for yourselves that 'these mental qualities are unskilful; these mental qualities are blameworthy; these mental qualities are criticized by the wise; these mental qualities when acted on lead to harm and suffering' then abandon them. When you know for yourselves that 'these mental qualities are skilful; these mental qualities are blameless; these mental qualities are praised by the wise; these mental qualities when acted on lead to well-being and happiness,' then keep following them.[4]

Surely, this encounter, in terms of the circumstances, the question posed and the response given is not about religion. Instead, we can see this has much to do with the freedom to think and freedom to express and more importantly, to have the choice and the right to do these things.

This is a state of logic and common sense that prevailed in the minds of thinking people in our region all these years ago. I find it very sad, when we talk of our past with much rhetoric and virulence these days, we often forget what was truly unique in our past and remember and recall only what might best be left in the haziness of the past and myth.

What the killings of today and the anticipated silence through these acts clearly show is a very radical shrinking of our public sphere and a relentless encroachment of our collective conscience and a dismantling of our collective intellectual traditions. What we see is an emergent fear of the plurality of ideas and intolerance of engaged and reflective dissent.

In these grim circumstances, when students of the Department of Sociology at South Asian University associated with the departmental students' blog, 'Rickshaw' organised a 'public meeting' on the theme, 'Muzzling Freedom, Killing Dissent: South Asian Scene', taking the killing of Avijit Roy as its point of departure on 5 March 2015,

---

[4] http://www.accesstoinsight.org/lib/authors/rosenberg/righttoask.html (accessed on 27 February 2015).

I wondered what it means for the university and by extension South Asian citizenship. I also wondered if it would mean anything at all going by the broader regional realities all of us are very familiar with. A handful of students and faculty members constituting a panel expressed what the incident and the larger issues it entails, mean to them. Some other students also took part in the discussion.

But obviously going by the student and faculty population in the university, most people clearly had other things to do, going by their absence. I have no doubt, for each individual whatever else they had to do, must have been important. But then, this is precisely what the larger South Asian polity's inactivity in the context of the regions' larger crises including the intolerance of ideas and dissent has also indicated. If issues such as the shrinking public sphere in our time do not touch our home, salary, scholarship, our right to buy a car and so on, it appears that killings and dismantling of collective conscience that is necessary to expand the singular truth in our time could be tolerated. We can, as we have seen in many parts of the region, be contended with gleaming highways, chandelier-hugging five-star hotels, urban beautification programmes and other manifestations of 'development'.

It seems to me this is the kind of reality my friend and poet, Rudramurti Cheran wrote in another context in his poem 'The Story of a Severed Leg' as 'the irresponsibility of distance'.[5] If so, this also means that the people perpetuating the intolerance of the plurality of ideas that has become endemic in our region are not merely religious and political extremists as often claimed. The silence of ordinary and often reasonable people is as culpable. So the small 'public meeting' held at South Asian University will not change the direction of South Asia's future or the way its citizens think for sure. But it indicates that our collective conscience still flickers on and off and sometimes can be seen above the long shadows of irrationality and disinterest.

[5] http://thepoeticheart.com/poems/dr-rudhramoorthy-cheran/the-story-of-a-severed-leg/ (accessed on 27 February 2015).

21

Reformulating South Asia

Artists' Travels and Possibilities of a New Cartography[1]

Sasanka Perera

As a matter of historical fact, at the height of Buddhism's considerable political power, its ideas and influence travelled throughout present-day South Asia from Afghanistan to Sri Lanka and within what constitutes contemporary India and Nepal as well and then went well beyond the region into the Far East.[2] In this kind of travel of ideas, practices and people that transformed civilisations in the long term, there was an obvious necessity to cross and re-cross borders that marked limits and beginnings of political power even through the nation states as we know them today with their militarised borders that had not emerged yet. South Asian cultural history is replete with these kinds of experiences over time and often much of these are now not even part of the region's collective consciousness. To put it quite simply, if explored, this almost forgotten reality referred to the shared culture and practices that constituted South Asia in the past that proponents of the idea of South Asia often refer to. Compared to this, however, today 'all the states in the region' seem to be 'trying to

[1] This chapter with minor changes is taken from a more complete version titled, 'Re-imagining and Re-narrating South Asia: Artists' Travel and the Practice Visual Art as a New Experiential Cartography' published in Dev Nath Pathak, ed., 2018, *Another South Asia!*, New Delhi, Primus Books. The author would like to thank Primus Books for their consent to republish this chapter.

[2] Sasanka Perera, 2014, 'Beyond History; Against the Present: Preliminary Thoughts on Reimagining South Asia,' in *India+Sri Lanka: Sethu Samudram—Sethu Book Art Project*, Colombo and Bengaluru, Theertha International Artists' Collective and 1 Shanthi Road, pp. xvi–xxv.

become copybook examples of garrison states'.[3] And in this context, travel is far more difficult for people in the region despite the great advances in technology and transportation.

I am not arguing that travel of people and ideas do not take place today but that it is a considerable effort. In that effort and through that experience, what is felt is not a South Asia that is well-connected or integrated and governed by the warmth of a responsive regionalism but the shrillness of parochial nationalisms competing with each other. In a sense, relatively easy inter-regional travel is perhaps the most obvious casualty of the failure of SAARC. Of course, there are some limited successes without any sense of reciprocity. For instance, Indian citizens can apply for Sri Lankan visas online via a very simple and efficient system if they had a passport and a credit card. But that privilege is not extended to Pakistani citizens by Sri Lanka. On the other hand, in its own peculiar wisdom, the Indian state still expects Sri Lankan citizens to apply for Indian visas via a cumbersome physical process at its embassy in Colombo and a number of regional offices or at the mandated private company in Colombo. It is in this kind of context where travel and cross-national association is difficult and with reference to his hope that India and Pakistan could enter into a treaty of peace, security and friendship, the former Prime Minister of India, Manmohan Singh observed in January 2007, 'I dream of a day, while retaining our respective national identities, one can have breakfast in Amritsar, lunch in Lahore and dinner in Kabul. That is how my forefathers lived. That is how I want our grandchildren to live.'[4] In a very similar context, Afghan President Ashraf Ghani was asked in an interview with CNN-IBN on 30 April 2015, what his thoughts on connectivity in the region were with reference to India and SAARC's proposed motor vehicle agreement. Ghani's answer went beyond mere connectivity within India: 'Of course. In India, you can have breakfast in Delhi, lunch in Peshawar and dinner in Kabul. That's the world

[3] Ashis Nandy, 2005, 'The Idea of South Asia: A Personal Note on Post-Bandung Blues,' in *Inter-Asia Cultural Studies*, Vol. 6, No. 4, p. 543.

[4] http://www.thehindu.com/todays-paper/breakfast-in-amritsar-lunch-in-lahore-hopes-pm/article1780445.ece (accessed on 4 May 2015).

we are seeking'.[5] Both leaders were expressing these views when they were heads of their respective states while recognising that relatively unhindered travel in their region was something essential to aspire for but was nowhere near reality.

Broader Possibilities of Art Organisations in South Asia

Would the ideas of cultural practitioners such as visual artists who travel in the region regularly and the work they do in the process, enable such an imagination as well? How would this become possible? Do they not face the same kind of difficult and cumbersome state-centric travel hurdles that other mortal citizens routinely face? Or is this possible at all? To provide some preliminary answers to these questions, I will explore the dynamics of travel in the region facilitated by the South Asian Network for the Arts (SANA) that connected regional art organisations in Delhi, Lahore, Dhaka, Kathmandu and Colombo. At another level, I will also explore the political dynamics of collaborative art projects that presuppose the necessity of artists or their works to travel across national borders. By this, I simply do not mean any exhibition or any artwork as such but projects that take as their point of departure the need to create a South Asian sensibility in some way.

In making these assumptions, I also assume that an artist, his or her work and collaborative projects if carefully thought out have certain subversive possibilities of transcending the routine limitations of nation states in South Asia. South Asian Network for the Arts formally functioned from 2004 to 2010 supported by the Ford Foundation. It was modelled on an earlier network of workshops called Triangle workshops established in New York by Robert Loder and Anthony Caro in 1982, which aimed to bring artists from different parts of the world to different workshops organised in various parts of the world on a regular basis.

[5] http://ibnlive.in.com/news/breakfast-in-delhi-lunch-in-peshawar-and-dinner-in-kabul-thats-the-world-we-seek-afghan-president-ashraf-ghani/542673-2.html (accessed on 4 May 2015).

The expectation was to increase artists' mobility thereby also increasing possibilities of global exposure and avenues for experimentation in environments of collegiality. I will not discuss the history of this initial network even though its impact on SANA needs to be recognised.[6] Despite this formal period of operation over six years from 2004 to 2010, informally, other related activities had been ongoing since 1997 from the time a regional artists' workshop was organised by Khoj International Association in India.[7] Speaking in Manchester in 2003, one year before SANA was officially established, Pooja Sood made the following important remarks on the establishment of the network as a person keen on 'developing deeper connections between art practitioners in the region' and also as an Indian which often carries the burden of India's perceived and real hegemony in the region irrespective of one's individual intentions: 'The premise for success in any intercultural work is one of underlying mutual respect and trust between the partners and I would like to believe that the trust and respect is in place.'[8] This issue of mutual respect and trust is a crucial consideration when we know that in practice, many regional forums attended by state functionaries including SAARC are in fact dominated by the hegemonic positions of larger powers. This is not only an issue that has to do with India but also with Pakistan, given its own interest to outplay India. It is precisely this rivalry and the inability of smaller states to intervene that has made SAARC relatively dysfunctional. As such, it is important that the initial efforts to establish the South Asia Network for the Arts took into account this crucial factor. History also indicates that the other country-specific organisations that were established as part of this initiative also paid considerable attention to this basic premise. In addition to Khoj International Artists' Association in New Delhi, the other regional organisations include Britto Arts Trust in Dhaka, Theertha International Artists' Collective in Colombo, Vasl Artists' Collective in Karachi and the short-lived Sutra Artists' Association in Kathmandu.

---

[6] For more details, please refer to Sood, 'Towards Building a South Asian Network for the Arts'.

[7] Facebook communication with Pooja Sood, 17 May 2015.

[8] Pooja Sood, 2009, 'Six Degrees of Separation,' in *6 Degrees of Separation*, p. 36.

At a fundamental level, the stated effort of SANA and its constituent organisations was not to help formulate a South Asian regionalism, consciousness or sensibility but to become more aware of the art practices in the region as it was recognised that most practitioners were oblivious of work that was going on across regional borders.[9] But my argument is that in the process of making this awareness possible which enabled artists' mobility in the region, a particular consciousness of the region also emerged which outlasted SANA itself and contributed to become a core ethos in some of the constituent groups such as Theertha International Artists' Association in Colombo as well as other groups that were not part of SANA such as 1 Shanthi Road in Bengaluru and many individuals who came into a broader system of circulation of people, ideas and collaborative projects across national borders. In this regard, Ifthikar Dadi notes that 'nonprofit initiatives' such as Britto in Bangladesh, Khoj in India, Theertha in Sri Lanka and Vasl in Pakistan have been able to develop not only 'local artistic and curatorial initiatives' but also to link 'peoples and ideas in innovative ways across South Asia'.[10]

> Before SANA was formally established in 2004, a number of regional artists' workshops allowed for the fine-tuning of the model, logistics and anticipated expectations. After the first Khoj workshop in India in 1997, some enthusiasm manifested among artists who had taken part in this workshop as well as in similar workshops in other regions of the world as part of the Triangle network to set up a similar network in South Asia. As a result of this enthusiasm, the first Vasl International Workshop was held in Gadani near Karachi in January 2001 while in September of the same year, Theertha International Artists' Association organised a similar workshop in Lunuganga in southern Sri Lanka. Britto Arts Trust held its first workshop in Tepantor, near Dhaka, Bangladesh soon after.[11] These workshops that attracted artists not only from the region but also from countries beyond the region,

9 Sood, 'Six Degrees of Separation', p. 36.

10 Iftikhar Dadi, 2012 (1 October), 'Curating South Asia,' in *Guggenheim UBS MAP.* http://blogs.guggenheim.org/map/curating-south-asia/ (accessed on 19 May 2015). http://blogs.guggenheim.org/map/curating-south-asia/ (accessed on 19 May 2015).

11 Sood, 'Six Degrees of Separation', p. 38.

> marked the first time relatively large scale mobility of artists in the region and beyond took place in the postcolonial era. As a result, a scheme of possibility was already firmly rooted on the ground before SANA actually took off ground formally in 2004.

The idea of individual workshops organised as part of the network was to 'function as an art laboratory that brings artists together from different parts of the country, from the subcontinent and from around the globe, setting up a cooperative, non-hierarchical work situation where dialogue, exchange and transfer of information, energy and skills can take place as an intensely lived experience' usually for about two weeks at a time.[12] Nevertheless, the format promoted by SANA also created tensions at various times. This is because the individuals who participated in workshops came with their own personal attitudes and above all, at times replicated the nationalist positions of their nation states. In such contexts, these nationalist positions were countered by other competing nationalisms. . But in the long run and as an overall exercise, exchange of ideas and skills did take place; and friendships were forged that lasted much beyond the duration of each workshop. Also, as the network was formalised under SANA, the pre-SANA two-week workshops were replaced by one-month long residencies.[13]

It is in this space of creativity and mutuality that the ability to imagine the region beyond the hurdles and hostilities of nation states and to work out an alternate experiential cartography of the region became possible. Nevertheless, what was planned and what was achieved had to be undertaken well within prevailing restrictions placed by nation states' imagination of themselves and their own formalised sense of enmity and suspicion of others. Sood notes that due to the political instability in the region and mechanisms instituted by governments undermined these governments' publically stated commitment of people-to-people contact, 'making inter-cultural work in the region extremely difficult'.[14] Taking the specific example of organising the network meeting, a public

[12] Sood, 'Six Degrees of Separation', p. 38.
[13] Sood, 'Six Degrees of Separation', p. 39.
[14] Sood, 'Six Degrees of Separation', p. 40.

forum and an exhibition of contemporary miniatures from Pakistan in New Delhi in November 2001, Sood notes that the visa regime in place was extremely difficult and more than 50 per cent of the time was spent on 'writing to individual country departments of Pakistan, Bangladesh etc. within the Ministry of External Affairs' in Delhi for clearance.[15] She also notes that visas involving India and Pakistan are even more challenging and require endless planning in both countries and the help from sympathetic colleagues.[16] Playing a similar role as Sood in the Sri Lankan context, Anoli Perera notes,

> looking at the past experiences of facilitating artists' mobility and being an artist myself, what I feel is that for most of us, nation state boundaries are mere technicalities of defining a land mass, and these do not seem to pose a boundary that confines our minds from connecting with an art scene beyond our countries. I think, we as artists imagine a larger geography where the boundaries are fluid—our cartography relies more on artistic possibilities and sharing of knowledge, connectivity etc. etc. to draw our own map of the artists' community and the extended realities within which they work.[17]

With reference to her experience in Pakistan, Huma Mulji notes that since about 1997, 'an institutional forum opened up "South Asia for South Asians"' in a situation where prior to this, as noted by Quraishi, it was only on rare occasions that South Asian artists collectively interacted in their local contexts.[18] This reference was made in the context of expanding possibilities towards formally setting up the South Asian Network for the Arts.

Referring to Colombo-based Theertha International Artists' Collective's location in SANA, Perera notes that the network offered a space for her colleagues in Sri Lanka to find their own 'peer community within a regional/international setting that understood

[15] Sood, 'Six Degrees of Separation', p. 40.

[16] Sood, 'Six Degrees of Separation', p. 40.

[17] Personal email communication from Anoli Perera, 17 May 2015.

[18] Fatima Quraishi, 2014. 'Collective Histories: Vasl and Pakistani Art,' in *South Asian Network for the Arts*, edited by Pooja Sood, New Delhi, Dhaka, Colombo and Karachi: Khoj International Artists' Association, Britto Arts Trust, Theertha International Artists' Collective, Vasl Artists' Collective, pp. 71–102, 95.

their anxieties, frustrations and aspirations and which, in a way, was being misunderstood' in her own country.[19] She also notes that in the context of evolving sociopolitical changes in the region, 'most of the experiences of groups within SANA had similar bearings' and 'art that was produced by them engaged in parallel themes and approaches.'[20] Significantly, it is through these practice sharing experiences in different South Asian locations that gave this collective art a certain regional identity in experiential and political terms which also impacted on the artists in evolving a certain kind of basic regional sensibility which had not hitherto evolved significantly in any other sector.

These experiences narrated by Sood, Perera, Mulji and Quraishi bring out an important aspect in this kind of travel and work environments and their difficulties as well as potentials. Clearly, the difficulty in overcoming the hurdles put in place routinely by nation states such as visas is extremely frustrating, which creates a sense of antipathy towards the idea of the state itself and has the potential to make individuals unaware of their extended neighbourhoods in political and cultural terms. At the same time, and in most cases, when participants experience and see the extents to which local organisers in different countries go to make their travel and cross border work possible, it is in that realm of cooperation which exists beyond the influence of nation states that possibilities of reimagining the region differently began to emerge. This is not a matter of delinking oneself from the shackles of nation states or suspending one's citizenship in preference to a South Asian citizenship that does not yet exist. But it is a matter of finding the best possible ways to negotiate one's existence within the nation and the region, which would allow for a broader experience of South Asia. As Perera notes,

> of course, this does not necessarily mean that I don't feel I am Sri Lankan, and that I have little recognition for its boundaries and its status as a nation. But within that national affiliation, my loyalties do not necessarily get anchored to the narrowly defined markers that

---

[19] Anoli Perera, 2014, 'Theertha: A Journey by a Collective of Restless Artists,' in *South Asian Network for the Arts*, pp. 117–136, 123.

[20] Perera, 'Theertha,' pp. 117–136, 125.

nation states usually promote or get hampered by the policies that they push forward to be exclusive.[21]

Compared to Perera's position on the ability and the necessity of artists to transcend the borders of nation states, Dadi, with reference to the emergence of nation states in the region notes, that 'the South Asian artist's status as a "national" figure remains key to situating her formative and ongoing concerns.'[22] For him, then, the point of departure for artists in the region and their creative obsession is mostly a matter of local prerogative. He also notes that 'the very supremacy of the nation-state has also led to the constriction of intellectual and imaginative horizons' and has also 'elided numerous regional and transnational connections....'[23] As such, any reimagining of the region remains a considerably uphill task.

I would like to explore these possibilities and concerns in the context of three art projects that came about as a result of these cross-border collaborations facilitated by SANA and its earlier and later incarnations. These are the '*Aar Paar* Project', the exhibition, 'Six Degrees of Separation' and the 'Sethusamudram Art Project'.

The *Aar Paar* Project

Let me begin with the meanings and nuances of the *Aar Paar* project which was a public art project and a collaboration with very clear political goals. In linguistic terms, *aar paar*, literally means 'this side, that side' in Hindi and Urdu, the politically dominant languages in Pakistan and India. At another level, it also refers to a decisive battle in both languages. The project self-consciously transgressed electronically and in the virtual realm the militarised and contested borders that separate India and Pakistan when both countries were experiencing significant political crises.[24] Karachi-based artist Huma Mulji and Mumbai-based artist Shilpa Gupta formulated and coordinated the project. Both had initially met in New Delhi in an art exchange programme in 1999.

---

21 Personal email communication with Anoli Perera, 17 May 2015.

22 http://blogs.guggenheim.org/map/curating-south-asia/ (accessed on 19 May 2015).

23 http://blogs.guggenheim.org/map/curating-south-asia/ (accessed on 19 May 2015).

24 Perera, 'Theertha', pp. 117–136.

The project was initiated in 2000. Its second phase continued into 2002. It came into being in the context of two major political crises of the time, the Kargil War in 1999 and the communal violence in Gujarat in 2002. Participating artists from India and Pakistan contributed digitally created photographs and graphic works that were exchanged by email between Karachi and Mumbai. The general theme of the works was focused on the idea, 'search for peace and understanding'. On both sides of the border, the electronic images were mass produced using cheap and widely available technology.[25] Later, these prints[26] were publically exhibited and competed for space among commercial advertisements, political posters and movie posters. They were seen in shop fronts and street corners. At another level, copies of these prints were also distributed with local newspapers, while others were distributed as handouts in public spaces.[27]

Despite widely prevalent political anxieties in both countries, the project made 'aesthetic intrusions' into selected public spaces in Mumbai and Karachi irrespective of the rhetoric of the two nation-states and their followers in the process of which a 'cross border conversation between two cities' was initiated.[28]

6 Degrees of Separation

If *Aar Paar* was a conversation across borders between two cities in India and Pakistan in a time of crises, '6 Degrees of Separation: Chaos, Congruence and Collaboration' was a more fuller conversation across South Asia involving fourteen artists from Bengaluru, Colombo, Delhi, Dhaka, Karachi, Kathmandu, Kottayam, Mumbai and Lahore. Singh has suggested that it was an exhibition that knitted together South Asian art worlds.[29] Initially proposed by Frigyes Karinthy in 1929 in the short story, *Chains*, 'six degrees of separation' is the notion that every

---

[25] Perera, 'Beyond History', pp. xvi–xxv.

[26] A total of 21 posters were mass-printed and distributed for the project.

[27] Perera, 'Beyond History', pp. xvi–xxv.

[28] Perera, 'Beyond History', pp. xvi–xxv.

[29] Kavita Singh, 2009, 'Towards Building a South Asian Network for the Arts,' in *6 Degrees of Separation*, p. 4.

individual in the world is likely to be 'connected to any other person on the planet through a chain of acquaintances that has no more than five intermediaries.'[30] In today's commonsensical usage, it is a reference to the superficiality of people's separation from others, which is also the point of departure of the exhibition. That is, in an ideal sense, the cultural connections in the region should be proximate and not distant. But as Singh has suggested, in the context of South Asia's quotidian realities within which this exhibition also took place, the conventional notion emanating from this specific linguistic usage could well be inverted to mean significant separation rather than proximity.[31]

Within this context, the exhibition's approach, logistics and its overall curatorial sensibility makes considerable symbolic and pragmatic sense. For one, the artists whose works had been selected for the exhibition had travelled to at least some of the countries in the region and many of the works in the exhibition were either produced or inspired by workshop experiences in South Asia that had been made possible due to improved inter-regional travel since the late 1990s.[32] Some of the artists focused on the very idea of travelling across borders and encountering places that are both alien and familiar.[33] Focusing on the themes of recognition and misrecognition, familiarity and unfamiliarity and the act of travel and movement, many of the works in the exhibition reflected upon meeting an 'other that is uncannily both like unlike oneself'.[34] Four simultaneous exhibitions on the same theme opened in four other countries.

Sethusamudram Art Project

The third event I have in mind is the 'Sethusamudram Art Project' launched in 2009, which was conceptualised by Colombo-based Theertha International Artists' Collective and Bengaluru-based

---

30 http://whatis.techtarget.com/definition/six-degrees-of-separation (accessed on 19 May 2015).

31 Singh, 'Towards Building a South Asian network for the Arts', p. 5.

32 Singh, 'Towards Building a South Asian network for the Arts', p. 4.

33 Singh, 'Towards Building a South Asian network for the Arts', p. 5.

34 Singh, 'Towards Building a South Asian network for the Arts', p. 5.

1 Shanthi Road as a three-year collaborative art project.[35] It is indicative of art collaboration moving beyond SANA in the sense Theertha International being one of the original members of SANA while 1 Shanthi Road was not. But this collaboration was made possible by the space that was created by SANA and the processes that lead up to it. The project, like *Aar Paar* was focused on addressing an issue between two countries and in this case between India and Sri Lanka. And instead of an issue of anxiety-ridden contemporary politics, the focus was on mythologies shared by the people in the two countries over thousands of years. Sethusamudram, of course, was the mythical bridge across the Indian Ocean between the two countries that is referred to in ancient texts such as *Ramayana*. Weerasinghe notes that '"Sethusamudram" as a concept, given its particular history, metaphorically embraced the connections and the splits, the similarities and the dissimilarities and the shared anxieties, emotions and histories between the two nations.'[36] To be more precise, he notes that by taking the metaphor of the bridge as the point of departure, the project attempted to 'engage with the contemporary dynamics of art and politics by traversing wide expanses of thoughts that included social, political, historical religious and mythological domains as relevant to our lived experiences as visual chroniclers and interrogators living in the "*souths*" of Sri Lanka and India.'[37] In this sense, what is mythological was only the project's point of departure while its process and content squarely consumed contemporary politics including violence, urbanisation, sexual identities and so on which made sense in both cities. The project involved two exhibitions in Colombo and Bengaluru and has led to considerable subsequent collaborations on an individual and institutional basis that involved Indian and Sri Lankan artists.

When one looks at these examples, it is obvious that they did not transform the broader nationalist politics, ground realities and the intellectual discourses in India and Pakistan in the case of *Aar Paar*.

---

[35] Jagath Weerasinghe, 2014, 'An Introduction: About the Sethu Art Project,' in *India+Sri Lanka*, pp. viii, xiii–x; Suresh Jayaram, 2014, 'Conversation across Cultures,' in *India+Sri Lanka*, pp. xii–xv.

[36] Weerasinghe, 'An Introduction', p. viii.

[37] Weerasinghe, 'An Introduction', p. viii.

Similarly, with regard to '6 Degrees of Separation,' the broader political landscape in South Asia was also not transformed. And 'Sethusamudram Art Project' also did not impact long term Indo-Sri Lanka relations. But in the processes and tools that were formulated, tested, fine-tuned and implemented to make these kinds of cultural practices possible, some of the dogmas of different variants of competing nationalisms and the shrillness of the nation's rhetoric was at least monetarily made mute. In that transcendent space, some contested geographies were perhaps redrawn and some were reimagined and yet others not visited, and the flow of ideas across boundaries became possible, at least momentarily. In other words, in a moment of liminality, perhaps a few fragments of what we so casually refer to as South Asia was thought of differently.[38]

Conclusion: Paths of Possibilities

What I have presented earlier are merely three examples of many such events in the South Asian cultural terrain that have emerged without the direct participation of the state. Beyond the end products, such as exhibitions and collaborative art projects which people actually see, what are far more crucial in this context are the processes that people do not see that nevertheless make possible what is finally seen. It is this often unseen realm of possibilities that the South Asia Networks for the Arts, its predecessors and decedents have introduced into the region's wider cultural practices. In much the same way Adajania describes the transformation of the context of operation of Khoj International Artists' Association from 'nation to region to planet,'[39] one can also expand that description to include other constituent groups in SANA as well as others that have emerged beyond the network. Each of these organisations has brought South Asia and the world into their national contexts and has transported their local practices of art to South Asia beyond their national borders.

[38] Perera, 'Beyond History,' p. xxi.

[39] Nancy Adajania, 2014, 'Probing the Khojness of Khoj,' in *South Asian Network for the Arts*, p. 4.

It seems to me, it is within these transformative possibilities that South Asia has been liminally redrawn and reimagined. Much of this has become possible through the act of travel within a discursive practice centred upon art production and delinked from the prerogative of the nation state. Structurally, the travels of these artists that have been made possible by organisations such as those linked to SANA are not too different from the pilgrimages in ancient 'India' that Diana Eck has described.[40] When Hindu pilgrims took it upon themselves to travel to their sacred places, they navigated across a 'sacred geography' that collectively constituted a 'part of a living, storied, and intricately connected landscape'.[41] The wonderings of these pilgrims painted on the ground, a much more different and nuanced cartography that was experientially rooted than the formal cartographic and political representations of these areas that we are now quite familiar with.

In today's contexts when artists travel from Delhi to Colombo to Male and beyond, they are navigating across a cultural landscape that had been under-known in the region for a considerable period of time. But in this form of travel, work and moments of respite, it becomes more possible to comprehend local anxieties, contradictions and nuances in evolving politics and in the way history is seen. It becomes more possible to reconstruct South Asia as part of a 'living, storied, and intricately connected landscape' in the manner suggested by Eck[42] unmediated by the nation state and its limiting prerogatives. In such a situation and over time, it might become possible to reconstruct the region emotionally, experientially and culturally, rather than in the dominant perspective of an amalgamation of garrison states.

---

[40] Diana L. Eck, 2012, *India: A Sacred Landscape*, New York, Harmony Books.

[41] Eck, *India*, p. 2.

[42] Eck, *India*, p. 2.

22

The Cultural Politics of Hatred in South Asia[1]

Ravi Kumar

Taufiq: *You know that religion column we have. I write Muslim, in Bold and Capital.*

Ajay: *That religion column you were talking about, we write 'Indian' in Bold and Capital there.*
[Dialogues from the popular action film titled, 'Baby' (2015)]

Aditi: *We require proof (of your patriotism) because your look doesn't reflect patriotism.*
For how long do you have this beard?

Ali M: *It has been around three years.*

Aditi: *Why?*

Ali M: *It is a religious custom.*

Aditi: *Have you ever thought about how a common patriot would differentiate between the bearded Ali Muhammad and those bearded terrorists from Syria, Afghanistan, Pakistan and Kashmir, whose photographs are printed in newspapers every other day? How would we know that they are the bad Muslims, and you are the good one?*
[Dialogues from a popular film titled, 'Mulk' (2018)]

These are only two examples of a very common trend that indicate how popular culture locates religion and nations. While the first dialogue

[1] I would like to thank Rama Paul in helping me in translating the songs.

clearly tries to pit religion against the nation and it is not surprising it is Islam versus India. No doubt the protagonist also talks earlier in the dialogue about how Hindutva[2] supporters were out there to kill innocent people. However, this invention of a perennial Muslim villain and linking this character to nations has been a global phenomenon. We can see Hollywood doing the same thing after the 'commie villains' vanished due to the collapse of the cold war. Mumbai-based Bollywood film industry did not have such a relationship with Islam as a religion, to begin with, when films like *Mughal-e-Azam*, *Mere Mehboob*, *Taj Mahal*, *Pakeezah*, *Bahu Begum*, *Umrao Jaan*, *Barsaat ki Raat*, *Nikaah*, etc., were made. One finds Muslims turning into villains mostly from the 1990s onwards. Even when a story revolving around Muslim characters is formulated, the content is dealt with in a way that creates stereotypes.

The second sequence of dialogues above creates stereotypes and the usual dichotomy between the good Muslim and the bad Muslim. It is also interesting how Syria, Afghanistan, Pakistan and Kashmir come up in one breath. Recent films have expanded the territoriality of the bad Muslims to Afghanistan and Syria as well, and Chapter 13 in this book focussed on universities and intellectuals and cites the examples of how students from Kashmir get beaten up in times of heightened tensions even when they say that they are not Afghanis. Something interesting is happening here that is transforming a religious identity within a nation (which is India here) into the *other* that then gets superimposed on certain nations by transforming it into a political category. Mamdani writes, 'by equating political tendencies with entire communities defined in nonhistorical cultural terms, such explanations encourage collective discipline and punishment—a practice characteristic of colonial encounters'.[3] Mamdani also terms this good and bad Muslim distinction as dehistoricised 'construction of political identities'[4] as we find the identity of Muslim being used as a political category.

---

[2] Hindutva refers to a political-cultural formation of exclusivist politics which privileges a narrow political interpretation of Hinduism over all other forms of faith in determining issues such as nationalism, patriotism, citizenship etc.

[3] Mahmood Mamdani, September 2002, 'Good Muslim, Bad Muslim: A Political Perspective on Culture and Terrorism', *American Anthropologist*, Vol. 104, No. 3, p. 767.

[4] Mamdani, 'Good Muslim, Bad Muslim'.

Interestingly, the same identity, if not in terms of good and bad Muslim, is made into a political category at the inception of the nation state itself. That is, religious identity is entrusted with the onus to build the new nation. This new nation is provided with contours on how it ought to locate the other social and cultural entities within itself vis-à-vis others. So, listening to the lyrics of songs from the film *Jagriti* on each Independence Day and Republic Day in India in conjunction with an outrageously dehistorised and manipulated piece of popular cinema called *Padmavat*[5] produces an extremely antagonistic and violent idea of the nation.

Consequently, Muslims are treated as anti-national[6] while north-eastern people feel alien in a city like Delhi the way it treats them.[7] Very often, Muslims are seen as favouring Pakistan in cricket matches and even get arrested for the same.[8] A Bangladeshi Muslim or a Rohingya[9] becomes a national security threat simply because historically borders have been created and they have crossed over those lines. These have successfully made religion into a political category and also into synonyms with nations. So, as part of its agenda, Bharatiya Janata Party (BJP) maintains that Bangladeshi

---

5 For critical reviews of *Padmavat*, see Rahul Aijaz (https://tribune.com.pk/story/1619600/4-padmaavat-review-not-historical-masterpiece/) (accessed on 12 March 2018) and Aparita Bhandari (https://www.theglobeandmail.com/arts/film/film-reviews/review-padmaavat-perpetuates-stereotypes-and-carries-a-dangerous-message/article37787050/) (accessed on 12 March 2018).

6 https://www.aljazeera.com/indepth/features/bigotry-normalised-modi-180411100651759.html (accessed on 15 May 2018); see https://freepresskashmir.com/2018/08/16/on-i-day-i-was-told-you-are-a-muslim-i-can-kill-you-and-get-away-with-it-jamia-student-on-alleged-assault/ (accessed on 1 September 2018); also see https://www.theguardian.com/commentisfree/2018/jul/20/mobs-killing-muslims-india-narendra-modi-bjp (accessed on 13 September 2018) for different colours nationalism takes.

7 https://www.indiatoday.in/india/north/story/report-says-north-east-residents-in-delhi-face-humiliation-132328-2011-04-18 (accessed on 12 June 2018); also see https://timesofindia.indiatimes.com/city/delhi/81-of-northeast-women-harassed-in-Delhi-Survey/articleshow/29270244.cms (accessed on 12 June 2018).

8 https://timesofindia.indiatimes.com/india/19-arrested-for-cheering-pakistans-champions-trophy-victory/articleshow/59243368.cms (accessed on 11 September 2018).

9 https://economictimes.indiatimes.com/news/politics-and-nation/rohingyas-are-national-security-threat-government-in-supreme-court/articleshow/60737138.cms (accessed on 23 September 2017).

Muslim immigrants to India have to be sent back, but Hindus from neighbouring countries will be provided citizenship in India. In 2014, Narendra Modi, before he became the Prime Minister of India, said, 'As soon as we come to power at the Centre, detention camps housing Hindu migrants from Bangladesh will be done away with.' He further said, 'We have a responsibility toward Hindus who are harassed and suffer in other countries. Where will they go? India is the only place for them. Our government cannot continue to harass them. We will have to accommodate them here.'[10] The BJP President Rajnath Singh had also said in 2014, 'If BJP comes to power, we'll institute an inquiry to find out how so many people of a particular community could enter the country illegally and settle down.'[11] Hence, what one finds is an interesting framing of the nation within religious boundaries. Interestingly enough, these tendencies are not completely new and have a long drawn history that begins in a concerted manner with the making of the post-colonial nation state. And India is not an exception. In a comparable sense, while both Pakistan and Bangladesh equate the nation with being Muslim, Sri Lankan and Bhutanese, the nation states' primordial political identity comes from their self-declared claim of being Buddhist.

When the British left South Asia it was also divided into new nations. Unfortunately, some of these territories were drawn along religious lines. More importantly, one finds ideological apparatuses in the newly created nation states imagining the new nation in different hues and colours. One such ideological apparatus was cinema. Hindi cinema demonstrated that it was conscious of the challenges that the new nation faced in terms of development, building a nation where caste needed to be challenged—as shown by the film *Sujata* (1959)—and preparing the new generation to commit themselves to the new values (which it tried to define as well). Sahir Ludhianvi, writing for the film *Didi* (1959) would lyrically present the challenges before the nation state as

[10] https://www.ndtv.com/india-news/hindu-migrants-from-bangladesh-must-be-accommodated-narendra-modi-551611 (accessed on 19 May 2018).

[11] https://www.business-standard.com/article/pti-stories/bjp-for-action-against-illegal-migrants-from-b-desh-rajnath-114033000430_1.html (accessed on 13 October 2017).

a dialogue between a teacher and his students in the song 'Humne Suna Tha Ek Hai Bharat' (We had heard that there was an India). Students ask the teacher that the India they confront in reality is not the same as they read in the books. It is rather about caste, religion, Brahmins and harijans and violence. The teacher responds that we were ruled by people who pitched us against each other in the name of religion and caste, and we fell into this trap. He explains that religion and knowledge have always been monopolised by the powerful and poverty and the plight of the marginalised were explained as the fate of *karma*. In *Hum Hindustani* (1960) Sunil Dutt presents the imagination of the new India in the song titled, 'Chodo Kal Ki Baatein' (Let go of old stories). The song talks of scripting a new story for the future as dynamite rips through mountains and mining goes on in the background alongside the marching images of police and military while jets fly by. On the other hand, it talks of how the nation needs to build many more Taj Mahals and Ajanta and Elloras. It appeals to Indians to make honesty their religion. These narratives go on while photographs of Nehru flashes across the screen completing the imagination of a Nehruvian nation.

While this image was being made part of the popular culture through cinema, there were other significant frameworks emerging simultaneously as well indicating the tensions and the faultlines along which the politics of the new nation were to be defined and played out. This framework based itself on an interpretation of history that was not based on facts. It was rather presenting myths as history. It was also not an explanation of history as a process but rather preferred to talk in terms of binaries between Muslims and Hindus, the former being an outsider and an oppressor. Post-colonial nation states began with the project of creating political categories of the other and this other was not only for internal consumption of the hegemonic social and economic forces, but this specific and vilified other was constantly invoked vis-à-vis all others who were somehow accommodated in systems of hierarchy and control. We have seen through the dialogues from recent films how these political categories of vilified others culminate into a performance of organised animosity among nation states.

The way films like *Baby*, *Mulk* and others have portrayed Muslims is not an anomaly. It is part of a process that began immediately after independence. They have always been othered. Kalyani Chadha and Anandam P. Kavoori argue that while Muslims have played a significant role in the Bollywood film industry historically, 'the portrayal of the community itself has nevertheless remained deeply problematic, with Muslims being othered in a sustained fashion in commercial cinema'. This othering has happened 'through a variety of strategies of representation ranging from exoticisation and marginalisation to demonization ...'. Exoticisation happened through films 'that were typically based on characters connected with the Mughal court ... or on storyline based on the reigns of various Mughal emperors ...'. Even the category of Muslim social films 'that centered their narrative on the Muslim community and issues related to it' explored a 'limited terrain' of the Ashrafs. They were limited not only in the sense of being restricted to a small group but even within that group, they did not talk of their socioeconomic or political issues. 'Instead, romantic relationships and family dramas constituted the bulk of their subject matter ...'. Marginalisation as a cinematic mode was present in the 'the casting of Muslim characters in limited roles, always subordinate to the leading players'. They became marginal to the narrative through a Muslim occupational stereotyping. By 1990s and 2000s, the Muslims again became prominent in the films but their 'substantive presence' was 'in a variety of negative roles' as criminals, corrupt politicians, police officials, and Pakistani, and Afghani aggressors etc.[12]

These politics of representation go back to times after independence. And the interesting part has been that India, as well as Pakistan both, began creating a narrative wherein religion and the nation were conjoined at their birth. This was reflected in the way someone like Jinnah and Golwalkar[13] both emphasised Muslims as being outsiders for their very different political agendas. In 1940, Jinnah said:

---

[12] Kalyani Chadha and Anandam P. Kavoori, 2008, 'Exorcized, Marginalised, Demonized: The Muslim "Other" in India Cinema', in *Global Bollywood*, edited by Anandam P. Kavoori and Aswin Punathambekar, New York, New York University Press, pp. 131–145.

[13] M.A. Jinnah was a leader of All India Muslim League and was the first Governor General of Pakistan. M.S. Golwalkar was the second Sarsanghchalak (Head) of the Rashtriya Swayamsevak Sangh (RSS). His two books—*Bunch of Thoughts* and *We or Our Nationhood Defined*—became very controversial for their extreme right-wing sectarian thought.

> The Hindus and Muslims belong to two different religious philosophies, social customs, and literature[s]. They neither intermarry nor interdine together, and indeed they belong to two different civilisations which are based mainly on conflicting ideas and conceptions. Their aspects on life, and of life, are different. It is quite clear that Hindus and Mussalmans derive their inspiration from different sources of history. They have different epics, their heroes are different, and they have different episode[s]. Very often the hero of one is a foe of the other, and likewise their victories and defeats overlap.[14]

M.S. Golwalkar considering these two groups to be different would go on to say that 'ever since that evil day, when Moslems first landed in Hindustan, right up to the present moment, the Hindu Nation, has been gallantly fighting on to shake off the despoilers'.[15] In fact, he calls Muslims as 'foreign hordes' in his famous book *Bunch of Thoughts*.

> This origins narrative has prompted contemporary violence, absolved it, and argued for a recognition of an always-there difference. The hero of one and the foe of another are at battle—'the civilization of conquest is also the civilization of defeat'—the two modes are in syncopation.[16]

Once these kinds of politics were conceived of and committed to, this idea of difference went all out to ensure that this is established as a perennial commonsense, and ultimately the nation mirrors this idea. What could have been better than employing one of the most powerful popular mediums—that of cinema—for this purpose?

In 1954, the film *Jagriti* (awakening) is released. It was designed as a pedagogical exercise where the relationship of teacher and taught is meant to communicate what would be the idea of the Indian nation. In one of its famous songs in the film, the teacher takes students on a tour of India signing a song some of whose lines read as follows:[17]

---

[14] Mohammad Ali Jinnah, 1947, *Some Recent Speeches and Writings of Mr. Jinnah*, Vol. 1, Lahore: S.M. Ashraf Publishers, pp. 174–180. (Quoted in Manan Ahmed Asif, 2016, *A Book of Conquest: The Chachnama and Muslim Origins in South Asia*, Massachusetts, Harvard University Press.)

[15] M.S. Golwalkar, 1938, *We or Our Nationhood Defined*, Nagpur, P.V. Belwalkar, p. 17. (Quoted in Asif, *A Book of Conquest*.)

[16] Asif, *A Book of Conquest*.

[17] I am thankful to Rama Paul for helping me with translations of the songs.

aao bachcho tumhe dikhaye jhanki Hindustan kee
iss mittee se tilak karo yeh dharatee hai balidan kee

[Come hither kids, (and) let me show you some of the visual delights of India, Smear this soil on your forehead, (for) this is the land of sacrifice.]

....

yeh pratap kaa vatan pala hai aazadee ke naaro pe
kud padee thee yaha hajaro padminiya angaaro pe

[this is where Maharana Pratap gave the clarion call for independence this is where thousands of Padminis (women) immolated themselves on pyre]

....

dekho mulk maratho kaa yeh yaha shivaji dola tha
mughalo kee taakat ko jisne talavaro pe tola tha
har parvat pe aag lagee thee har patthar ek shola tha
bolee har har mahadev kee bachcha bachcha bola tha
yahan shivaji ne rakhee thee laj hamaree shan kee

(Look at this land of Marathas where Shivaji thrived
His sword tested the might of the Mughals
Each mountain was on fire and each stone was blazing
Every kid was chanting and invoking Lord Shiva
This is the land where Shivaji defended our honour)

The song through its cinematography and superimposed locations of historical monuments narrates to a group of school children the story of the grandiose of India, appealing to them to smear the soil of the land on their forehead because this land of sacrifice needs to be worshipped. When it takes them to Rajasthan, it is portrayed as the land of Maharana Pratap, who is glorified as somebody who fought against the Mughals for 'freedom', and that of Padmini (a mythical queen) who jumped into a fire to save her honour from Alauddin Khilji, a Muslim warlord.

The song does not stop here. It takes the children to the land of Marathas and tells them the story of Shivaji who fought against the Mughals and defended the dignity of Indians. It mystifies this sense of 'valour' by saying that everyone was fighting the Mughals with the clarion call of 'Har Har Mahadev', which is an invocation of the Hindu god Shiva. Mughal rule is portrayed as colonisation and Maharana Pratap and Shivaji are portrayed as freedom fighters who saved Indians from shame.

Interestingly, a film titled, *Bedari* was released in Pakistan in 1956. It was a completely plagiarised version of *Jagriti*. The Indian leaders were replaced with Pakistani leaders such as in the case when Jinnah replaced Gandhi. The music was the same but the lyrics changed. Instead of Indian singers such as Mohammad Rafi, Lata Mangeshkar and Asha Bhosle who sang the songs of 'Jagriti', Saleem Raza and Munawwar Sultana sang for the Pakistani version. The film was a huge success in the initial weeks like the Indian counterpart. In fact, Nazir Rizvi, who acted under his screen name Rattan Kumar acted in both the films as the leading protagonist. However, very soon a public uproar against the plagiarised version forced Pakistani Censor Board to ban the film.

The song mentioned earlier was replaced with 'Aao Bachchoun sair karayen tum ko Pakistan ki' and its subsequent line like the Indian version talks of sacrifices made for the land. Playing along the same ideological lines of trying to build a historical narrative on how Muslims fought against the cruel Hindus, it talks of how Muhammad Bin Qasim, the general of Umayyad Caliphate who fought against the last Sindhi Brahmin king called Raja Dahir. So, that is celebrated in this song as Indian song celebrated those who fought against the Muslim Mughals.

Aao Bachchon sair karayen tum ko Pakistan ki
Jis ki khatir ham ne di qurbani lakhoon jaan ki

[Come hither kids (and) let us explore Pakistan
as millions have laid down their lives for her.]

.....

Daikho yeh hay sindh yahan zalim Dahir ka tola tha
Yaheen Mohammad Bin Qasim Allahu Akber bola tha

(Regard the land of Sindh where ruthless Dahir reigned
It was here that Muhammad Bin Qasim bellowed 'Allah O Akbar')

> When the Gandhi's contribution is celebrated in the Hindi film with lines such as 'Sabarmati ke sant tune kar diya Kamal' (O! the saint of Sabarmati you have done wonders), the Pakistani film celebrates the contribution of Jinnah and says,
>
> *yun dee hamein azadi ke duniya huee hairaan*
> *ae quaid-e-azam tera ahsaan hai aisa*
>
> (The way you clinched our independence astounded the whole world
> O! Quaid-e-azam thank you for the favour)
>
> *Bedari* presents Jinnah as a soldier of Mohammad (*deen-e-mohammad ka sipaahi*) who was carrying the flag of Islam (*islam ka jhanda liye aaya sar-E-maidan*) and attributes the freedom that Muslims enjoy to him. In fact, the militancy of the songs of *Bedari* is clearly reflected in one of the songs when it says,
>
> *Tum rahto aaram ke jhule mein mat jhulo*
> *Kanto pe hai chalna mere haste huye phulo*
> *Lena abhi Kashmir hai ye baat mat bhulo*
> *Kashmir pe lehrana hai jhanda uchchaal ke.*
>
> (Do not rest at the moment
> as you tender ones will have to walk on the bed of thorns
> Do not forget that you still have to seize Kashmir
> And hoist the flag atop Kashmir.)

What we come across in these examples is an interesting case wherein the idea of the nation is being conceptualised vis-à-vis some *other* identity, who is being created as the enemy. Colonialism appears as one of the enemies. But more prominently and since more recent times, it is the *other* nation that has become the enemy. The cultural politics all along had this orientation and it is this orientation that has fuelled hatred not only towards other nations in the region but also towards other religions. So, the enemy resides in *people* following a certain religion that is different from one's own and are part of a nation that is different from one's own.

The power of electronic media—like television, Internet-driven services and cinema—is not only omnipresent today but all-powerful as well. The attention paid by political formations of a different kind to this medium and the amount spent on it is a reflection of its power. Cinema, as exemplified previously, has become a powerful means to vilify the *other* as well as generate a meaningless and xenophobic love for the nation. It is not a coincidence that when elections approach (as in 2019) one finds films like Uri, which also gets a mention by the ruling party (BJP) during the budget session of the Parliament. One also finds a dangerous trend towards mutilation of history and creating an ahistorical imagination of nation on television as an idea of India is invoked through television serials like 'Chakravartin Ashoka Samrat', 'Porus', 'Chandragupta Maurya', '21 Sarfarosh—Saragarhi 1897' and so on. A sense of past, a false image of past, which is made to look as real as the real, creates a false notion of the nation and this notion is always pitted against people across borders. Hence, the cultural logic produces a populace not without a sense of history and historical past but with a manipulated sense of past.

In such a situation, it becomes extremely difficult to talk about a region because of the hatred that has already been created through a variety of ways, cultural instruments being one of them. That is, the idea of the region and even the cultural terrain within each nation is fragmented on the basis of these divisive representations. The animosity that exists today among nations and the people of South Asia is very difficult to undo because hatred and distrust over other nations and other people is something that we are socialised into since our birth and it becomes tenacious because of the linkages between religion and nation.

Index

Note: The letter 'n' following locators refers to footnotes.

D

About the Authors

Sasanka Perera teaches Sociology at South Asian University, and is the founding professor of the university's Department of Sociology. He has researched on the thematic issues of contemporary visual art in Sri Lanka, violence and memory, religion and politics. He is the Editor of *Society and Culture in South Asia*. Some of his recent publications include *Warzone Tourism in Sri Lanka: Tales from Darker Places in Paradise* (2016), *Violence and the Burden of Memory* (2015), *Culture and Politics in South Asia: Performative Communication* (co-edited, 2018) and *Sociology, Social Anthropology in South Asia: Histories and Practices* (co-edited, 2018) and *Intersections of Contemporary Art, Anthropology and Art History in South Asia: Decoding Visual Worlds* (co-edited, 2018).

Dev Nath Pathak teaches Sociology at South Asian University, and is a founding faculty member of the university's Department of Sociology. His current research interests include popular culture (music, cinema and performance) and South Asian studies. He is Reviews Editor of *Society and Culture in South Asia* (the journal of Department of Sociology, South Asian University, co-published with SAGE India). Some of his recent publications include *Living & Dying: Meanings in Maithili Folklore* (2018), *Another South Asia!* (2018), *Culture and Politics in South Asia: Performative Communication* (co-edited, 2017), *Sociology and Social Anthropology in South Asia: Histories and Practices* (co-edited, 2018) and *Intersections of Contemporary Art, Anthropology and Art History in South Asia: Decoding Visual Worlds* (co-edited, 2018).

Ravi Kumar teaches Sociology at South Asian University and is a founding faculty member of the university's Department of Sociology and its Chairperson. He is also Associate Editor of *Society and Culture in South Asia* and serves on the editorial board of *The Journal of Critical*

Education, Policy Studies and Critical Education. Some of his recent publications include *Contemporary Readings in Marxism: A Critical Introduction* (2016), *Neoliberalism, Critical Pedagogy and Education* (2016), *Social Movements: Transformative Shifts and Turning Points* (2014), *Education and the Reproduction of Capital: Neoliberal Knowledge and Counterstrategies* (2012) and *Sociology and Social Anthropology in South Asia: Histories and Practices* (co-edited, 2018).